ALSO BY VICTORIA PRINCIPAL

The Body Principal

The Beauty Principal

The Diet Principal

Living Principal

VILLARD V NEW YORK

Living Principal

....

LOOKING AND FEELING

YOUR BEST AT EVERY AGE

Victoria Principal

All rights reserved under International and Pan-American Copyright
Conventions. Published in the United States by Villard Books, a division
of Random House, Inc., New York, and simultaneously in Canada by
Random House of Canada Limited, Toronto.

VILLARD BOOKS is a registered trademark
of Random House, Inc. Colophon is a trademark of
Random House, Inc.

Library of Congress Cataloging-in-Publication Data

Principal, Victoria.
Living Principal : looking and feeling
your best at every age / Victoria Principal.
p.   cm.
ISBN 0-375-50488-5
1. Women—Health and hygiene.   2. Beauty, Personal.   3. Exercise for
women.   4. Longevity.   5. Principal, Victoria.   I. Title.

RA778 .P91455   2001
646.7'042—dc21   00-053401

Printed in the United States of America on acid-free paper

Villard Books website address: www.villard.com

2 4 6 8 9 7 5 3

First Edition

Book design by Barbara M. Bachman

THIS BOOK IS DEDICATED TO ALL THE WOMEN

IN MY LIFE . . . GIRLFRIENDS, WIVES, MOTHERS,

DAUGHTERS, WORKING WOMEN, ATHLETES,

ARTISTS, AND GODDESSES.

YOU INSPIRE AND SUPPORT ME THROUGH

THIS JOURNEY.

First say to yourself what you would be;

then do what you have to do.

—EPICTETUS

ACKNOWLEDGMENTS

With gratitude to the following individuals for helping bring
Living Principal to life:

Dan Strone of Trident Media Group for his wise, caring literary
representation; Bill Sobel for his dedicated legal expertise and
friendship; Pamela Cannon for her editorial passion and
precision, and everyone on the team at Villard/Random House
for their hard work; Silki Hernandez, my indispensable
assistant; Vivian Turner for lending us her amazing expertise;
Jeff Katz for the artistry of his photography; Jeremy Mariage,
Cathy Highland, Lisa Tarlow, Teresa Flores, Mery Garcia, and
Richard Salcido (our book shoot team); Mim Eichler Rivas,
collaborator and friend extraordinaire; my beloved Harry; and
the book angels in the ladies' room, whoever you are!

And special thanks for the important contributions to
Living Principal from the following medical experts: Allen S.
Cohen, M.D., Harry Glassman, M.D., Soram Singh Khalsa,
M.D., Peter Pugliese, M.D., Uzzi Reiss, M.D., Carsten R.
Smidt, Ph.D., F.A.C.N.

CONTENTS

THE GENESIS OF

LIVING PRINCIPAL

Angels in the Ladies' Room

AGE AFFECTS EVERYONE DIFFERENTLY, AND DIFFERENT AGES CAN AFFECT EVERYONE DIFFERENTLY TOO. FOR me, forty-two hit dangerously hard, like no age had impacted before. It was as though the realization that I had entered my forties had just dawned on me—two years later!

This was starting to become a pattern for me. From the time I became an adult, every year that there was a number two attached to my age—twenty-two, thirty-two, and now forty-two—it seemed, like clockwork, I entered into a downward spiral, overcome by a sense of mourning for the loss of the younger me. In the past, I had weathered these passages with important, life-altering decisions that helped me move forward, allowing me to ultimately rebound—stronger, wiser, and happier than before.

Given my pattern, maybe I should have been more wary, but forty-two really caught me off guard. I admit that in my late thirties, the notion of turning forty did bring with it a certain awareness—especially of the "m" word—*middle* age. Intellectually, I could accept that forty is indeed the midpoint in a healthy eighty-year life span. But emotionally, the idea brought with it a variety of conflicting associations.

As a baby boomer, I grew up in an era when the image of middle age, at least to me, was of someone who was losing interest—in life and in herself—and someone who was less interesting to others. Middle-aged people, as I perceived them, were weary. They'd been around, they'd seen enough of life, and it was time for their kids to live and for them to settle into their decline toward old age. When I was a teenager coming of age during the youth revolution of the 1960s, the prevailing attitude said that you might as well be dead as middle-aged. Back then, thirty was considered over-the-hill.

But in spite of some apprehension, I sailed into my forties—literally—when I celebrated my fortieth birthday by jumping off the third highest mountain in Switzerland, and paragliding to a safe and ecstatic landing. And when forty and forty-one turned into banner years in every respect, I relaxed, thinking that the aging process had somehow magically passed me by.

That's when I got slammed by forty-two. All of a sudden, the woman whose face I knew from my own mirror was changing. For the first time, I could see the physical signs of aging. Up until this point, they hadn't been an issue, thanks to good genetics and earlier commitments I'd made to taking care of myself. But suddenly, I found that I was all too human and not at all immune to aging.

If the changes had been only physical, I doubt I would have been thrown for such a loop. The real shock was finding that I was not immune to ageism within the entertainment industry. Whether overt or covert, the practice of ageism is rampant in many fields. The powerful potential of workingwomen in their forties, fifties, and sixties is particularly overlooked, and in show business it is most visible in our very lack of visibility.

All of a sudden, I turned forty-two and experienced what I had heard about for years but hadn't yet really encountered. After nine fantastic years as Pamela Barnes Ewing on *Dallas,* I had successfully made the transition to a thriving film and TV-movie career, starring in as many as three movies a year. But when I hit forty-two, my acting career abruptly dropped off the face of the earth. From my perspective, it was shockingly unfair. I was just hitting my stride, with that much more training, experience, and emotional depth to offer as an actress. For years I'd been warned not to be so open about my age. I always ignored those warnings, wondering why my career would change if I got a year older. But, to my surprise and dismay, it did.

Other concerns I'd never even contemplated began to overtake me. Would my aging change the way my husband looked at me? When we married, he thought of me as the girl next door; would he be disappointed now that my feet were firmly planted on the other side of girldom and think, *This isn't my wife, where did the girl go?*

Before I knew it, my inner voice, usually a source of reason and comfort, went into panic mode, warning me of every kind of worst-case scenario. *Well, Victoria,* said my cruel internal voice, *you've had your good times, and it's never going to be that good again.*

At that point, I realized I needed help. For starters, I needed to have a talk with my inner voice. I needed to rethink my attitude toward aging, toward change, and toward myself. I needed to understand that I hadn't quit acting but that acting had quit me; understanding that, I needed to become creative in carving out a new professional direction. I needed to talk to, and be reassured by, my husband, Harry—who, by the way, is my best friend and confidant, as well as the love of my life. I also needed input from my close women friends, both older and younger.

What I really needed was this book, or something like it. But at the time, I found nothing to address my many questions and concerns (although *Passages,* by Gail Sheehy, was insightful). So, in the spirit of true self-help, I set out to gather my own information and inspiration. The result of that search is that today, at fifty, I feel happier, healthier, busier, and more fulfilled than ever—in my career, my marriage, and as a human being.

The idea to compile the practical and philosophical guidelines that served me so well didn't happen right away. Much of what I discovered came in the form of reminders or adaptations of the principles of good health that I had covered in my earlier books: *The Body Principal,* my guide to exercise; *The Beauty Principal,* my guide to skin care, makeup, and hair care; and *The Diet Principal,* my weight-loss and nutrition guide. As a matter of fact, I had always felt that my "trilogy" was complete.

By my early forties, however, I realized that there were important aspects of living I hadn't touched upon—at the time, I hadn't had the experience or the need to address them. Plus, the world had changed, offering us new ways to look and feel healthier.

So, by my late forties, as I approached another major age milestone, I felt that there absolutely needed to be another book. This new book, I decided, would be a combination and update of my earlier principles, together with what I'd learned in the interim—simply from the process of living and aging, and from the monumental discoveries in science and technology.

Even though I had come to this conclusion, *Living Principal* was not actually born until one evening when I met up with a pair of book angels. You may laugh, but that's exactly what they were. I met them in the ladies' room of a restaurant in Philadelphia, after excusing myself from dinner with Harry.

Seconds after I entered the otherwise empty ladies' room, two women, both lovely brunettes, came in. One appeared to be in her mid- to late forties, and the other about ten years younger. They recognized me immediately and introduced themselves as sisters.

"I have all three of your books," said the older sister. "I love them so much, I've worn them out."

What author doesn't love hearing that? I thanked her wholeheartedly.

"I wanted to buy them myself," the younger sister explained. "But I was told they were out of print." So instead, the sisters told me, the younger woman and her friends had been borrowing the books to copy.

"You should reissue them," said the younger sister.

"Funny you should say that," I replied. "I'm thinking about writing another book."

Both sisters were eager to know if I would cover some of the same topics—mainly diet, exercise, and skin care. I assured them that I would, but not in the same way I had fifteen years ago.

The older sister said excitedly, "If you're going to write this book, there are some things I really would like you to cover." She went on to mention several things—aging in today's youth-driven society, the relationship between hormones and aging, and the subject of how to dress. One of her biggest concerns, she said, was feeling she had to give up the way she had always dressed to avoid looking inappropriate.

The younger sister had questions about women's health issues; whether plastic surgery was advisable in her thirties; how to find time to work out and release stress while juggling a full-time job, taking care of the house, and finding time for her family.

So there in the ladies' room, *Living Principal* was virtually outlined for me. Thrilled, I hurried back to tell Harry about my encounter with the bathroom book angels. I announced, "You're not going to believe what happened—I'm ready to start my next book." Before Harry could respond, it dawned on me that I'd forgotten why I'd gone to the ladies' room in the first place. "Excuse me," I said, laughing, "I've got to go to the bathroom!"

Within the week, I started making notes. It's important for me to remind readers that I'm not a guru or an irrefutable authority. I'm a woman who has struggled to achieve good health—physically, emotionally, and spiritually. Because what I do for a living depends partly on my looking good—and, just as importantly, on feeling good—these guidelines have been essential for me. I'm partial to solutions that simplify my life and to advice that is sane, safe, and straightforward. What I offer you is the hope that what has worked positively for me will also work for you.

Because I intend to cover ground that sometimes exceeds my personal experience, I will from time to time use examples and lessons from friends and colleagues. I'm also privileged to present information I have gleaned from the medical experts who have generously contributed to portions of this book.

So you're ready to get started and you want to know where to begin? Guess what, you've already begun! You may not see instantaneous results, but by opening your mind to the possibilities that life can offer, you've already embarked on a new path. Let your creative mind and a life-affirming attitude go to work for you. A fundamental of *Living Principal:* If you truly desire to better yourself, you have the ability to create the solutions that will work, not as a quick fix but, I hope, as a lifetime fix.

My suggestion is that you start by focusing on one area you'd like to change—whether it's losing weight; committing to exercise; practicing what I call Ten Minutes of Joy; having your hormones checked; starting a new skin, hair, and nails regimen; exploring plastic surgery; getting in touch with your spiritual side; balancing your emotional and physical health; taking a vacation . . . or piercing your navel! It's a good idea not to do everything at once. Allow yourself time to incorporate changes in different areas so they become realistic and substantial parts of your lifestyle.

In the chapters that follow, I'll be reminding you, very simply, to remember to breathe.

I urge you not to overcomplicate the wonderful opportunity we have every day of our lives to renew, restore, revive, and rekindle our love affair with living. Whether or not you take advantage of the opportunity is up to you. But you don't have to stress and strain and worry that you won't do it right. Just be open to change and growth.

I can assure you that by reading this book you will have altered your life. You will live differently by becoming aware that a day without joy isn't living and that joyful moment-to-moment living is the secret to youth everlasting. Simply by going on the journey that follows, you'll be arming yourself with knowledge you didn't have before that will allow you to make changes at a pace that's right for you.

And remember: Breathe.

Living Principal

Focusing our attention—
daily and hourly—
not on what is wrong,
but on what we love and value,
allows us to participate in
the birth of a better future,
ushered in by the choices
we make each and every day.

— CAROL PEARSON

CHAPTER ONE

YOUR INTERNAL VOICE—

TAKING CHARGE

OF YOUR ATTITUDE

Beyond the Dash

Early in the process of outlining this book's goals, I realized that it would be less about aging and more about living. It's about living fully as we are aging, not about putting life behind us. It's about living happily and well as we invoke our feminine strength, our womanliness, to be not only as much as we always were, but very possibly more. After all, if we live and learn as we go, we will have those wonderful perks called hindsight and wisdom to guide us. Now we can *live*.

We also can benefit from new ways the world has to offer us to be more youthful at a mature age, allowing us to attain something I think of as youthful maturity.

Not to be silly or inappropriate, not to strive to be twenty-one again (something I don't think I'd want!), but to feel and look and be our very best at every age.

Let me add that, in the world we inhabit now, there are more choices than ever available for who we want to be and what life roles we want to play. We don't have to fit a cookie-cutter mold of what any particular age is supposed to look like or be. The shoulds and the musts no longer apply. Our choices are now about what we can do to be our best selves—by our own individual standards.

In the past, many of us thought that once we turned forty, life was a ticking clock, ticking into old age and death. Now, because of improvements in the care we take of our health and the advancements of science and technology, the clock isn't ticking so loudly at forty, fifty, sixty, even at seventy! The very process of aging, once considered absolutely inevitable, has begun to be seen as a treatable disorder. Some scientists have even predicted that there may come a time when the causes of death will be eliminated.

Aside from the ethical and population-control issues this possibility raises, it brings into question our cultural attitudes about the "curse" of dying. My take on death happens to be different. To me, it's part of the natural order, a necessary phase of the life cycle.

Because I was raised in an Air Force family who moved frequently overseas, while growing up I was exposed to less fearful cultural attitudes toward aging and dying. Here in the United States, the time I spent on my grandmother's farm in Georgia made me a firsthand witness to the cycle of birth, life, and death, then a breath before the cycle started once more. I saw it not only in plants, fruits, and grains, but in cattle, pigs, chickens, cats, and dogs.

Instead of fearing older age and death, my thought is that we should fear *not* living. Sadly, there are a lot of people walking around not living—that's much more frightening. Instead of feeling that our best years are behind us, wouldn't it be better to focus on what's in front of us?

Those attitudes were important reminders to me when I was forty-two and found myself buying into the idea of the ticking clock. In hindsight, I know how foolish that was. At the time, however, I was listening to a worried inner voice telling me that the clock was running down and life wasn't ever going to be as much fun, and that I wasn't going to be as enthusiastic, attractive, and interesting, and that everything was going to be less. When I finally examined my fears, I saw that I had a few options. I could respond by retreating into denial, pretending that this age thing was just a bad dream. I could give in to fear and prepare for a lesser life. Or I could put my emphasis not on the fact that I was dying but on the fact that I was living: the quality of my life.

I chose to emphasize what some people call "the dash," the mark on tombstones between the dates of birth and death. Contained within that little mark is an entire lifetime. Until science cures mortality, we all know with certainty that we are going to die. That is the one promise made to each of us the moment we're born. What we don't know is when. So none of us can ultimately determine how long our dash is going to be; what we can shape is its quality, the quality of our life. That, I believe, starts with attitude.

Once I shifted my focus to life's journey, rather than its ultimate destination, what had been a terrible depression became an astounding revelation. Out of that downward spiral came a turning point at forty-two—my life became more than before, not less or worse, but fuller and more joyful than it had ever been.

It helped me see what's important to me about my life—that I make it count for something and not waste its precious opportunities; that I have the courage to face my fears; that I have generosity of spirit not only for others but for myself; and that I keep my mind open to the possibilities that each year brings.

Living that way hasn't always been easy. Sometimes in a desire to move ahead at full throttle, I forget the adage about stopping to smell the roses. In fact, I had to consciously train myself to do just that—the daily practice I call Ten Minutes of Joy, which we'll explore later on. For me, the art of living in the moment is one of the most powerful ways to rejuvenate yourself—in practically no time and without spending a penny.

Living Principal means that you can create the life you want and the self you want. At this writing, all of us will eventually go, gentle or raging, into that good night; but now we have the option of going more slowly, at a later date. Instead of denying or fearing the process of aging, my choice is to embrace it, to try to do it both gracefully and intelligently.

"Grace" is such a beautiful word, one that for the most part has been lost from our vocabulary. I love reading books like Jane Austen's, about eras when grace was considered a vital quality. Grace really is admirable, defined not only by what we see on the outside but by what we sense from the inside. It's a manner in which one carries oneself—externally and internally. As we age, we have the option to carry ourselves inside and outside in such a way that we do it with grace.

Wouldn't most of us rather see someone age with grace than with fear? Few of us are attracted to the face of fear—the person who is desperately trying to make herself into her twenty-year-old incarnation. We may empathize with it, we may sympathize with it, but it's not attractive. It's not enticing. It's not something you're drawn to. Grace is attractive. It's universally admirable. It is appealing to all of us.

Think of famous older women who are beautiful in their totality: That is grace. Women like Katharine Hepburn, Catherine Deneuve, Audrey Hepburn, Sophia Loren, Judi Dench, Tina Turner, Helen Mirren, Jacqueline Bisset, Candice Bergen, Diane Sawyer. Those women have inspired me, as have women like Shirley Temple Black and Vanessa Redgrave, whose accomplishments beyond professional work have enhanced their beauty as they have aged. Now a new generation of public women—like Oprah Winfrey, Susan Sarandon, Michelle Pfeiffer, and Katie Couric—has come along to exemplify grace and intelligence as they pass from one life stage to the next.

When I say aging with intelligence, what I mean is moving through the years not thoughtlessly but with foresight and care, using the knowledge we have and resources that we may seek out. I hope that's what *Living Principal* will offer you—an intelligent resource as you determine who you want to be and how you want to live.

LESSONS FROM THE PAST

What about the instances in our lives when we confront circumstances beyond our control? At those times, the words of writer John Homer Miller are relevant: "Your living is determined not so much by what life brings to you as by the attitude you bring to life; not so much by what happens to you as by the way your mind looks at what happens."

When I was going through my aging crisis and struggling to find a healthier attitude, I discovered that one of my most valuable resources came from my own past—from crises that came before, misfortunes that befell me, mistakes I had made—and from what I had learned in the process.

So when I took the time to reflect on two earlier crises, I was able to remind myself of a few priceless life lessons. At the age of twenty-two, incredible as it sounds, I found myself washed up on the shores of Hollywood. A year before, I had been launched into stardom in *The Life and Times of Judge Roy Bean* with Paul Newman. When I was twenty-two, my second film, *The Naked Ape,* came out. To say it was a bomb is to be generous. Every door that had opened for me was now locked. I was a twenty-two-year-old has-been. In real time, I was the epitome of youth; in show-business age, I was about to pass my prime.

Everyone I knew made it painfully clear that it could take many years for me to retrieve the acting image I had tarnished, and that by then it might be too late. The prevailing attitude in Hollywood was that you needed to "make it" as young as possible, and if you didn't "hit" within the first three to five years, you probably never would. For me to have hit and failed so quickly made it unlikely that I was going to ever hit again.

To pay the bills, I lived on my meager savings and continued to study acting while trying to get my career back on track by following the advice of industry people whom I considered knowledgeable. In those days, my dark Italian-American looks were considered too "exotic." My figure, I was told, was too voluptuous. Trying to fit the mold, I became a blonde and dieted myself into a stick. Though I worked sporadically, in decent films, my self-esteem remained crippled. In periods of inactivity, I comforted myself with the delicious food I loved and had been denying myself and, of course, gained weight—as much as an extra forty pounds at one point. That was when I realized I was trapped in a destructive cycle and that I needed to change the way I lived. I had created the trap; I could free myself.

After three years, I threw myself a life preserver. I didn't want to live as too thin, too fat, too blond, too exotic, too anything other than who I wanted to be—myself. I decided to stop listening to the ways everybody else was trying to reinvent me. Instead, I would reinvent myself, using my own standards. To do that, I chose to leave acting and become a talent agent. For the first time in my life, my career didn't depend primarily on how I looked. Being a successful agent depended on other skills—intelligence, intuition, sense of humor, flexibility, verbal and people skills, and a determination to win. Those qualities weren't ones I necessarily thought that I possessed, but I worked hard to cultivate them. Working behind the scenes, going to bat for other actors and actresses, I revived my sense of self-worth. So after three years, when the *Dallas* opportunity came my way, I was able to reinvent myself again and return to acting on my own terms.

Of my many lessons from this period, I was most empowered by the discovery that *it is possible to re-create oneself.* I think women's innately creative sensibilities make us eminently suited to the task. Most women must play several roles in their lifetime, often at the same time. Reinventing your life, I found, doesn't have to be a mysterious, daunting process. Sometimes it's as simple as changing your hair color, rearranging your furniture, wearing a new perfume, or going for a walk after dinner instead of watching TV; sometimes it's as subtle as calling a friend you haven't seen in a long time, reading a book that transports you to new possibilities, or taking a class in a subject you feel passionate about. Or you may need to make more dramatic changes, as I did. You may need to change your job or pursue it in a different way. You may need to end a relationship that isn't working. You may need to move to a different home or even to a different city.

I learned the tough way that however you decide to change yourself, what matters, above all, is that you *do it for you.* I saw how destructive it was when I lost weight to satisfy people who seemed more knowledgeable than I, or when I tried to live up to some media vision of beauty. I had to learn how to be comfortable with my weight for myself. When I chose to do it for me, I decided to do it in a way that was healthy but allowed me to eat the foods I loved. That policy has been a faithful friend to me throughout the years.

Whenever I hear a woman say that she's going on a diet because her husband or lover has been making digs about her weight, I am concerned for her. The fact is that when you change yourself for somebody else, you are giving up a piece of yourself. It is hard to give up pieces of yourself and expect to be a whole person—a vital part of what makes someone attractive and keeps a relationship healthy.

Now, on the other hand, loving partners, spouses, family members, and friends can make thoughtful suggestions that are definitely worth exploring. If the suggested change is something a loved one would enjoy, it might be a positive change for you as well.

If, for example, your husband says to you, "I love you as much as I always have. But I'm disappointed that you let your hair go silver. I so loved the color of your hair when I met you."

In that case, why not consider changing your hair back to that color—at least temporarily. If you don't like it, you can let it grow out to silver again. Incidentally, this compromise works both ways. If a woman wants to enliven her romantic self and her relationship, she might go to her husband and lovingly remind him how much it turned her on when he wore his hair down to his shoulders. She might say, "I know you're older and feel you should wear it short, but would you try doing it for me?" Or she might suggest other changes: Would you pierce your ear? Would you start jogging with me?

The other lesson I learned in my twenties about my ability to re-create myself by my own choosing was that *real change takes place on the inside*. Dyeing my hair back to its natural dark brown and changing my job were external changes. The real change was the way I began expressing myself with my internal voice. Once I began to speak to myself with respect, encouragement, awareness, and generosity, I began to flourish. The difference in the way I began to talk to myself was reflected in the way I began to feel about myself. Instead of inflicting blame and self-reproach for not living up to the expectations of others, my internal voice became my best friend. The upshot was a consciousness shift. My attitude enabled me to take the risks that ultimately led to success.

When I turned thirty-two, my age crisis had nothing to do with professional disappointment. On the contrary, with *Dallas*'s popularity at an all-time high, my career couldn't have been better. The problem was that I had become a classic workaholic—always striving toward a goal, never living in the moment. Because of the stress, the isolation, and the overworking, I was physically and emotionally unhealthy—weakened to the point that I couldn't enjoy anything. When I looked in the mirror, I saw a weary, lonely woman.

After being despondent and unable to muster the energy to do anything about it, I decided that since I was going to be thirty-two whether I liked it or not, I'd better do something positive. But I didn't know what to do until a change was suggested by a dear friend. In her brutally honest manner, she said, "What is the deal with you? You are beat, you are tired, you are stressed—you look terrible. Why don't you take a vacation?"

My initial reaction was: A what? Because of my work ethic, I suppose, I had never given myself a vacation. Perhaps on some level I didn't feel that I deserved one. Or maybe the notion of not working seemed frivolous. Or if I wasn't working, I ought to be resting. But not resting in a location with coconut drinks! What if somebody called and I missed a job?

"A vacation?" I asked my friend. "Where would I go?"

"Are you joking?" she said. "You can go anyplace in the world."

She convinced me that I had every right, opportunity, and resource to offer myself a vacation. When I asked her where she would go if she was planning a vacation, she answered, "Well, I've never been to Hawaii."

"Great," I said, "we're going to Hawaii." Since she had been so thoughtful about my well-being, a month later I thanked her by taking us both to Hawaii for ten days. While I was there, I ate three healthy meals a day, worked out, and caught up on my sleep. But we partied too. We had so much fun. I took to vacations like I'd always taken to work. I gave myself permission to *have a good time*. I truly relaxed, indulging in every moment—sunbathing, swimming, going for walks, talking, reading books, and occasionally dancing all night.

I came home and back to work renewed. I had learned that before you can shift your attitude out of a depression, the best thing you can do for yourself is *positive motion.* Not motion as in running away from the problem, and not just frivolous motion, but motion to move you out of the depression. Motion that leads to a better place. The motion to take a vacation was life-changing for me, because it spurred me into some decisions about my lifestyle. I resolved that taking care of myself— body, mind, and spirit—was as important as my work ethic; in fact, I needed a living ethic. I decided that no matter what I did to improve myself, I would approach everything with the goal of *having fun.*

Back at work on *Dallas,* I still worked as hard as I always had, but I made some changes about the way I spent my weekends. Instead of watching the show by myself, I began having friends over every Friday night, and would prepare chili and corn bread. I began hiking and exploring trails in the nearby canyons. I began going to the movies. I started going to a park every weekend with my dogs. Maybe I'd invite a friend to go with me; maybe I'd throw a ball for the dogs; maybe I'd take a book. The important part was that I was getting out in the fresh air, doing things that nurtured my soul. Instead of feeling guilty that I wasn't accomplishing a specific task, my internal voice was gently reminding me, *You deserve it.*

Thirty-two became one of the best years of my life. By the time I turned thirty-three, I could really depend on my best friend—me.

These lessons served me well when forty-two came along. I wanted and needed to reinvent myself again, but I had to do it for me, not for show business. If it meant fighting harder for fewer roles, I would do that. If it meant throwing myself more fully into my work as a producer and into the skin-care company I had launched, I would do that. And if it meant taking classes in areas of acting that I hadn't pursued before, I would do that. After six years of studying comedy and auditioning, the effort paid off in acting jobs. The effort had already paid off in every other way, because I enjoyed all six years.

The moral of this particular story is simple: When what you're getting from life isn't what you want, then you must make changes within yourself. Life isn't going to change for you. Making the changes may challenge you or take time. But examine your own wealth of experience and review the lessons you've learned from the past, and I'll bet you'll be pleased to discover powerful resources at your disposal.

The answer lies within you.

Sometimes making an external change can trigger an internal one, as I learned earlier in my life. Sometimes the change that takes place on the inside starts there, with a shift in attitude. The fact is that when you *feel* you're fat, ugly, and over-the-hill, you'll *act* fat, ugly, and over-the-hill. Or perhaps you'll *pretend* you don't think you're fat, ugly, and over-the-hill. Neither is a healthy way to be. As I discovered when my own voice was taunting me with derisive adjectives, you have to make friends with yourself.

If I had thought that my internal voice was destructive and cruel, I was surprised and dismayed to find out I wasn't alone. This was painfully demonstrated to me in an airport ladies' room when I was traveling a few years ago. Bathrooms, you may have noticed, seem to figure heavily in my life!

For whatever reason, I am approached more often in rest rooms than in any other place—by women who want to ask my advice, who have read my books or seen me on TV; who want to confide something they may never have told anyone, not even their lover, best friend, sister, or mother.

Whether they're asking about skin care or makeup or weight loss or exercise, they often turn to look at themselves in the mirror—right in front of me—and say something nasty about themselves. One woman, a few years my senior, said, "You know, I've been telling myself to do something about these wrinkles and I've just been saying, 'Fix your skin, you fat old crow,' but I just don't do it."

I turned her around to face me and said, "Excuse me. You call yourself a fat old crow? You say this out loud?"

"Oh, no," said the woman, "I don't say it so anyone can hear, just to myself."

"So," I asked again, "you say to yourself in your mind, 'you fat old crow'?"

She'd been calling herself a fat old crow, as I understood it, since she was in her mid-thirties. That was something I couldn't fix for her, I explained. And if she didn't start by addressing her negative internal voice, no skin-care product, surgery, weight loss, or any other improvement effort was going to help.

Clearly, if you're that mean to yourself in your mind, I pointed out, then you're sending a message to your whole body. To your whole self. How do you surmount "you fat old crow" every morning? How do you go out in the world and have a great day after that?

Then I asked, "If you got up in the morning and I happened to be in your bedroom and I said, 'You fat old crow, get up and go to work,' what would you say?"

The woman replied, "I'd say, 'How dare you!'"

That was my point. "If you wouldn't allow anyone else to talk to you like that, why would you speak to yourself that way?"

She had never thought about that before. I encouraged her to try a kinder way to speak to herself—even to wake up in the morning and greet herself in the mirror with *Hello, I sure love you.*

Instead of calling herself fat, I suggested she say to herself, *I love me and I weigh more than I want to . . . so today I'm going to begin a better way of eating.*

When my internal voice got stuck on over-the-hill, I opted to say to myself, *Yes, I am older, but I love me and I still feel youthful and I hope the whole world can see who I really am.*

If you've lost weight by changing your eating habits, and then you've gone on a binge, here's another suggestion for your internal voice: *I ate like a pig last night! I know I did. But you know what I'm going to do? Instead of eating more to console myself, I'm going to eat really well today. Every time I feel bad, instead of eating more, I'm going to hug myself, even if it's in my imagination. I'm going to console myself. I'm not a bad person. I'm somebody who ate too much last night and I don't have to eat too much today to make it better; that'll just make it worse.*

Or if you always look tired, no matter how much rest you get, try not to call yourself haggard; you might say: *You know what? I'm going to save my money, and I'm going to a good doctor to get my eyes done, because I've done everything else I can do, and I can't solve this on my own. I need professional help. I would really like to do this for me.*

Or if you feel your libido has suddenly flattened out—or completely disappeared—rather than labeling yourself sexless, suggest to yourself: *It's time to go and have my hormones checked and see what I can do naturally, or with medicine, to restore the sensual me I know and miss.*

Whatever the issue is, you need to understand that if you call yourself names that you wouldn't let anyone else call you, then you are abusing yourself. You need to say: *I'm not going to call myself names anymore. And if I can't stop, I'm going to seek out a therapist to help me.*

If you've made a habit of not loving yourself, learning how to break it may take time. But practice can make a world of difference. Practice being as courteous and kind to yourself as you would be to the people you love or even to a stranger. It has to start with you.

When you face disappointment, acknowledge it, then practice letting it go; practice forgiving yourself. If you hang on, it'll turn into baggage so heavy that you're doomed to keep disappointing yourself. On the flip side, don't rationalize destructive behavior and make it okay when it's not. When you make a mistake, take responsibility for it and try to find a better response for next time so you don't repeat the same mistakes.

Rather than using your internal voice as a built-in critic, practice pointing out qualities and accomplishments that make you feel proud. Instead of saying, *After having three babies, I just let my body go to hell,* congratulate yourself on motherhood and thank your wonderful body for making and nurturing your beautiful babies. Now use some of that nurturing on yourself.

Strive for excellence, not perfection.

Practice being a good friend to yourself. Cheer yourself on. Pass yourself in a mirror and give yourself a smile. Give yourself a compliment: *What a warm, sincere, nice woman you are.* Don't be shy: *What a warm, sexy, attractive woman you are!* If you're starting out on a new lifestyle plan, be your own inner coach: *I can do it. I've already made a commitment. I'm strong and determined. I am woman.* If failure or skepticism rears its head, face it and encourage yourself: *I'm trying very hard to do this, and most of all I need my own support.*

Many women are relieved to know they're not alone in the self-critical way they talk to themselves. In contrast, I've found that most men have wonderfully encouraging and supportive internal voices. When facing challenges, their attitude is often a self-confident *I know I can do it*. One senses that even when dealing with defeat or disappointment, men usually direct their energies toward doing better the next time, not calling themselves unkind names.

Regardless of gender, people who know how to talk to themselves supportively usually like themselves as human beings.

Practice liking yourself. If you've haven't taken an inventory of the things you like about yourself lately, I heartily recommend that you sit down and make a list of qualities that you admire about yourself before you go on a crusade to change the things you don't like. Maybe you like the color of your eyes. Maybe you appreciate your sense of humor, the quality of your voice, or your kindness to others. Maybe there was a challenge in your life that you handled well or an event where you carried yourself with grace and intelligence.

And while you're listing the qualities you like about yourself, you might want to include things you like in general—the pleasures in life that you cherish and that make you feel alive. Interestingly enough, often what we love in the world around us and in others is a reflection of what we love in ourselves.

To give you some ideas, here are a few loves and likes that are on my list: *I love the garden. I love the feel and smell of the earth. I love the fragrance in the summer an hour after sunrise, when everything begins surrendering to the warmth. I love the word "very." I love breezes on my face and in my hair. I love the sun on my skin, with clouds passing through it. I love the smell of puppies. I love driving fast with the music too loud. I love being alone when the sun is setting. I love the face of every child. I love two A.M. when everyone is in bed safe and sound. I love reggae, UB-40. I love Vivaldi. I love Celine Dion. I love good food: I'd rather have a meal than dessert. I love a good joke. I love warm rain or an unexpected storm. I love books and movies. I love grace and intelligence. I love a good, long shower. I love this planet. I love life.*

Practical Steps for
Taking Charge of Your Attitude

The following reminders may be helpful in getting you started on the path of looking and feeling your best, or in fueling your progress if you've already begun. Remember, even if you choose to take action with only one of these practical steps, that one change may significantly improve your life. Rather than thinking of these exercises as tasks, you might look at them as gifts—opportunities to discover the wealth and riches you already have within yourself. Open them at your own pace and enjoy the fun surprises they may hold.

COMMIT TO LIVING BEYOND THE DASH

The first step to change begins with an awareness of your current attitudes. I recommend noticing and possibly writing down observations you may make about your attitudes toward aging and the way you live day to day. Questions you might ask yourself: *Do I embrace the aging process as a means of growth that is fundamental to my journey in life? Do I resent or dread the aging process? Do I remember to live each day fully, focusing on the journey rather than the destination?* As you sharpen your awareness about these attitudes, try making a verbal or written commitment, a personal mission statement about how you wish to live, then consciously work to alter or let go of unhelpful attitudes.

INVOKE THE POWER OF YOUR OWN WISDOM

Take this opportunity to do an inventory of the life lessons you've learned. When in your life has an experience clued you in to the secret of your own success? Can you remember other instances when you made an attitude adjustment that empowered you? How have you successfully weathered earlier life occurrences by re-creating aspects of yourself?

EMBRACE THE IDEA OF HAVING FUN AS IMPORTANT TO HEALTHY LIVING

If you're carrying around so many shoulds and musts that you're overwhelmed by the thought of attempting even one new thing, no matter how positive, take this opportunity to dump those old attitudes—literally. Write down all those tired ideas that self-improvement has to be serious backbreaking work and throw them out. Now give yourself permission to have fun on your journey toward looking and feeling your best.

TAKE CHARGE OF YOUR INTERNAL VOICE

Today, right now, begin to attune your awareness to how you speak to yourself. If you are being overly self-critical and unsupportive, make it your goal to change your internal voice to that of an encouraging friend. Include in your notebook or journal a list of suggestions for better ways to speak to yourself, particularly in situations where you tend to be judgmental.

FOCUS YOUR ATTENTION ON WHAT YOU LOVE AND VALUE, NOT ON WHAT'S WRONG

Make a list of your likes, loves, and passions—from colors to books, singers to favorite cities or heroes. Then make a list of what you love about yourself.

There is a choice you have to make
In everything you do.
And you must always keep in mind,
The choice you make, makes you.

— AUTHOR UNKNOWN

CHAPTER TWO

THE MIND-BODY LINK—

COMMITTING TO WHOLE-HEALTH

Best-Kept Secret for Living:
Your Primitive Guide

IT'S MY GUESS THAT EACH OF US HAS EXPERIENCED ONE OR MORE OF THE FOLLOWING SITUATIONS, PERHAPS COUNTLESS times. Do any of these sound familiar to you?

It's nighttime and you find yourself walking to your car alone in a dark parking structure. All of a sudden, even though you appear to be completely alone, "something" tells you that you're not. You're breathing hard, and your heart begins to race. The hair on the back of your neck and your arms stands up. You get to your car, jump in, close and lock the door. And then you see a man darting away in the shadows.

You meet someone and you have an immediate "sensation" that you cannot trust this person. Perhaps you honor that instinct and guard yourself, and discover soon enough that you were right. Or maybe, because of your social training to ignore those "kinds of feelings," you don't listen.

You sit down in a chair at a beauty salon and your hairstylist touches your hair and acts in a certain way that gives you the sudden sense— "Oh, no, this stylist is going to ruin my hair today."

Although each of these situations emphasizes only feelings, we are wise to listen to them. These feelings serve as a guidance system, warning us of danger, protecting us from driving too fast so that we avoid a collision, or directing us in traffic when we're lost.

What many refer to as a sensation, a feeling, or a "something" that directed them to make a choice about a current urgent situation, I choose to call our "primitive guide."

Over our lifetime, we've often heard of women's intuition. That intuitive sense is universal. While it may sometimes communicate with us in a kind of voice, it should not be confused with the internal voice that we've already discussed. Unlike an internal voice, which is an ongoing two-way conscious dialogue inside the mind, the primitive guide functions more through feelings—both physical and emotional—speaking in a one-way communication.

Your primitive guide can be seen as the voice of your subconscious. You could say that it is your body's voice. Whatever we call it, my deep conviction is that this unsolicited guidance system is our umbilical cord to a happy, healthy life. It is our trustworthy guide to what is right or wrong for each of us. And when we use its wisdom, mentally and physically making the choices it directs us toward, we engage our mind-body link—making better choices and living better lives.

We hear our primitive guide very clearly when we're children. But unfortunately, over time, most of our cultural rearing teaches us to suppress it. We're taught not to listen to that impulse at the moment when it says, *No, don't do that,* or, *Yes, do that right now!* Because we want to be socially appropriate, or because it's easier not to rock the boat, not to be different or contrary or strange, as we become adults we start to suppress and ignore our primitive guide's messages—until we can no longer recognize them.

Somehow, during the course of becoming an industrialized society and supposed civilization, we have individually and collectively lost the ability to respect and understand the importance of listening to our primitive guide. Instead, what we register all too often, given the demands to keep up with the high-speed pace of our technological times, is the voice of fear, even panic. I want to stress that it's imperative not to mistake anxiety for our primitive guide.

When you're on an airplane and your breathing accelerates as your blood pressure soars and you think, *Oh my God, what if the plane crashes?*, you should know that's anxiety talking and not a true message from your primitive guide. The best way to discern the primitive guide from the anxious voice is to ask where the fear started. Did it start with a message in the brain, a thought, or was it a feeling that came to you naturally and organically? If the former, let your internal voice gently assure you that you are all right; if the latter, then allow your guidance system to steer you to safety. Sometimes, you may have noticed, when that feeling tells you to be on alert for real danger, your body and mind seem to automatically shift into a state of heightened awareness in order to make the right decisions.

Obviously, the disconnection so many experience from this innate survival mechanism isn't healthy and can put us at significant risk in all kinds of situations. Therefore, getting in touch with our primitive guide can be a real longevity secret. Just think—if you had a built-in navigational system that sent you signals about what choices were right and wrong for your whole-health, wouldn't you want to take advantage of that information? Well, you can—provided that you tune or re-tune yourself to receive the signals.

Before I realized I needed to reconnect, I often had to turn to friends after I'd made wrong choices and say, "I knew I shouldn't have done that. Something told me that I shouldn't." After enough of these experiences, I recognized that it wasn't "something" telling me what I needed to hear: It was me. I had to learn to trust, a process that has changed the course of my life for the better on more than one occasion.

Even though most of us lose contact with this amazing primitive intelligence, I believe that if we make a conscious effort and practice enough, we can regain access. In fact, just by choosing to reinstate your relationship with your primitive guide, you will soon detect it, perhaps vaguely at first, then more and more clearly. Then you can begin using it.

I want to point out that the power of your attitude—as expressed through your internal voice—can strongly help or hinder how you're able to access your primitive guide. Remember, your cells are listening.

By the way, our primitive guide can tell us what is right and wrong not only for basic survival, but for many situations we encounter—whether in response to an opportunity or challenge, another person, a food, a job, a lifestyle change, or a medical choice. No matter what our aging options are, without the use of our primitive guide, we can't make those choices in a *whole* way.

MAKING WHOLE CHOICES: AGING INTELLIGENTLY

When the reality of my own aging first threw me into such a tailspin, I didn't realize I had any say in what was happening to me. Of course, as I recounted earlier, my first lesson was discovering that I could change my attitude and feelings of helplessness by embracing the notion that I did have some options. Then I had to decide which ones were right for me.

In the relatively short time since I began to look at those different choices, there has been an explosion in the sheer number of aging options. Science has also taken a quantum leap. Ten years ago, living until the age of seventy-five was considered a healthy average life span. Today, theorists propose that an ordinary life span can extend to 120! The body's slowing down brought on by the aging process was previously understood to be natural and inevitable, but experts now tell us that we can postpone much of that slowing down. With breakthrough evidence that establishes aging as a disease, these experts suggest that it is not inevitable that we age.

We're learning that disorders of the cells such as Parkinson's disease can be treated with fetal tissue stem-cell transplants that can actually reverse the symptoms of the disease. Likewise, a disease-free elderly person can be given stem cells that multiply to give him or her the cognitive ability of a person up to ten years younger—within a year.

In fact, the products I've developed for my skin-care line—purely over-the-counter topical treatments—have been shown to reverse the aging action of the cells within the skin of the face, by as much as five years.

However old or young I might appear right now, if I choose to take advantage of the choices that are now or will soon be available from the field of anti-aging, there is every chance that my appearance will have changed far less when I'm sixty-five. It will be up to me to continue to work out, to maintain healthy nutrition, and to practice my other whole-health principles. What this means is that in fifteen years, I could look as I do now and also have the same mental ability, energy resources, muscle tone, and possibly the same amount of elastin and collagen in my skin.

Choices will be arising about all of the most common aging symptoms: problems with hair loss or graying, slowing down of memory, decline of hand-eye coordination, wearing out of joints, decrease of tissue plumpness, disorders of the digestive process, loss of bladder control, decrease of the ability of the liver to process toxins. We'll face decisions about the body's increasing vulnerability to diseases, its lowered resistance to common pollutants in tap water and poor-quality air, the depletion of energy due to the thyroid's deceleration, and diminished sex drive.

In the chapters that follow, some of the leaders in the antiaging field will elaborate on the causes and treatments that are available now, in the foreseeable future, and beyond. They're exciting and somewhat daunting, but I hope you feel motivated and encouraged by the knowledge that you have options. What's also important, I discovered through trial and error, is to make those choices in whole. By that I mean not just developing an action plan to address the aging process in visual terms; instead, plan to develop a whole-living plan that addresses your visual appearance along with your energy level and capacity, your memory, and your emotional and spiritual growth as a human being.

There are plenty of examples you might see around you right now of individuals treating their aging process just on the basis of their appearance. That's a choice, if that person says to herself, I'm going to look great, whatever I have to do. If I have to take a pill every day, if I have to take human growth hormone shots every day, if I have to go to Europe and get sheep shots every year, I'm going to do it so I look great.

She will no doubt achieve a better-looking, younger-looking, and possibly even longer life. But, boy, it's going to be pretty shallow. Because then she'll be living in fear of the day that those things run out. She isn't using her additional time, younger looks, health, or energy and ability to fulfill herself as a human being.

Making whole-aging choices is based on the assumption that if we can live longer, we should grasp that the quality of life must be a priority. Otherwise, it's just going to be a longer, miserable life!

This is not to say that there's anything wrong with wanting to look better. As I confessed earlier, the first signs of aging that really shook me up were the ones I saw in the mirror. That forty-two-year-old woman looked fatigued. She looked stressed and anxious. And I was. Lines that I never had before were developing. My skin, for the first time, looked thin; I later learned that it had lost its plumpness because of a decrease in collagen. I had also lost my color, caused in part by poorer circulation and thinning skin, as well as more dead surface cells hiding my natural color. My usually olive complexion had an almost gray cast.

These visual signs of aging were the ones I chose to address first. As a matter of fact, that was the main impetus behind developing anti-aging skin-care products—to help myself. After all, if they could help me, I could share them with other women.

But just looking better and looking younger weren't enough; nor is living longer what it's all about. Again, I had to examine what quality of life I wanted. In the end, I made the decision that if I don't live a day longer than I would have without any anti-aging help, that's fine with me. I simply want to live better. For my whole-health, I have decided that the options from anti-aging will offer me a better quality of life in my old age. When all is said and done, I do intend to have an old age. And I know that I'm going to die. My choice is to have a better, happier, healthier life until that moment—whether I'm hit by a bus tomorrow or I'm ninety-five years old in my garden, bent over my flowers, trying to decide which one to pick.

BASICS OF WHOLE-HEALTH

Since I'm a woman who has long sought information about just what constitutes healthy living, my bookshelves reveal such a vast array of materials that I would probably need two more lifetimes to peruse them all. (Sound familiar to anyone?) From the many that I have read, I've gained a good deal of helpful knowledge. At the same time, a majority of health guides tend to make the process of getting and staying healthy seem far too arduous. In response, I've tried to simplify the process for myself and to define my own goals. Very simply, my concept of whole-health is that we do our very best to stay in touch with all the senses that we were given.

According to *Webster's Dictionary*, our five senses—sight, hearing, smell, taste, and touch—are each a "specialized animal function or mechanism basically involving a stimulus and a sense organ," each function "constituting a unit distinct from other functions (as movement or thought)." In other words, connection to our senses is the foundation for the health of our bodies, minds, and emotions.

Take the ability of the body to move. Your senses give you the primary command to let you know when you may need or want to move. Your senses also give meaning to the act of motion, connecting you to what's going on outside and inside of you. Take, for instance, what's known as a runner's high. If you've ever experienced it, you may be aware that your heightened state of well-being is caused by chemicals in the brain that are triggered by your senses: your tactile senses that let you feel the wind on your face and your heart and lungs pumping, along with the sights, smells, and sounds inside and around you. The exhilaration of being sensually connected in this fashion is that it continues to feel good when you stop running.

Staying in touch with my senses has shown me the importance of the mind-body link by involving me as a whole person—helping me attune my awareness to how I'm feeling physically, mentally, emotionally, and spiritually. And with a whole awareness of how I'm really doing, I'm able to better care for myself and my health, using my senses, my primitive guide, and my internal voice to make decisions about what specifically will work for me—and what won't.

These innate capacities that we've been discussing make up your very own whole-health first-aid kit.

If you aren't feeling well or are in need of general preventative health advice, I would always recommend that you seek professional medical guidance. At the same time, I'm concerned when I hear about women who have placed the entire control for their well-being in their physicians' hands. The fact is, as the best doctors and surgeons are known to say, patients who take an active role in their own healing will heal more quickly and more successfully than those who don't.

The bottom line is that in every area of your health, *you are the best authority on you.* For that reason, I've made an effort over the years to know what a doctor is looking for when, for example, he or she gives me a particular test, to know what it means when she or he checks my blood pressure or cholesterol. If you don't know such things, always ask. And when you go in for your regular physical or gynecological exam, feel free not only to ask what the findings mean, but also to volunteer any information about aspects of your health that the doctor may not ask about. Ask for the free brochures available to answer your questions; almost every medical office has them.

Many of us recognize the value of such regular physical checkups, but to my knowledge, no one in the health community has yet instituted an annual checkup that assesses all the areas of our lifestyle. This is in spite of the fact that so many experts are looking at the mind-body link as a basis for good health. Fortunately for us, until such an official exam is developed, I've got a do-it-yourself whole-health checkup which has served me well over the past twenty years and which I'm happy to pass on.

Since my birthday falls a few days after the New Year, at a traditional time for reflecting on the past year and looking toward the future, I developed the annual habit of sitting down with pen and paper as early as mid-November. Taking as much time as I need in the year's remaining four to six weeks, I do an inventory of my life, a checklist of what's working and what isn't. Often I'll begin just by writing down how I'm feeling in general. Then I'll focus in on different areas and list those that I'm pleased about, and those that I'm not, and from there I'll make decisions about what I can and can't change, which choices are feasible and which aren't.

Of course, when things aren't working, I don't let them slide until November; on some level, I try to check in with myself throughout the year. But this annual process allows me to look at the big picture, so that by January first, I will have made a list of anywhere from one to five priorities—things that I may stop, start, or continue doing. These are usually significant life decisions.

What counts in this process is to assess how I feel, not how someone else wants me to be. Am I okay with this aspect of myself? Do I accept myself as I am? If not, can I accept that I'm going to work slowly and determinedly to change it?

In my twenties, I used this approach to get in touch with my feelings about others telling me how I should look and about the importance of taking care of myself—for myself. When I entered my thirties, I made a list of some of my habits and quirks that had been fun, interesting, and perhaps charming in my twenties but that I didn't think were going to continue to work for me—and chose to discard them from my lifestyle. One of the first things to go, thanks to the realization that I wanted to quit—and my husband's comment about how unpleasant it was to see me smoking—was cigarettes.

As I entered my forties, another mannerism I let go was my hearty use of choice four-letter words. When I was younger, my family, friends, and coworkers found it absolutely charming that I looked and acted one way but spoke another. Harry used to call me his foul-mouthed Mary Tyler Moore. But for a forty-something-year-old, use of such salty expletives wasn't so amusing, especially given my goal of learning to age with grace and intelligence. My habit was still probably surprising, but no longer as charming. As a result of consciously deciding to forgo some colorful parts of my vocabulary, I have expanded my knowledge and passion for the beauty of the English language and its amazing range of descriptive ways to communicate.

(Recently, filming a television series, I must confess that my abstaining from "picturesque" four-letter words suffered a serious setback.)

Then there was my previous tendency to get up in the midst of any restaurant, anyplace in the world, and tell some of the bawdiest jokes ever heard on the face of the earth, often entailing minutes of detail. No mere one-liners, some of these jokes could go on as long as seven or eight minutes. When I did my annual checklist a few years ago, I made the decision not to stop doing something I truly enjoy, but to be a little more conservative about when and where I choose to share these jokes. I couldn't stop altogether, because my husband—who used to be concerned about my uninhibited joke telling—requested that I resume it. He discovered that any initial embarrassment he had felt was overshadowed by the enjoyment of sharing my humor with others.

My annual checklist has covered everything: the way I feel about my body, energy, health, work, and friendships; what's working in my daily routine; whether the extra projects I've undertaken are fulfilling me or draining me; whether my internal voice is empowering me or not; how connected I feel to my primitive guide; whether I'm doing my best to stay in touch with my senses; how I feel about what I'm giving to others and what I'm getting back.

Several good friends have adopted the use of the annual checklist. As for its timing, some start before the holiday season, in keeping with New Year's resolutions; others like to do it in conjunction with their birthdays. You can do it as part of spring cleaning, when you may be going through closets to oust things that don't work for you any longer. Or, like some of my friends who are mothers, you may choose to start your list in the summer and begin your action plan in September, the beginning of the school year. Or, by all means, you can start it today.

Just as I have learned so much about myself from this process, I have been very lucky to learn from my friends who have shared their feelings and concerns after doing their own inventories. One friend then in her late forties (who happens to be in the entertainment industry) found that the industry's demands that she look, act, and be younger were no longer working for her. Since she is very stylish and has always taken great care with her exercise and nutrition, her figure and overall demeanor were as youthful as ever. But in spite of good skin care and protection, her face was showing visible signs of age. On the one hand, she was uncomfortable with doing anything cosmetic or artificial in response to industry pressure; on the other hand, she recognized the reality of winning in a business that puts such a high premium on the appearance of youth and youthful energy. The issue was affecting her work, her income, and her self-esteem.

"What do you think I should do?" my friend asked. "Should I have cosmetic surgery?"

As gently as I could, I gave her my honest opinion that if surgery was something she wanted to do for herself, now was a good time to do it. But to do it for the business alone was a bad idea. As we talked more, she agreed that, for the longest time, she'd been looking tired, no matter how much rest she got; she didn't like the way she looked even to herself.

She decided to investigate her options. Eventually, she chose cosmetic surgery for her eyes and was overjoyed to say that she felt and looked like herself again—from a decade earlier.

Another dear friend, in her late fifties, showed me the lengthy hit list she had made for cosmetic surgery. When she asked for my input, it was the opposite of what I'd told my other friend. What she was contemplating was way too much all at once, like she was having a knee-jerk reaction to the aging process. In fact, my recommendation was not surgery at all. In an effort to stave off aging, my friend had dieted too much, trying to be as thin as she was in her girlhood. She had used dieting as a fix-all without exercising because, she admitted, she didn't like going to the gym. As a result, she looked gaunt and weak—not just because she'd gotten older but because she had lost so much weight. After we talked over her options, she decided to slowly put some weight back on, enough so that she looked and felt healthier.

During that process, she also started taking vitamin and mineral supplements, something she had ignored before. Instead of going to the gym to work out, she took up yoga and started a dance class. Within six months, she was utterly rejuvenated. Her skin regained its youthful tone, her hair grew in thicker and shinier, and her eyes sparkled with health, energy, and strength. She looked phenomenal and felt better than ever. Her whole-health had transformed.

Later on, when this particular friend was in her mid-sixties, still in fantastic shape, she decided that she was ready for some plastic surgery. Agreeing with my "less is more" philosophy, rather than going through multiple major procedures, she chose only to have her eyes done, later having laser resurfacing of her face along with a chemical peel of her neck and décolleté. She was thrilled with the outcome, not to mention the saving of time and money that she could devote to some of the creative and charitable projects she had been undertaking with her new-found reservoir of well-being.

Another girlfriend, a working mother in her late thirties, confided that when she sat down to do her annual inventory, although she was pleased with almost every area of her life, she had a strong sense at the end of every day that something was missing. She felt good about her work and marriage, about her role as a mother and friend. She felt happy about her home and community, about the helping projects that fulfilled her spirit, and, for the most part, her health and appearance. But her senses were connecting her to a feeling of melancholy—as if there was something she had forgotten to do for herself.

It helped my friend to hear that what she was feeling is virtually universal for mothers, especially those with younger children. Almost every mother I know, as well as many women I know who are caregivers by nature, feel that they keep ending up last on the list of priorities, even when they make a concerted effort to do otherwise. While this situation may feel like one of those things over which we don't have much control, these women often confess to a sense of growing discomfort that could turn into rage.

To pinpoint where she was coming up short, my friend then returned to her list and went into further detail about each area of her life. What was missing, she concluded, was enough time in the day to accomplish what she needed to do for others and for herself. The best fix for her—and for every mother I know—is the daily practice of Ten Minutes of Joy, which we'll talk about later on. My friend was very skeptical that ten minutes a day were going to make much of a difference. To her astonishment, the daily practice of taking out that little amount of time, completely for herself, immediately brought her more satisfaction—whether she used it to curl up in a hammock in her backyard, stroll through her favorite bookstore, dance hip-hop alone in her living room, or have her morning coffee outdoors with the sunrise. Before long, the vague feeling that something was missing was no longer there. She said she felt a wholeness that she hadn't experienced since her early twenties. For my friend, Ten Minutes of Joy became a life-changing experience.

Whether an annual personal checkup will change your life or not, it will definitely heighten your awareness of such issues as self-image, body image, health level, job, relationships, marriage, sex life, family, financial status, and emotional and spiritual life.

With that awareness, you may want to make priorities for change. And to do that, you might find the following tool helpful.

THE 1 TO 10 SCALE

I run my life with the 1 to 10 scale. It's easy and just about foolproof, as long as you are completely honest. Any time, you can rate your feelings about choices that may range from the mundane to the vital. Here are examples of some basic daily living questions:

- On a scale of 1 to 10, how much do I want to stay home for dinner? How much do I want to go out to dinner?
- On a scale of 1 to 10, would I prefer pasta for dinner? Or would I prefer chicken?
- On a scale of 1 to 10, would I prefer to go to sleep early? Or would I prefer to stay up an hour later and read a good book?
- On a scale of 1 to 10, how much do I want to cut my hair? On a scale of 1 to 10, how pleased am I with the way it is now?

When Harry and I select a movie to see, we use the 1 to 10 scale. When deciding what to order in restaurants, I ask waiters to tell me which entrée they prefer on a scale of 1 to 10.

Few tools have saved me as much time and stress as this exercise. I might ask myself: On a scale of 1 to 10, do I want to wear the blue dress or the lavender? Maybe I thought of the lavender first, but on a 1 to 10 scale, the lavender is a 7 and the blue is a 9.

This approach also helps you to get in touch with how you're feeling. Have you been blue lately? Have you been for a while, or is it temporary? Ask yourself on a 1 to 10 scale: How happy am I—in general or at this moment?

This exercise works as well for the day-to-day easy decisions as it does for the more meaningful decisions, such as: On a scale of 1 to 10, how pleased am I with the life I've lived so far? And the ultimate 1 to 10 question: How much do I like myself? Evaluate your answers, and if you're not satisfied with the number, think about taking steps to change how you're feeling about that particular situation.

LIVING CEREMONIES

The idea of having a daily or regular routine may seem less than glamorous. But to me, my daily rituals not only give me structure and organization, they also make my life sweeter and more meaningful. Rather than seeing my routine as boring or mundane, I think of it in terms of ceremonies and celebrations.

Although those words may be better suited for bigger occasions, I use them in connection to all my regular habits—whether they take place daily, weekly, monthly, or annually. I have so many ceremonies that have become an integral part of how I live, I'm often not always aware of them.

It was my husband who brought my waking-up ceremony to my attention. My routine is to greet the day quietly and slowly. First I like to open the curtains and let in only natural light. Then I open a door or window to feel the breeze on my face, the temperature and movement of the air. For a few moments, I enjoy simply inhaling and exhaling to connect with place and time. As my senses awaken, I next like to put on music that makes me feel good. After that, I'm ready for the rest of my morning. Starting the morning like this sets the tone for the rest of the day. No matter how busy and crowded my schedule, my early-awakened feelings of calm and appreciation tend to stay with me. Even when crises come from nowhere—and they do—when I've established the right tone, instead of bolting out of bed and hitting the ground running, I'm better equipped to respond.

Shared rituals are some of my favorites. As I mentioned earlier, when I was single, the highlight of my week was my Friday-night celebration with a regular group of six or so friends to watch *Dallas*. Every week, I made the same chili and corn bread. Offering another menu would have been sacrilege.

Happy couples often report that one of the keys to a successful marriage is in certain activities that may seem absolutely banal to outsiders, even downright boring, but give them an abundance of peace and comfort. For Harry and me, not a week goes by that we don't have sushi on Sunday nights. We have turned down the most lavish invitations because we hate to miss our sushi ceremony. If you asked us what's so great about it, we'd be hard-pressed to explain. And yet we anticipate the event with great excitement, relishing it with no less pleasure than the previous week.

One night a week, usually Wednesday, we go out to dinner to socialize with friends, and one night a week, usually Saturday, we go out on a romantic date, just the two of us. Typically we choose dinner and a movie. It's not so much what we do that makes our date night special but the fact that we give this time to our relationship once a week, every week. It's one of the best ways we have to keep our marriage fresh and new. In fact, after over a decade and a half of marriage, we've frequently had strangers mistake us for newlyweds.

Sunday brunch is another of my loves. I enjoy cooking and having family and friends over. In the summer, I especially like to gather in the garden, enjoy a good meal, and relax the afternoon away.

One of my other rituals, at least once a month, is a facial on Saturday and massage on Sunday. For me, these are professional necessities. (The practice of getting regular massage, for both women and men, is prevalent throughout most of Europe, by the way.) When it comes to whole-health, facial and body massage are terrific for you on every level—stimulating your circulation, cell growth, muscle tone, and energy, at the same time totally relaxing you and allowing your body to release toxins. Great for your body, mind, and spirit, massage is one of the best things you can do for yourself on a regular basis.

There is much debate about which style of massage is most beneficial. The answer is going to depend on personal preference and individual health histories, and it's one that your primitive guide can best provide. Remember: It's essential that the person touching you be someone you're comfortable with. If you prefer a woman instead of a man, feel free to request it. If you prefer someone with a strong touch rather than a softer touch, by all means ask for it. Within a minute of lying down on the table and being touched, if you get a feeling that you don't like, give yourself permission to get up and say, "I'm so sorry, this isn't working." I have done it more than once. Is it embarrassing? Yes. But I'd rather do that than make nice for an hour while someone touches me and I feel unpleasant, uncomfortable, and unhappy.

If treating yourself to regular massages isn't in your budget, you might offer to trade massages with a friend or partner. Let your senses enjoy the giving as much as the receiving.

Considering how hard so many of us women work in our professions and in taking care of everyone around us, we should each try to pamper ourselves in daily, regular ways whenever possible. Pampering doesn't have to cost a cent. One of my dearest passions is reading literary fiction. Since most days I do a lot of reading for work—whether it's scripts for acting jobs or scientific journals for skin-care research—snuggling up with a good novel is a holiday. If left to my own devices, I can stay up all night reading.

The idea of having a regimen, or a regulated course of activity, might seem an imposition. Yet because I have chosen them, none of the daily ceremonies I have for taking care of myself feel imposed on me. If for any reason I'm unable to do a part of my routine—such as my three skin-care steps or my workout—I feel that I'm missing something.

Many of the details of the following routines are contained in subsequent chapters. For the moment, I'd like to offer some examples of how I incorporate whole-health principles into a typical day:

- Upon waking: Every morning after rising, I do my regular three steps of skin care.
- Stretching: Every morning, early, I do yoga. Even if I can't continue into my full workout, every morning of my life, whether I'm in a hotel room, my home, or someone else's home, I do the yoga-like routine that I created for myself, incorporating stretch and dance movements.
- Exercise: Anywhere from three days a week to every day, I do a resistance workout with cords. After that, two to three times a week, I power-walk outside or on the treadmill. Whether I do cords and the treadmill in the morning may depend on that day's schedule, although I always do my yoga ceremony early in the morning. And I breathe.
- Breakfast, lunch, dinner, snacks: When it comes to eating, I avoid restrictive rules, generally following the guidelines of the *Diet for Life* (see page 65) that have been my mainstay for twenty years. What's important is that I take the time to enjoy and savor the food and to make sure that I listen to my body—eating when I'm hungry, not eating when I'm not, and putting down my fork when I've had enough. For my midmorning or midafternoon snacks, I might have a handful of almonds or treat myself to one square of dark, pure chocolate.
- Supplements: I take vitamins and minerals during breakfast and lunch. Some people take supplements either before or after their meal. My theory—which has been successful so far—is that if I take them with food, I'll be less likely to upset my stomach.
- Getting in touch with the world: Every day, if I have the time, one of my long-loved ceremonies is having breakfast and then quickly reading the newspaper. On days when I don't catch the morning paper, I watch the news on TV at some point before the day is over. (I try not to watch TV news just before going to sleep because it can leave me agitated.)

- Staying in touch with friends: Each day, no matter where I am in the world, no matter how hard I'm working, I call one friend who isn't a business associate. Because the entertainment business is so competitive and self-involving, it's far too easy to isolate yourself from the people you really care about.

- Making contact: Once or twice weekly, in addition to my daily phone call, I'll call another friend whom I haven't seen in a while and say, "I'm coming over to hug you." That's all I do. I'll pull into my friend's driveway, leave the engine running, and jump out; we'll hug, acknowledge how much we miss and care for each other, and then say good-bye until the next time when we can hang out. It's my way to experience that sense of having a village or neighborhood, which we all need.

- Food for thought: At some point in every day, I take a few minutes to read a paragraph from *A Manual for Living,* a recent interpretation and translation by Sharon Lebell of the teachings of the ancient philosopher Epictetus. He was a freed Roman slave whose practical wisdom never fails to connect me to the values I hold most dear.

- Gratitude: At one meal during the course of each day, I take a moment to give thanks for that meal. Which meal varies from day to day, but every day I like to acknowledge that this food and the life it supports, mine, are true gifts.

- Ten Minutes of Joy: Every day, wherever, whatever, whenever, however.

- Before retiring: Just as I do upon waking, I take three minutes for skin care.

It probably won't surprise you that I also believe in celebrating the big, important events and passages in life. That goes for somber and sad occasions marking a good-bye or a loss, just as it goes for holidays and festivities.

Earlier I described how I use the occasions of my birthday and the New Year for doing a checklist to get in touch with myself. I do something else every year to celebrate this passage from the old to the new that occurred by happenstance about fifteen years ago. Not intending to create an annual event, I got the idea that it would be fun to do something for my birthday that I'd never done before—to experience something totally new. From that year on, I planned something different every year. Each event had to be invigorating, thrilling, and actually age-defying. Every year, how I choose to spend the beginning of the year and my birthday sets the tone for the remainder of the year.

I have mentioned how, for my fortieth birthday, I trained and jumped off a mountain in Switzerland, paragliding down to a field at the base. For one birthday, I was one of the first civilians to go down the Olympic bobsled course with a gold-medal bobsled driver. Two years ago, I went up with a pilot in a P-52 Mustang—an old fighter plane with an all-Lucite cockpit—and did barrel rolls at 300 miles an hour off the coast of Malibu. In an earlier year, I went soaring for thirty minutes in a glider—a plane without an engine but with an expert pilot—over the Mojave Desert.

Doing things that are physically challenging certainly makes me continue to feel young and strong. But there have been years when I've wanted to be more low-key and have decided to simply go out to the desert, watch the sun come up, and be reflective. Once I hired a hot-air balloon to go up in the dark early morning so that I was above the mountains as the sun rose on the first day of the New Year. I loved that.

Rather than making me feel like another year has come and gone, these ceremonies rarely mark endings. Instead, they herald what's to come. Doing things that I've never done before allows me to experience them with all my senses, much in the way that children look at the world—with fresh eyes. We rarely forget our firsts: our first rainbow, our first pony ride, our first kiss, our first airplane ride. As adults we don't get as many firsts; we get jaded and desensitized. The rush of having an experience I haven't done, seen, heard, smelled, or felt before allows all my senses to renew themselves.

In setting a tone for the year to come, my annual celebration helps me keep fresh eyes during all the seasons ahead. This way, I'm better able to see the color of the sky, hear the birds in the trees and the rustle of the leaves, smell all the different scents, taste all the tastes, and, above all, really experience, enjoy, and connect to the people I love.

As you can see, routines can take on extraordinary properties when you turn them into ceremonies. You not only can set the tone for the day, week, month, or year ahead, but during tough times—anyplace, anytime—you can invent on-the-spot ceremonies to switch the energy. Feeling down? Rather than fighting it, you can actually embrace it—perhaps by taking yourself to an old-fashioned tearjerker and having a good cry. Or you can use my daily practice of calling one friend. If you don't have a friend with a spare shoulder, create a dialogue with your internal voice that will give you space to feel what you're going through and offer yourself encouragement.

Stressed? One of the best ways to shift the energy of a day that's gone downhill is to grab a favorite CD, go for a drive, and sing at the top of your lungs. If you don't have time for that, try skipping for five or ten minutes. Skipping, you should know, is no secret at all to younger generations. You're never too old to skip. Or if that's not for you, a scenic walk can help, too.

If you have only five seconds, do what I do when I need to link body and mind for dramatic results. It's known as a deep cleansing breath: Stand up straight, shoulders down, arms relaxed at your sides, and take in a slow, deep breath, filling your lungs and holding the breath for a slow count of ten. You may feel some discomfort right before you finish counting. That's okay. On ten, slowly release the air, breathing out through your mouth. Two or three cleansing breaths and you will probably feel an immediate improvement in your sense of well-being.

Breathing for energy is a whole-health requirement. Try doing one sit-up without inhaling or exhaling. Then try inhaling through your nose before you move, and exhaling through your mouth as you sit up. The breath supports and energizes you. Often, people who dislike exercise are not breathing. When they start to breathe properly, it changes their whole attitude.

Taking time to breathe in the aroma of your food before you eat, and in between bites, not only helps you enjoy the eating experience, it should also slow down how fast you eat your food and help you control portions. Besides, like water, air is calorie-free. A perfect segue to weight loss—our next chapter's topic.

Practical Steps for Committing to Whole-Health

As we review the main ideas from this chapter, I offer reminders of practical suggestions you may wish to explore for taking action. The attainment of whole-health is, without a doubt, an ongoing process. Therefore, these steps can be taken slowly, perhaps by trying one new approach now and another down the road. Feel free to be creative and improvise on their themes.

ACCESS THE WISDOM OF YOUR PRIMITIVE GUIDE

First choose to honor this universal, innate capacity we all have. You may want to recall, perhaps in writing, the ways in which you have connected to your primitive guidance system in the past. Then simply acknowledge your primitive guide and be thankful for it. Consciously remind yourself to notice its messages in the days and weeks to come. Practice trusting and believing that your primitive guide can help you on a day-to-day basis.

MAKE CONNECTING TO YOUR SENSES YOUR TOP HEALTH PRIORITY

As an exercise, take one day a week to honor one of your five senses.

TAKE A WHOLE VIEW OF YOUR HEALTH

Begin to identify aspects of your living that may be impacted by the choices you make on your whole-health path. Right now, it's unnecessary to judge or assess how you're doing in these regards; just identify different areas for which health matters to you. Examples: body, mind, emotions, spirit, family, friends, romance, sex, marriage, home, finances, career, parenthood, creativity, fun, leisure, adventure, connections to culture, community, and the world, etc.

GIVE YOURSELF A WHOLE-HEALTH CHECKUP

Take as many days or weeks as you need to look at those areas that matter to you, then make a checklist of what's working in your life and what isn't. Spend some time identifying, in writing if you prefer, how you're feeling in general. In which areas do you have a sense of well-being and health? In which areas would you like to see improvement? Make sure that this is how you truly feel, not how someone else might wish to see you improve. To do that, see if you are at peace with that aspect of yourself. If not, do you accept that you're going to work slowly and determinedly to change it? Choose anywhere from one to five priorities for change—things that you are going to consciously stop, start, or continue doing in a new and better way.

SEEK PROFESSIONAL HELP AS NEEDED

If you're overdue for your annual physical checkup, regular gynecological exam, or mammogram, make those important visits part of your whole-health plan. If emotional or psychological issues have been raised for which you can use help, make finding a supportive therapist one of your priorities.

SIMPLIFY YOUR LIFE WITH THE 1 TO 10 SCALE

You can utilize this tool for important assessments and decisions or the smaller time-consuming details that can overburden the daily grind. Try it—you'll like it.

TURN ROUTINES INTO LIVING CEREMONIES

What are the activities of your typical day? As you think them over or as you travel through your day, you might want to want to make note of daily events that you enjoy, anticipate happily, or would miss if you didn't have. If you have never thought of these points in your day as ceremonies, use your imagination to find ways to acknowledge them as such by including small touches. You might use candles when serving a meal, choose a chair you love to sit in for reading time, even find special words you can say every day to a loved one. The next step is to add to your ceremonies those daily tasks and duties that you may not particularly relish. (Examples: flossing your teeth, housecleaning and cooking meals, chauffeuring kids, paying bills and handling correspondence, commuting in traffic, daily responsibilities on the job, taking care of needy or ailing family members.) Again, can you come up with ideas for making these mundane chores less burdensome and more enjoyable? (Examples: flossing as part of a beauty self-care regimen; listening to music while cleaning house or driving; wearing a special outfit for housecleaning that includes gloves and an apron with pockets for all your cleaning products and tools; taking a cooking class to focus the meal on artistry rather than duty; investing in computer software to make bill paying and money management less onerous and more interesting and fun.)

CELEBRATE YOURSELF AND LOVED ONES WITH CEREMONIES ON A WEEKLY OR MONTHLY BASIS THROUGHOUT THE YEAR

As you begin this step, note the weekly and monthly special events that are currently part of your life. Next, make a list of a few rituals you'd like to incorporate on a regular basis. Maybe you can establish one day a week as your beauty-care day: Get a massage from a professional or from a caring friend; have a home facial you give yourself or get one from an aesthetician, or with a visit to the hair or nail salon. Maybe you and your spouse want to establish one night a week as "date night." You may opt to establish one day a week as personal or family time for being out in nature. Because so many of our rituals are culturally built upon food, my suggestion is to make these regular celebrations less about what you're going to eat and more about what you're going to do and experience.

As you look over your calendar for the year ahead, make a list of birthdays and holidays that you enjoy. In planning traditional feast days, you may also wish to note some of the other senses you can pay tribute to. As you plan for your own birthday this coming year, instead of focusing on the notion of getting a year older, use it as an opportunity to set the tone for the year that will follow. Allow yourself to fantasize about what your dream birthday celebration might be—whether it's a party that you've always wanted or an experience that you've never had before. After you've spent some time fantasizing, can you come up with a realistic plan to celebrate yourself that embodies the same spirit?

 ## INCORPORATE RITUALS FOR SETTING TONES AND SHIFTING ENERGY

While none of us has a crystal ball to predict the many ways in which life doesn't run according to plan, take this opportunity to make a list of some of the more predictable situations that can and do arise to throw you off course during the day. Now bring your awareness to the ways you tend to cope that are either helpful or self-destructive. If you see consistent choices that aren't working for you, list them alongside an alternative course of action. Let the list of helpful methods become your arsenal. If you need ideas, review some of the suggestions in this chapter or ask friends what they do to successfully get out of a funk. Next, explore some ways to set a positive tone even before situations become stressful. (Examples: creating a morning ritual that lets you start your day with a smile; taking a few moments before going to sleep to review the good things in your day about which you feel grateful; drifting into sleep as you savor hopeful thoughts of tomorrow; picking a ritual for the first day of the week or month that sets a happy tone for the rest of the week or month.)

CREATE YOUR OWN RITUAL FOR REMEMBERING TO BREATHE

Pay attention to your breath, whether it's deep and cleansing or natural in and out.

One can spend a lifetime assigning blame, finding a cause "out there" for all the troubles that exist. Contrast this with the "responsible attitude" of confronting the situation, bad or good, and instead of asking, "What caused the trouble? Who was to blame?" asking, "How can I handle this present situation to make the best of it?"

ABRAHAM MASLOW

CHAPTER THREE

SAYING YES!—A DIET AND

SUPPLEMENT PLAN

Best-Kept Diet Secret: You

FOR ALL OF US WHO SUCCESSFULLY TAKE CHARGE OF A PARTICULAR ASPECT OF OUR LIVES, WE OFTEN EXPERI- ence a defining moment that first motivates a decision, then spurs action, and continues over time to keep us committed to our cause.

My defining moment in taking charge of my weight came when I was in my mid-twenties and I caught a glimpse of myself—forty pounds overweight—as I passed a full-length mirror in my home.

This coincided with the time in my life during which I'd left my acting career, in part to distance myself from an industry that required me to live up to standards of beauty that weren't right for me. During my time off, I was so relieved not to have to look a certain way for the approval of others that I lost control with food. In the process, I managed to ignore the pounds as they crept on incrementally. Oh, sure, I knew I'd put on a few pounds—five, seven, ten, even twelve or thirteen pounds. But I always thought that if I put my mind to it, I could lose the weight without a problem. I had the best intentions to get around to doing that . . . but always in the future. Inevitably, a sumptuous meal would call my name, and I kept putting it off for days, weeks, and months.

The shock of suddenly observing myself in that full-length mirror was devastating. No longer could I be in denial that it was just a few extra pounds. No longer was it going to be as easy to lose it as I'd once assumed.

Shame and anger filled me. How could I have done this to myself? The next thing I knew, my internal voice was off to the races, punishing me with derogatory adjectives like "lazy," "loathsome," "indulgent," "trapped"; telling me that I didn't have the willpower to lose the weight. In a word, I was "bad." My primitive guide, on the other hand, sent me a different message. Not concerned with doling out blame, it began then and there to direct me to what was best for me—for my health, my work, my self-esteem. I began that process by changing my internal voice. I stopped beating up on myself and instead offered myself encouraging yet firm words that it was time to change the way I'd been eating. My first piece of sound advice to myself was to go to a nutritionist.

At the time, the reality that I had a weight problem was a very painful awakening. Looking back, I'm immensely grateful for that experience, because I was able to confront myself in the mirror in that defining moment and acquire the tools that allowed me to take charge of the issue—not just at twenty-five, but for the rest of my life. In my thirties and forties, whenever I've put on weight—I give myself a five-pound leeway—I acknowledge that I've been eating and living in a way that has contributed to the weight gain. Then I skip the blame game and take action.

Let me stress that being overweight does not make you a bad person. Being overweight may make you a potentially unhealthy person. The burden on your internal organs increases the risks of respiratory disease, heart disease, high blood pressure, high cholesterol, clogged arteries, diabetes, kidney disease, and varicose veins. External bodily effects—such as fatty deposits on thighs and rear end, flabby upper arms and back, protruding stomach, swollen and sagging breasts, and a double chin—may make you look unhealthy. Moreover, obesity is second only to smoking in accelerating your aging process. That news is according to all the latest anti-aging theories as reported in *The Disease of Aging: How Not to Grow Old Before Your Time,* by Hans Kugler, Ph.D., who writes:

> Life-shortening factors like smoking cigarettes or being overweight will not just eliminate a few years but will condense the entire aging process, making us older earlier. On the other hand, factors that increase lifespans will also delay aging, rather than simply add years.

The leading life-extending factor, says Kugler, is the cessation of smoking, if you're a smoker. The second life-extending factor is maintaining normal weight—through good nutrition, supplements, and exercise.

When I was in my twenties, my defining moment with my weight came from the visual effects I saw in my mirror. Although that image continued to motivate me in my thirties and forties, I became increasingly aware of the importance of maintaining healthy weight for my overall well-being and ultimate longevity. That's been helpful, especially because, as we age, putting on weight can be easier and the process of losing it harder than when our bodies were younger and more resilient.

Again, blaming yourself for being out of shape won't get you very far. Anyone can gain weight. Being heavy may be a result of genetics and habits that started as early as infancy. Or, with age and a sedentary lifestyle, it may happen over time. For others, putting on weight may occur intermittently—due to circumstantial changes like pregnancy and childbirth, cessation of regular exercise because of injury or illness, or other marked changes in one's lifestyle—with pounds vacillating up and down between a healthy medium and a significant gain or even an unhealthy loss.

Whatever your particular pattern, overeating rarely has to do with genuine hunger or a natural drive to nourish your body. Eating too much often stems from other, more emotional reasons: depression, anger, stress, boredom, feelings of insecurity and fear, or as a way to rebel. Sometimes in our natural drive to experience pleasure—and food is a primal pleasure—we overeat privately or socially, not stopping when we're full because we don't want the party to end. Other reasons include eating on the run or dining out most of the time because of travel and work. Then there are those of us who eat unconsciously. If you eat a meal or snack at your desk at work, in front of the television at home, or while you're on the phone, you can consume two to three times as much food as you need simply because your brain hasn't registered that you've eaten. Have you ever gotten up in the middle of the night and stumbled half asleep into the kitchen to eat almost a whole carton of ice cream without even thinking about it, then wondered later why you're having such a hard time losing weight?

No matter how we got to the extra pounds, to long for the magic cure is virtually universal. You probably know what I'm talking about. Haven't we all, at one time or another, wished for that new pill or procedure or gadget or breakthrough diet that would give us effortless, overnight weight loss? If that weren't the case, the trillion-dollar diet industry would soon be out of business. How many times have you bought the latest diet and started it with the total conviction that this time was finally going to be *it*? And in no time, whether you lost a little in the interim or not, the diet stopped working. Whatever its magical secret was—high-protein/low-carbohydrate meals or food combining or exchange counting or wheat-grass shakes—was so restrictive that you couldn't live that way.

The real secret, one that hardly gets mentioned, is that the success of a diet doesn't depend on what you eat, it depends on *you*. In my own weight-loss journey, that was the most powerful lesson I had to learn. It was incredibly helpful to gain an awareness of why I was overeating and to start changing those habits. It was extremely valuable to educate myself about good nutrition and to have a nutritionist assist me in developing a way of eating that was sensible, safe, and satisfying. But without my own commitment, none of that would have mattered. The power had to lie within me.

Guess what? Once you accept that you are your own best-kept diet secret and that the magic cure lies within you, not only will you be more likely to lose the weight and keep it off, you will probably do it in a quicker, less stressful fashion. The beauty of this secret is that no matter how many diet gimmicks have failed you in the past, *starting right here and now, you're in charge, and you already have everything it takes to be successful.*

One minor hurdle for me was my antipathy to the word "diet." To be sure, it has fallen so far out of favor that it seems to have become a four-letter word. In the past, the idea that one was going on a diet brought up all kinds of restrictive connotations, right in sync with the notion that overeating made one bad. Going on a diet was like being sent to jail, where servings of lettuce passed for meals. The word conjured visions of obsessive behavior, of great longing for untouchable foods, of need, hunger denial, even starvation. This wasn't just my ignorance. After all, I'd been on grapefruit-and-coffee crash diets before, and they were pretty miserable.

For my own purposes, I have made peace with the word. A diet, as I use the word, is simply a nutritious way of eating. Instead of seeing it as a jail term full of imposed rules and regulations, I see it as a range of delicious food in intelligent portions. Instead of having to say, "No, I can't eat that now, I'm on a diet," I'm able to choose food that's better for me and say, "I'm going to eat this—because 'diet' is what I eat." Though I may choose to avoid certain foods or ample quantities, I am saying yes to the joyful process of creating the me I want and life I want.

Three variations on a nutritious way to eat follow. The first is an updated version of the *30-Day Diet to Lose,* which I use whenever extra pounds have crept on and can be repeated for as many months as necessary. Because our bodies and metabolisms are all unique, it is not realistic to set a precise number of pounds that each individual can expect to lose in the first thirty days—although anywhere from five to ten pounds has been commonly reported, even higher in the first month for those who are significantly changing their eating habits. If one continues the *30-Day Diet to Lose* for subsequent months, a consistent loss of five pounds per month can be reasonably expected.

Seven sample days of my updated *Diet for Life* are also included. For maintaining healthy weight after the *30-Day Diet to Lose,* the *Diet for Life* has been more than a way of nutritious eating for me; it's been a way of life.

Finally, if you have a lot of weight to lose and want to jump-start the process—with your doctor's permission—or if you need to quickly get rid of a five- to ten-pound weight gain, you'll find the one-week *Bikini Diet.* With very low calories and high fiber, the *Bikini Diet* is highly effective, and for those seven days, you will not be deprived nutritionally. It should not be followed any longer than the one week, however, and should not be used more than once a year.

One of the problems with diets that restrict you from eating certain kinds of food is that by making them taboo, you end up craving and consuming them even more than if you allowed yourself to eat them in modest proportions. That's the reason I no longer believe in a list of forbidden foods. My motto is never say never. Instead, I prefer to classify different foods and food groups into two basic categories—those we need and those we don't.

You're probably aware that food is fuel for the body. Without it, the body cannot function or survive. Consider the analogy of treating your body as you might a prized sports car: You would always choose the high-premium fuel that keeps it in greater running order, as opposed to the lower-grade fuel that might cause poor performance and breakdowns, wouldn't you? Therefore, it makes sense, and is a caring thing to do for ourselves, to eat the foods that give us more of what we need.

You may be familiar with the "big six," the basic nutrients found in food: vitamins, minerals, proteins, fats, carbohydrates, and water. Simply stated, when digested and metabolized, these nutrients interact with our bodies' enzymes and coenzymes to produce energy, along with other healthy actions such as cell and tissue growth.

Proteins are considered the building blocks of our cells, containing the amino acids our bodies require for building and maintaining healthy blood and tissues, fighting disease, and repair. Foods that give us complete proteins from animal sources—like poultry, fish, beef, pork, and dairy products—are said to be the most efficient suppliers of the amino acids that proteins deliver. At the same time, foods that give us incomplete proteins from vegetable sources—like nuts, soybeans, lentils, and other legumes—can be combined with other food sources of protein, such as whole grains and other complex carbohydrates, to become complete and effectively nourish us.

In spite of the bad rap given to carbs in recent years, you should know that they top the list of what we need, as our main source of fuel for energy and endurance. Our central nervous system and brain functions rely heavily on nutrients from carbohydrates. Food sources include vegetables, fruits, cereals, breads, pasta, potatoes, and rice. Granted, not all carbohydrates rate high on the scale of what we need. Broken down into three classifications, the most needed are those that are called complex (vegetables, fruits, legumes, high-fiber grains); followed next by simple starchy carbs (potatoes, rice, pastas, and breads and cereals made with natural ingredients); and then the least needed type, processed carbohydrates (white breads, white-sugar-sweetened food, cookies, chips, colas, etc.). Complex and simple carbs give us vitamins, minerals, and roughage in their most natural form and convert into blood sugar more slowly. The processed, refined carbs, on the other hand, are rapidly converted into glucose, which can cause blood-sugar imbalance, mood swings, and other ailments that range from tooth decay to diabetes to heart disease. While the refined carbs should be minimized, we should also use good judgment about our portions of even necessary carbs.

Another much maligned but essential nutrient is fat. Besides supplying us with the proper insulating material to keep out the cold, fat helps us produce the natural oils in our body that assist in digestion and elimination and help prevent our skin from becoming dehydrated. The digestion of fat allows chemical messages to flow to the brain and tell our bodies that we're sated. All of that said, let me note that much of the fat we require daily is routinely available in the nutritious foods we eat, such as lean animal protein, fattier fish, and vegetable sources.

All fats, however, are not equal. We generally don't need saturated fats (fats that are solid at room temperature), like those from fatty meats, cream, butter, and cheese. You may already know that consuming too much saturated fat results in an increase of your LDL cholesterol (the harmful form of cholesterol that we all need to keep low), potentially leading to blocked arteries and heart disease. We also don't need any artificially produced fats that have words like "hydrogenated" or "partially hydrogenated" on their label. Not only are they often saturated, but many contain trans-fatty acids. If you think about how these products are made—heated with processes that include being chemically and molecularly altered after having ions shot through them—you can imagine what they do in your body.

Fats we do need come in the form of monounsaturated fat, which is liquid at room temperature (olive oil, canola oil). These fats have single bonds in their chemical composition and break down naturally in our bodies. More complicated is the metabolic processing of polyunsaturated fats (safflower, corn, and soy oils), which have double bonds and can break down in our bodies in ways that may not help fend off free-radical formation (more on that in a moment). We'll talk about other fats we do need with our experts.

Although I advocate a low-fat diet—as the *30-Day Diet to Lose,* the *Diet for Life,* and the *Bikini Diet* are—I must offer a word of warning about some packaged products that tout themselves as low-fat or nonfat. In order to taste good, many of these products compensate with high levels of sugar or unnatural additives that you don't need. If you check the food label and don't know what half of the ingredients mean, it's a good bet that by consuming them you're losing whatever health benefits you might have gained from going low-fat. At the same time, some low-fat and fat-free products that are made with a minimum of chemicals—such as low-fat cream cheese, low-fat or fat-free sour cream, and fat-free mayonnaise—offer benefits of calorie reduction and good taste.

All natural food sources contain varying amounts and types of vitamins, minerals, and water. We'll soon hear from two experts about some of the ways that vitamins and minerals serve to regulate the metabolic process, aiding in the development of tissue and bone as well as the chemical reactions in our cells. Water, which makes up 70 percent of our body weight, is what transports all these wonderful nutrients to our cells, tissues, and organs. Interestingly, our bodies' water composition matches that of the earth—which is likewise 70 percent water. In fact, the salinity (or salt content) of our blood and other bodily fluids mirrors the salinity of the sea. Water flushes toxins and waste from our cells and is needed for nearly all our bodies' processes. Without adequate water, our cells would basically suffocate.

Because our need for water far exceeds what we get from food, it is essential to drink more of it—eight or more glasses (eight ounces each) a day. Twenty-five years ago, I instituted the habit of drinking a glass of water a half hour before mealtime and either hot or iced tea with each of my meals. In addition to letting me feel full and quenching my thirst, fluid intake is great for my skin, digestion, and for hydrating during exercise. Although caffeinated coffee falls on my list of things we don't need, you have to drink really strong tea to feel the effects of its caffeine; there are also many decaffeinated and herbal teas to choose from. Tea is a staple beverage for all three of my diets.

Carrying a sports water bottle with you can be a handy reminder. Or, if you're around the house or in the office a lot, do what I do and find a lovely glass to sip from. The operative word, by the way, is sip. That's because the faster you drink the water, the faster you eliminate it; the more slowly you sip, the longer your body holds on to and benefits from it. Plus, sipping throughout the day is much more comfortable than throwing down a glass of water in a couple of gulps.

30-DAY DIET TO LOSE

Some basic guidelines may be helpful before you get started. Think of them not so much as rules but as suggestions to support your efforts in saying yes to good health.

- Although the *30-Day Diet to Lose* has been approved by the Food and Drug Administration and recommended by a host of doctors and nutritionists, always check with your personal doctor or a nutritionist before embarking on this or any diet. Use that visit to have your cholesterol and blood pressure checked, which will allow you later to see the improvement you have made. Ask your doctor what your ideal weight should be, and together come up with a realistic goal for your first month's weight loss.

- Most current weight-loss programs suggest that you weigh yourself only once a week. If you are obsessed with the numbers on the scale, I agree. If gauging your weight loss motivates you, then every three days is fine. Every day is too often, since hormonal or water-retention fluctuations will not give you an accurate reading.

- Follow the diet closely, with as few substitutions as possible. It has been designed to offer you taste, variety, and balance so that you don't have to worry about how to choose your next meal. Weekends are not vacations from the diet: If you have social obligations that might throw you off, try to arrange them so they don't include meals. Exercise control. Again, saying no to pizza for thirty days doesn't mean you will never again enjoy its pleasures. It means that pizza isn't what you need *now*. But if you do find yourself on a hamburger-and-fries binge one night, skip the guilt and get right back on the diet the next day.

- Foods that come in tin cans are high on my list of what we don't need. Tuna and salmon packed in water are the exceptions. Otherwise, say yes to kicking the can.

- Pamper yourself with extra sleep, especially when starting on this diet. And don't forget to breathe!

- Avoid distractions like watching TV or reading during meals. Eat with all your senses. You can make your dining ceremony special to celebrate your commitment to a nutritious way of eating. Set a beautiful table with flowers and candles—even at breakfast. You might be dining alone, but why not use your best china, crystal, silverware, and linen? Since your portions may be smaller than what you've been eating, you might want to select smaller plates. If you're sharing your meal with family or friends, make the ritual of eating together full of warmth, fun, and interest. Take longer to chew your food. Lay down your utensils in between bites.

- You may be missing your favorite foods, but instead of feeling cheated, acknowledge to yourself how grateful you are for the healthful foods you are able to eat.

30-Day Diet to Lose—Days 1 to 5

DAY 1	DAY 2	DAY 3	DAY 4	DAY 5
Morning cereal† and 1 cup strawberries Nonfat milk Hot tea or decaf coffee	1 egg, poached or boiled 1 slice wheat toast, dry 2 slices tomato Hot tea or decaf coffee	Fruit and yogurt breakfast I* Hot tea or decaf coffee	Whole-grain cereal and 1 cup blueberries† Nonfat milk Hot tea or decaf coffee	1 slice banana bread* 1 slice melon and ⅓ cup nonfat yogurt Hot tea or decaf coffee
Spinach-mushroom salad* Turkey slice, white meat 2 melba toasts Beverage	California vegetable salad* 2 medium bread sticks Beverage	Open-faced tuna sandwich— wheat toast with cucumber slices, lettuce, and ½ cup water-packed tuna Beverage	Chicken salad* Beverage	Garden green salad* 2 melba toasts Beverage
Lemon halibut with fresh dill* ½ cup cooked brown rice Steamed broccoli Beverage	Aromatic marinated chicken* ½ steamed potato Steamed zucchini 1 melba toast Beverage	Steamed vegetable plate* with tomato dressing* 2 slices wheat toast, dry Beverage	Pasta with vegetables* 2 bread sticks Beverage	Broiled herb-garlic chicken* Steamed broccoli Beverage

*Recipe to follow

†When breakfast is listed as "morning cereal," I'm referring to low-sugar brand-name cereals such as Cheerios, Total, Special K, or Kashi. Choose what you love or have a variety. Whole-grain cereals are those you buy at the health-food store; they're low in sugar and fat as well and offer a mix of grains. Limit serving size to single portion as indicated on cereal packaging.

30-Day Diet to Lose—Days 6 to 10

DAY 6	DAY 7	DAY 8	DAY 9	DAY 10
2 salt-free rice cakes with all-fruit spread 1 cup mixed berries Hot tea or decaf coffee	Mini omelette* 1 slice wheat toast, dry ½ orange Hot tea or decaf coffee	1 slice melon 1 slice wheat toast, dry Hot tea or decaf coffee	1 egg, poached or boiled 1 slice wheat toast, dry 1 glass prune juice Hot tea or decaf coffee	Whole-grain cereal† and 1 cup strawberries Nonfat milk Hot tea or decaf coffee
Salade Niçoise* 1 slice wheat toast, dry Beverage	Garden green salad* Beverage	Chinese sesame-chicken salad* Beverage	Spinach-mushroom salad* Beverage	Open-faced turkey sandwich—wheat toast with cucumber slices, lettuce, and 2 slices turkey with low-fat mayonnaise Beverage
Steamed vegetable plate* with grated Parmesan Beverage	Fish-broccoli rolls in wine sauce* Sliced-tomato salad* Beverage	Steamed vegetable plate* with grated Parmesan 2 bread sticks Beverage	Broiled fresh salmon steaks* ½ cup cooked brown rice Sliced-tomato salad,* no dressing Beverage	Steamed vegetable plate* with tomato dressing* Beverage

30-Day Diet to Lose—Days 11 to 15

DAY 11	DAY 12	DAY 13	DAY 14	DAY 15
Fruit and yogurt breakfast I* Hot tea or decaf coffee	½ melon 1 salt-free rice cake with all-fruit spread Hot tea or decaf coffee	Morning cereal† and 1 cup mixed berries Hot tea or decaf coffee	Mini omelette* 1 slice wheat toast, dry 2 slices tomato Hot tea or decaf coffee	2 salt-free rice cakes with all-fruit spread 1 cup mixed berries Hot tea or decaf coffee
Garden green salad* 2 melba toasts Beverage	Chicken salad* Beverage	Spinach-mushroom salad* Beverage	Garden green salad* Beverage	Salade Niçoise* 1 slice wheat toast, dry Beverage
Steamed snapper with scallions and ginger* ½ cup cooked brown rice Steamed green beans Beverage	Steamed vegetable plate* with grated Parmesan Beverage	Baked skinless/ boneless chicken breast 2 melba toasts Sliced-tomato salad* with dressing Steamed broccoli Beverage	Lemon halibut with fresh dill* ½ steamed potato Steamed green beans Beverage	Pasta with vegetables* Beverage

DAY 16	DAY 17	DAY 18	DAY 19	DAY 20
1 egg, poached or boiled 1 slice wheat toast, dry 2 slices tomato Hot tea or decaf coffee	Fruit and yogurt breakfast I* Hot tea or decaf coffee	1 slice banana bread* 1 slice melon and ½ cup nonfat yogurt Hot tea or decaf coffee	Whole-grain cereal† and 1 cup strawberries Nonfat milk Hot tea or decaf coffee	Mini omelette* 1 slice wheat toast, dry ½ orange Hot tea or decaf coffee
California vegetable salad* 2 medium bread sticks Beverage	Open-faced tuna sandwich— wheat toast with cucumber slices, lettuce, and ½ cup water-packed tuna Beverage	Garden green salad* 2 melba toasts Beverage	Open-faced turkey sandwich— wheat toast with cucumber slices, lettuce, and 2 slices turkey with low-fat mayonnaise Beverage	Garden green salad* Beverage
Aromatic marinated chicken* ½ steamed potato Steamed zucchini 1 melba toast Beverage	Steamed vegetable plate* with tomato dressing* 2 slices wheat toast, dry Beverage	Broiled herb-garlic chicken* Steamed broccoli Beverage	Steamed vegetable plate* with grated Parmesan Beverage	Fish-broccoli rolls in wine sauce* Sliced-tomato salad* Beverage

30-Day Diet to Lose—Days 21 to 25

DAY 21	DAY 22	DAY 23	DAY 24	DAY 25
Fruit and yogurt breakfast II* Hot tea or decaf coffee	Morning cereal† and 1 cup blueberries Nonfat milk Hot tea or decaf coffee	1 egg, poached or boiled 1 slice wheat toast, dry 2 slices tomato Hot tea or decaf coffee	Fruit and yogurt breakfast II* Hot tea or decaf coffee	½ melon 1 salt-free rice cake with all-fruit spread Hot tea or decaf coffee
Shrimp salad* 2 melba toasts Beverage	Open-faced turkey sandwich— wheat toast with cucumber slices, lettuce, and 2 slices turkey with low-fat mayonnaise Beverage	California vegetable salad* 2 medium bread sticks Beverage	Garden green salad* 2 melba toasts Beverage	Chicken salad* Beverage
Curried chicken* ½ cup cooked brown rice Broiled tomato halves with garlic* Beverage	Steamed vegetable plate* with tomato dressing* Beverage	Aromatic marinated chicken* ½ steamed potato Steamed zucchini 1 melba toast Beverage	Steamed snapper with scallions and ginger* ½ cup cooked brown rice Steamed green beans Beverage	Steamed vegetable plate* with grated Parmesan Beverage

30-Day Diet to Lose—Days 26 to 30

DAY 26	DAY 27	DAY 28	DAY 29	DAY 30
1 slice banana bread* 1 slice melon and ½ cup nonfat yogurt Hot tea or decaf coffee	Whole-grain cereal† and 1 cup mixed berries Hot tea or decaf coffee	1 slice melon 1 slice wheat toast, dry Hot tea or decaf coffee	Mini omelette* 1 slice wheat toast, dry ½ orange Hot tea or decaf coffee	Fruit and yogurt breakfast II* Hot tea or decaf coffee
Garden green salad* 2 medium bread sticks Beverage	Spinach-mushroom salad* Beverage	Chinese sesame-chicken salad* Beverage	Garden green salad* Beverage	Shrimp salad* 2 melba toasts Beverage
Broiled herb-garlic chicken* Steamed broccoli Beverage	Broiled fresh salmon steaks* ½ cup cooked brown rice Sliced-tomato salad,* no dressing Beverage	Steamed vegetable plate* with tomato dressing* 2 medium bread sticks Beverage	Fish-broccoli rolls in wine sauce* Sliced-tomato salad* Beverage	Curried chicken* ½ cup cooked brown rice Broiled tomato halves with garlic* Beverage

When you first get started on the *30-Day Diet to Lose,* you may find yourself craving things you don't need that are not included on the diet. If you regularly consume significant amounts of substances such as caffeine, sugar, sodium, and alcohol, as well as red meat, cheese, colas and diet colas, butter, fatty, salty, sugary snack foods, or packaged products with lots of additives, you may actually go through a physical withdrawal when you discontinue them. On the other hand, many of us have discovered that once we get over the psychological shock, we feel better than ever when we don't eat those very things.

By the same token, if giving up your morning cup of coffee is going to take away a true joy in your life, that quantity of caffeine isn't going to endanger your health. But stick to that *one* cup. Better yet, try making your cup of coffee half de-caffeinated and half caffeinated. If you're one of those people who revs up on four cups of leaded coffee in the morning, two double lattés in the afternoon, with diet colas for lunch and dinner, you probably already know it's not good for you. Besides the jittery, jangled nerves and upset stomach it can cause, caffeine has been shown to contribute to cysts in women who are prone to them; it's also a diuretic and may dry out your skin. Plus, it's addictive.

If you are ready to embrace the tea habit, here is a handy rule of thumb for brewing black tea or tea with caffeine—steep the bag for fifteen to thirty seconds tops. That's plenty. If you're brewing loose tea, be careful not to let too many stray tea leaves linger too long in the water, which would result in a higher caffeine potency. Of course, if you're opting for herbal or green teas, steep away. Feel free to add lemon or a dash of nonfat milk and, if you desire, a teaspoon of raw sugar or artificial sweetener without aspartame. For fresh iced tea, make the hot tea and pour it into a glass or pitcher, adding sliced lemon and orange—which may make it sweet enough for your liking. If not, stir in artificial sweetener or a combination of raw sugar and sugar substitute to taste. Once the tea has cooled, pour over ice and enjoy.

In terms of artificial sweeteners: I make the best educated compromise I can. I steer away from using aspartame, preferring the occasional use of saccharin-based sugar substitutes. Sweetener made from the natural plant Stevia is a low-calorie option that can be purchased in most health-food stores. Most days I sweeten a steaming cup of herbal tea with a teaspoonful of whole organic sugar un-refined, unbleached, and not separated.

Another compromise you may note in the recipes for the *30-Day Diet to Lose* is the option to use either unsalted butter or a lower-fat butter substitute that says "partially hydrogenated" toward the end of the ingredients list. Butter tastes better but has fat, calories, and cholesterol; the substitute has less fat, fewer calories, and no cholesterol but does contain chemicals. This is a personal choice.

When it comes to harmful additives in food, I am most zealous about avoiding meat, poultry, and eggs from creatures that have been hormone-fed. Studies examining the effects of these hormones on our health and the aging process are alarming. Research suggests a link between accelerated growth and premature onset of puberty in children, as well as linkage to accelerated aging in adults. Therefore, I look for the words "hormone-free" on the protein sources I buy. Like-wise, I try to buy organic produce whenever possible. Because we have overplanted much of our land, without allowing for fallow periods so that the soil can replenish itself in between harvestings, many of our crops are being grown in soil that has been chemically boosted—not to mention the pesticides and other agents being used to get the fastest, largest yield.

Above all, allow your own whole-health instincts to make dieting a positive experience. If you feel a need for extra nourishment on the *30-Day Diet to Lose,* have an apple, orange, or a teaspoon of almond butter or peanut butter on a whole-grain rice cake. Remember, you're not in jail. The structure the *30-Day Diet to Lose* provides does take the guesswork out of what, when, and how to eat. What counts is that you're creating a healthy work of art—you—so bring your powers of creative thinking and problem solving into this process.

If you have more weight to lose at the end of the thirty days, it is safe and sound to continue with the diet plan for another thirty days or however many months you need. If you are ready to work at maintaining your weight, now you can easily transition to the looser structure of the *Diet for Life*.

Seven days of sample meals follow. In designing your own menu beyond that first week, you might want to use the list that guides me in my own kitchen:

- **What we need—*Diet to Lose* guidelines:** nonfat milk, eggs, high-fiber whole wheat bread, melba toast, bread sticks, rice cakes, tomatoes, hot tea and iced tea, salads, low-calorie dressings, homemade dressings in small portions, tamari sauce, all vegetables, turkey, chicken, veal (optional), fish, grated Parmesan cheese, herbs, spices, melons (not watermelon because of high sugar), no-sodium chicken broth, berries, low-sugar cereals (whole-grain, bran, Kashi, Total, Special K, Cheerios), lentil pasta, brown rice, prune juice, all-fruit spread

- **What we need to say yes to occasionally—*Diet for Life* guidelines (including the above):** low-fat milk and yogurt, potatoes, all fruits, all fish, liquor, wine, and light beer (in moderation), oatmeal, unsalted nuts, unsalted whole-grain crackers, unsalted whole wheat pretzels, bacon (if you love it), sauces without cream, homemade soups and stews, olive oil (sparingly) and low-fat mayonnaise, reduced-fat almond butter and peanut butter (small amounts), homemade light fruit desserts, pure dark chocolate

- **What we don't need most of the time:** whole-fat cheese, cream, ice cream and other high-fat dairy products, red meat and cured meat, olives, salt, butter, mayonnaise, cola drinks, chips, sugar, candy, cookies, brownies, cakes, sugar cereals, white bread, white rice, canned anything, pizza, fries, fast food, any fried food

Diet for Life—Seven Sample Days

DAY 1	DAY 2	DAY 3	DAY 4
Banana and walnut breakfast* 1–2 slices wheat toast, dry 1 glass nonfat milk Hot tea or decaf coffee	Whole-grain cereal ½ melon filled with mixed berries Nonfat milk Hot tea or decaf coffee	Good-for-you French toast* ½ melon 1 glass nonfat milk Hot tea or decaf coffee	Vegetable omelette* 1 slice wheat toast, dry Nonfat milk Hot tea or decaf coffee
Tuna salad with Dijon vinaigrette* Whole-grain crackers Beverage	Open-faced chicken sandwich—lettuce, mustard, 2 slices fresh roasted chicken Sliced-tomato salad* Beverage	Cold salmon plate— fresh salmon or ½ cup flaked canned salmon, sliced cucumbers, and tomatoes Beverage	Italian vegetable salad* Whole-grain crackers Beverage
Broiled herb-garlic chicken* Steamed broccoli Sautéed cherry tomatoes* Small green salad, light oil and vinegar Beverage	Grilled swordfish* 1 cup cooked brown rice Steamed spinach Beverage	Chicken salad* 1 honey apple* Beverage	Veal scallops in tomato sauce* Baked potato Steamed spinach Sliced-tomato salad* 1 orange, sliced Beverage

*Recipe to follow

DAY 5	DAY 6	DAY 7
1 slice banana bread*	1 popover*	1 small bagel, dab of
1 slice melon and ½	Fruit salad	light cream cheese
cup nonfat yogurt	1 glass nonfat milk	Sliced tomato and
Hot tea or decaf coffee	Hot tea or decaf coffee	onion
		Hot tea or decaf coffee
Tomato stuffed with	Shrimp salad*	Garden green salad*
chicken salad*	Whole-grain crackers	Sliced turkey
Whole-grain crackers	Beverage	Beverage
Beverage		
Steamed vegetable	Veal piccata*	Marinated bass
plate* with grated	Spaghetti	teriyaki*
Parmesan	Asparagus	Brown rice
1 cup pasta	Green salad, light oil	Broccoli
Bread sticks	and vinegar	Banana-berry dessert*
1 peach, sliced	Bread sticks	Beverage
Beverage	Beverage	

You'll note that I haven't suggested exact amounts or portion sizes for some of the items on these sample daily menus. In those cases, I'm leaving it to your best judgment to determine what a healthy serving of that food is for you at this time. Because this is a diet to maintain healthy weight and not to lose, you probably have attained healthy eating habits and know what foods you may want to limit.

Named for the time when I had put on a few pounds and had to fit into a bikini for a photo shoot one week later, this diet will definitely get results. Or it can be a kick-start if you have a lot of weight to lose. Again, it should not be used more than once a year, and your doctor's permission is a must.

Bikini Diet—Days 1 to 7

DAY 1	DAY 2	DAY 3	DAY 4
Scrambled egg white* 1 slice wheat toast, dry Hot tea or decaf coffee	1 glass prune juice 1 slice wheat toast, dry Hot tea or decaf coffee	1 sliced whole tomato on dry wheat toast with low-cal Italian dressing Hot tea or decaf coffee	Scrambled egg white* 1 slice wheat toast, dry Hot tea or decaf coffee
Salad made with any vegetables except tomatoes 1 slice turkey Beverage	Salad made with lettuce, tomato, ⅛ cup tuna, low-cal dressing Beverage	Chicken salad* 2 melba toasts Beverage	1 cup any steamed or raw vegetables Beverage
Steamed vegetable plate* Beverage	1 cup chicken broth Steamed celery 1 slice chicken breast Beverage	Steamed vegetable plate* Beverage	Broiled fish 2 melba toasts 1 cup steamed zucchini Beverage

*Recipe to follow

DAY 5	DAY 6	DAY 7
1 glass prune juice 1 slice wheat toast, dry Hot tea or decaf coffee	½ cup cut-up melon or sliced strawberries 1 slice wheat toast, dry Hot tea or decaf coffee	½ tomato, sliced 1 slice wheat toast, dry Hot tea or decaf coffee

Salad made with
   lettuce, tomatoes,
   mushrooms, and
   ½ cup shrimp—low-
   cal dressing optional
Beverage
	1 cup diced chicken
	   on a bed of sliced
	   tomatoes
	1 melba toast
	Beverage
		1 cup tuna salad with
		   Dijon vinaigrette*
		Beverage

Steamed vegetable
   plate*
Beverage
	Broiled fish
	½ tomato with low-cal
	   dressing
	Beverage
		Broiled chicken
		Steamed broccoli or
		   cauliflower
		2 melba toasts
		Beverage

Recipes for

30-Day Diet to Lose,

Diet for Life,

and Bikini Diet

BROILED HERB-GARLIC CHICKEN

Diet to Lose: Days 5, 18, 26

Diet for Life: Sample Day 1

Note: When meals or recipes call for cold chicken, use left-over from this recipe.

1—2 lb. broiler chicken, quartered and skinned

2—3 garlic cloves, pressed

Fresh ground black pepper to taste

½ tsp. dried tarragon

1 c. hot water

2 tbs. unsalted butter or lower-fat/cholesterol substitute
    such as I Can't Believe It's Not Butter! Light

2 tbs. chopped fresh parsley

1. Rub the meat with the pressed garlic, reserving garlic after you're done.

2. Brown chicken in a broiling pan under preheated broiler—5 minutes each side.

3. Remove chicken to a baking dish and lower oven temperature to 350 degrees.

4. Season chicken with pepper, tarragon, and the garlic you used to rub chicken.

5. Bake for 20 minutes, basting regularly with mixture made from hot water, butter or butter substitute, and parsley.

•• *Serves 4*

—

AROMATIC MARINATED CHICKEN

Diet to Lose: Days 2, 16, 23

1 garlic clove, chopped
1 large onion, chopped
Dash ground ginger
½ tsp. ground coriander
Fresh ground black pepper to taste
1 tbs. lemon juice
¼ c. vinegar
1 tbs. olive oil
3 tbs. water
¼ tsp. raw sugar
⅛ tsp. cinnamon
½ tbs. low-sodium beef bouillon
6–8 pieces chicken (breast halves, whole legs), skinned
1 tbs. chopped fresh parsley

1. In your blender or food processor, combine all the ingredients except the chicken and parsley and blend to a smooth paste.

2. Place the chicken in a shallow baking dish and pierce all over with a fork.

3. Spread with the paste and refrigerate overnight.

4. Preheat your oven to broil.

5. When it's ready, place the baking dish with the chicken on broiler rack and broil for 15 minutes on each side or until chicken is brown, basting occasionally with pan juices.

6. When brown, remove chicken from oven, garnish with parsley, and serve.

•• *Serves 4*

—

CURRIED CHICKEN

Diet to Lose: Days 21, 30

1½ lbs. chicken, skinned and cut into pieces or 1½ lbs.
    skinless boneless chicken breasts
½ tsp. fresh ground black pepper
1 tsp. garlic powder
½ tbs. Dijon mustard
⅓ c. water
2 tbs. lemon juice
2 tbs. honey
1 tbs. curry powder
½ large onion, sliced
2 carrots, peeled and sliced

1. Preheat your oven to 350 degrees.

2. Place the chicken pieces in a roasting pan and sprinkle half the pepper and garlic powder on top.

3. In a bowl, combine the mustard with 3 tablespoons of the water.

4. Stir in the lemon juice, honey, and curry powder.

5. Pour half the curry mixture over the chicken and scatter the onion and carrots around it.

6. Pour the remaining water over the vegetables (enough to cover) and bake for 30 minutes.

7. Turn the chicken over and sprinkle with the remaining pepper and garlic.

8. Pour on the remaining curry mixture. If needed, add more water to the pan.

9. Bake 45 minutes more, or until the chicken is brown.

•• *Serves 4*

—

CHICKEN SALAD

Diet to Lose: Days 4, 12, 25
Diet for Life: Sample Days 3, 5
Bikini Diet: Day 3

1¼ c. diced cooked chicken, white meat unsalted

1 large apple, diced

2 tbs. nonfat plain yogurt

½ tsp. curry powder

⅛ c. chopped unsalted almonds (optional)

4 lettuce leaves for garnish

1. Combine chicken, apple, yogurt, and curry. Garnish with almonds, if desired, and serve on a bed of lettuce.

•• *Serves 4*

—

CHINESE SESAME-CHICKEN SALAD

Diet to Lose: Days 8, 28

2 tbs. sesame seeds

2 c. finely shredded cooked chicken breasts

1 tbs. Dijon mustard

¼ tsp. ground ginger

1½ tsp. garlic powder

1 tsp. onion powder

¼ c. orange juice

1 tsp. low-sodium soy sauce

2 c. chopped celery

2 c. scallions, cut into 1½-inch lengths

2 tbs. finely chopped red bell pepper

5 c. shredded crisp iceberg lettuce

Orange slices and tomato wedges for garnish

1. Toast sesame seeds until lightly browned by placing them in a small pan in a 300-degree oven for two minutes.

2. Remove and let cool.

3. Put the shredded chicken in a bowl and sprinkle with mustard, ginger, garlic and onion powders, orange juice, soy sauce, and sesame seeds; toss well.

4. Place the chicken in the refrigerator to marinate and chill, at least 15 minutes.

5. Meanwhile, prepare the celery, scallions, red bell pepper, and lettuce.

6. When the chicken is chilled, stir in the celery, scallions, and red bell pepper.

7. Arrange the lettuce on a platter and top it with the chicken salad.

8. Garnish with orange slices and tomato wedges.

•• *Serves 4*

LEMON HALIBUT WITH FRESH DILL

Diet to Lose: Days 1, 14

You Can Use This Recipe for Bikini Diet Broiled Fish.

2 halibut fillets (cod, sole, or trout are fine)
Fresh ground black pepper to taste
1 tsp. chopped fresh dill (or ¼ tsp. dried)
2 tbs. dry white wine
2 tbs. fresh lemon juice
2 tsp. unsalted butter or lower-fat/cholesterol substitute
    such as I Can't Believe It's Not Butter! Light

1. You can broil or bake the fillets. If broiling, preheat the broiler. If baking, preheat oven to 350 degrees.

2. Wash and dry the fillets. Place in a glass baking pan.

3. Sprinkle with the other ingredients, finishing off with a teaspoon of the butter or butter substitute on each fillet.

4. If you are baking, bake for 15–20 minutes. If you are broiling, do so for 8–10 minutes; be careful not to overcook (the fillet will start to curl and brown).

•• *Serves 2*

FISH-BROCCOLI ROLLS IN WINE SAUCE

Diet to Lose: Days 7, 20, 29

Wine Sauce:

>   ⅓ c. water
>
>   ¼ c. dry white wine
>
>   ¼ c. bottled white grape juice
>
>   1½ tbs. lemon juice
>
>   ½ tbs. plus ½ tsp. Dijon mustard
>
>   1 tsp. coarsely chopped capers, drained
>
>   ¼ tsp. onion powder
>
>   ¼ tsp. garlic powder
>
>   1 bay leaf
>
>   ⅓ c. chopped scallions

2 fillets of sole, 3–4 oz. each

4 broccoli spears, with bottoms cut off

4 lemon slices for garnish

1. Combine all the sauce ingredients except the scallions in a skillet.

2. Cook over medium heat, stirring frequently, until thickened.

3. Stir in the scallions.

4. Roll each fillet around the stem of a broccoli spear; lay the rolls in the sauce, seam side down, and baste with spoonfuls of sauce.

5. Cook, covered, over medium heat for 12 minutes.

6. While the fish rolls cook, steam the other two broccoli spears until tender, just a few minutes.

7. When the fish rolls are done, transfer to a serving dish and pour the sauce over them.

8. Arrange the steamed broccoli spears around the fish rolls, garnish with the lemon slices, and serve.

•• *Serves 2*

—

BROILED FRESH SALMON STEAKS

Diet to Lose: Days 9, 27

2 salmon steaks
2 tbs. lime juice
1 tsp. unsalted butter or lower-fat/cholesterol substitute
     such as I Can't Believe It's Not Butter! Light
Fresh ground black pepper to taste
2 tsp. chopped fresh tarragon or ½ tsp. dried
½ c. dry white wine or dry vermouth

1. Preheat broiler.

2. Place the salmon steaks in a shallow baking pan.

3. Sprinkle with half the lime juice and dot with the butter or butter substitute.

4. Season with the pepper.

5. Sprinkle with half the tarragon and pour the wine or vermouth around but not over the salmon.

6. Broil for 10–15 minutes, basting often during the last 5 minutes.

7. Turn the salmon, season with the remaining ingredients, and broil about 5 minutes longer.

8. Baste again when done, then remove the steaks to serving dish.

9. Pour the sauce over the steaks and serve.

•• *Serves 2*

—

STEAMED SNAPPER WITH SCALLIONS AND GINGER

Diet to Lose: Days 11, 24

1–2 lb. snapper or 2 snapper fillets

1 tbs. sesame oil

1 tsp. white vinegar

2 tsp. mustard powder

1 tbs. white wine

⅛ tsp. ground ginger

8 scallions, minced

2 tbs. low-sodium beef bouillon

1. In a large skillet or wok, pour water to a depth of ¾ inch.

2. Place a steamer over the water and bring to a boil.

3. Place the fish in a glass casserole set on top of the steamer.

4. Lower the heat, cover tightly, and cook for 15 minutes.

5. Just before the fish is done, combine and heat remaining ingredients.

6. Remove the steamed fish to a serving dish and stir the remaining pan juices into the sauce.

7. Pour the mixture over snapper and serve.

•• *Serves 2*

—

MARINATED BASS TERIYAKI

Diet for Life: Sample Day 7

2 tbs. low-sodium soy sauce

2 tbs. water

4 tsp. dry sherry

1 clove garlic, minced

¼ tsp. ground ginger

4 bass fillets, about ¼ lb. each

1. In a small bowl, combine soy sauce, water, sherry, garlic, and ginger.

2. Arrange the fillets in an 8″ × 8″ lightly buttered glass baking dish and pour the teriyaki mixture over them.

3. Turn the fish over to coat the other side.

4. Cover dish and refrigerate for 1 hour.

5. Bake fillets at 350 degrees for 20 minutes.

6. Remove to a platter and pour sauce over them.

•• *Serves 2*

GRILLED SWORDFISH

Diet for Life: Sample Day 2

2 swordfish steaks, 1 inch thick

2 tbs. unsalted butter or lower-fat / cholesterol substitute
such as I Can't Believe It's Not Butter! Light

1 tbs. lemon juice

½ c. plain nonfat yogurt

½ tbs. chopped fresh dill or ¼ tsp. dried

1. Preheat broiler.

2. Combine the butter or butter substitute and lemon juice.

3. Brush each steak with the mixture, then broil 5 minutes.

4. Turn, brush with the butter and lemon, and broil for 5 minutes.

5. Cream the yogurt in a blender or food processor or by hand, then mix in the dill by hand.

6. When the fish is done, top with the dill-yogurt sauce and serve.

•• *Serves 2*

VEAL PICCATA

Diet for Life: Sample Day 6

. . . .

2–3 veal scallops, about ½ pound altogether

¼ c. flour

½ c. low-sodium chicken bouillon

½ tsp. dried oregano

⅛ tsp. dried sage

⅛ tsp. dried rosemary, crushed

1–2 tsp. Dijon mustard

1 tbs. olive oil

2 tbs. unsalted butter or lower-fat / cholesterol substitute
*   such as I Can't Believe It's Not Butter! Light*

3 tbs. marsala wine

3 tbs. lemon juice

Chopped fresh parsley

1. If your butcher hasn't already pounded your veal scallops, place them on a wooden cutting board, cover with wax paper, and pound with a wooden mallet or the back of a serving spoon until thin.

2. In a bowl, combine the flour, chicken bouillon, and all the herbs.

3. Spread the mustard on each side of the scallops, then coat with the flour mixture.

4. Heat the oil and butter or butter substitute in a large skillet over medium heat.

5. When the butter (or butter substitute) has melted, brown the veal quickly, about 3 minutes on each side.

6. Add the wine and simmer 5–7 minutes.

7. Add the lemon juice, scraping the bottom of the pan to mix the ingredients.

8. Remove the meat to a serving platter, sprinkle with the chopped parsley, and pour the sauce over it.

•• *Serves 2*

—

VEAL SCALLOPS IN TOMATO SAUCE

Diet for Life: Sample Day 4

12–14 veal scallops

2 tbs. unsalted butter or lower-fat / cholesterol substitute
    such as I Can't Believe It's Not Butter! Light

2 medium onions, chopped

¼ lb. button mushrooms, sliced (optional)

1 tbs. cornstarch

½ c. dry white wine

4 c. canned Italian plum tomatoes, drained and chopped

½ tsp. chopped fresh basil

1 tsp. chopped fresh oregano or ½ tsp. dried

1 tsp. chopped fresh sage

½ tsp. fresh rosemary, crushed

1 tbs. fresh ground black pepper

1 tbs. capers

1. If your butcher hasn't already pounded your veal scallops, place them on a wooden cutting board, cover with wax paper, and pound with a wooden mallet or the back of a serving spoon until thin.

2. In a skillet, melt the butter or butter substitute and sauté the onions and mushrooms, if using.

3. Remove from pan and brown the scallops quickly, about 2 minutes on each side.

4. In a small bowl, mix the cornstarch with 3 tbs. of the wine and pour over the scallops.

5. Continue cooking the veal until most of the liquid has evaporated. Remove to a serving platter.

6. Return the onions and mushrooms to the skillet. Add the tomatoes, herbs, and pepper and simmer about 5 minutes.

7. Add the scallops to the tomato mixture, spoon sauce over the veal, and add the capers.

8. Remove to a platter and serve.

•• *Serves 8*

SHRIMP SALAD

Diet to Lose: Days 21, 30

Diet for Life: Sample Day 6

....

1 head red-leaf or Boston lettuce (also known
as butter lettuce)
8 medium shrimp, cooked and cut into pieces or left whole
2 tbs. chopped scallions
½ cucumber, peeled and sliced
2 tomatoes, quartered
4 tbs. Homemade Vinaigrette (see p. 95)

1. Wash and dry the lettuce, tear into bite-size pieces, and put in a salad bowl.

2. Add the other ingredients, toss, and enjoy.

•• *Serves 2*

—

SALADE NIÇOISE

Diet to Lose: Days 6, 15

....

1 head iceberg, red-leaf, or Boston (butter) lettuce
1 7-oz. can water-packed tuna
½ lb. green beans, steamed

½ red onion, sliced, or small white onion, sliced

1 tomato, sliced

½ green bell pepper, seeded and cut into strips

½ red bell pepper, seeded and cut into strips

2 hard-boiled egg whites, sliced

2 small potatoes, boiled, skinned, and sliced

2–4 tbs. Homemade Vinaigrette (see p. 95)

2 tbs. grated Parmesan cheese (optional)

1. Wash and dry lettuce in a lettuce dryer or with paper towels.

2. Tear each lettuce leaf in half; line a salad bowl with the leaves.

3. Drain the tuna, flake with a fork, and place around the bowl on the lettuce. Then add each of the ingredients in turn.

4. Mix the whole salad with just enough dressing to coat but not soak the ingredients. Sprinkle with Parmesan cheese, if desired.

•• *Serves 2*

—

TUNA SALAD WITH DIJON VINAIGRETTE

Diet for Life: Sample Day 1

Bikini Diet: Day 7

Salad:

½ 7-oz. can water-packed tuna, drained and flaked

1 c. chopped bean sprouts, uncooked or lightly steamed

½ c. chopped celery

¼ c. chopped green bell pepper

1 small scallion, chopped, or ¼ c. finely chopped
    white onion
1 hard-boiled egg white, chopped
1 tomato, sliced
1 large apple, peeled and grated
Dressing:
¼ c. Homemade Vinaigrette (see p. 95) mixed with
    2 tsp. prepared Dijon mustard

1. Combine salad ingredients in a bowl and chill well, at least 15 minutes.

2. Mix the dressing and pour over the salad, tossing gently.
Use for sandwiches, for stuffing tomatoes, or on a bed of lettuce.

•• *Makes 2 cups*

—

ITALIAN VEGETABLE SALAD

Diet for Life: Sample Day 4

4 tomatoes, quartered
½ cucumber, peeled and sliced
1 small green bell pepper, seeded and sliced
¼ lb. button mushrooms, sliced
2 tbs. red wine vinegar
1 tsp. olive oil
Fresh ground black pepper to taste
1 tbs. chopped fresh parsley

1 tbs. lemon juice
1 hard-boiled egg white, sliced
½ head iceberg, red-leaf, or Boston (butter) lettuce

1. Put the tomatoes, cucumber, green bell pepper, and mushrooms in a salad bowl and toss with the vinegar, oil, and black pepper. Refrigerate for 15–30 minutes.

2. When chilled, add the parsley and toss.

3. Sprinkle the lemon juice over the top, garnish with the egg-white slices, and serve over the lettuce.

•• *Serves 2*

—

STEAMED VEGETABLE PLATE

Diet to Lose: Days 3, 6, 8, 10, 12, 17, 19, 22, 25, 28

Diet for Life: Sample Day 5

Bikini Diet: Days 1, 3, 5

Choose any combination or all of the following vegetables:
broccoli, potatoes, zucchini, tomatoes, carrots,
squash, fresh spinach leaves (cleaned well)
2–4 tbs. chopped fresh parsley
2 tbs. grated Parmesan cheese

1. Peel and/or slice the chosen vegetables into bite-size pieces.

2. Place them in 1 inch of water in a pot (or in a steamer if you have one) and cook on your stove over a low flame until vegetables can be pricked by a fork but are not too soft. (After years of over-steaming, I've developed a method for the madness and usually start with potatoes, carrots, and broccoli, then after three or four minutes, add the squashes, spinach, and tomatoes.)

3. When they're done to your liking, remove from the stove and transfer to a serving dish, sprinkle with the parsley and Parmesan, and serve.

•• *Serves 2*

—

BROILED TOMATO HALVES WITH GARLIC

Diet to Lose: Days 21, 30

2 large ripe tomatoes, washed
1 tsp. butter or lower-fat/cholesterol substitute such as
    I Can't Believe It's Not Butter! Light
1 clove garlic, minced
¼ tsp. summer savory
¼ tsp. dried thyme
¾ c. fresh coarsely grated Parmesan cheese
1 small yellow or green squash, sliced and steamed
4 parsley sprigs

1. Preheat broiler.
2. Cut the tomatoes in half vertically and arrange on a baking sheet, cut side up.

3. Melt the butter or butter substitute, then mix with the garlic and herbs and spread the mixture onto the cut tomatoes.

4. Sprinkle thickly with the cheese.

5. Place under broiler, cook until the cheese is melted and golden-brown, 10–12 minutes.

6. Garnish with squash and parsley sprigs.

•• *Serves 2*

—

SAUTÉED CHERRY TOMATOES

Diet for Life: Sample Day 1

1½ tsp. olive oil or 1 tsp. unsalted butter or
    lower-fat/cholesterol substitute such as
    I Can't Believe It's Not Butter! Light
1 clove garlic, crushed
½ lb. cherry tomatoes, washed
2 tbs. chopped fresh basil or ¾ tsp. dried

1. Heat the oil or melt the butter or butter substitute in a skillet over medium heat.

2. Add the garlic and sauté for 30 seconds, careful not to burn.

3. Add the tomatoes and sauté quickly, continuously shaking pan and tossing the tomatoes, making sure not to break the skins.

4. Add the basil and sauté another minute.

•• *Serves 2–3*

CALIFORNIA VEGETABLE SALAD

Diet to Lose: Days 2, 16, 23

. . . .

Choose any combination or all of the following vegetables:
     broccoli, green bell peppers, zucchini, mushrooms,
     tomatoes, carrots
1 head Boston (butter) or red-leaf lettuce
¼ c. chopped scallions
1 tbs. chopped fresh parsley
2 tbs. low-calorie, low-sodium dressing of your choice

1. Clean as many of the vegetables as you want, and cut into small pieces.

2. Wash and dry the lettuce, tear into bite-size pieces, and put into a salad bowl.

3. Add the scallions, parsley, and prepared vegetables.

4. Toss with the dressing and serve.

Serves 2 for lunch or 4 as a dinner side dish

—

SPINACH-MUSHROOM SALAD

Diet to Lose: Days 1, 9, 13, 27

. . . .

½ lb. fresh spinach leaves
¼ lb. button mushrooms, sliced
2 tbs. chopped scallions

¼ tsp. low-sodium soy sauce

2 tbs. Homemade Vinaigrette (see p. 95)

1 hard-boiled egg, sliced

1. Soak the spinach in cold water for 5 minutes, then rinse under running water and dry in a lettuce dryer or with paper towels.

2. Place in a salad bowl and add the mushrooms and scallions.

3. Add the soy sauce to the vinaigrette, pour over the salad, and toss well.

4. Garnish with the egg slices and serve.

•• *Serves 1–2*

—

GARDEN GREEN SALAD

Diet to Lose: Days 5, 7, 11, 14, 18, 20, 24, 26, 29

Diet for Life: Sample Day 7

1 head lettuce of your choice, or 3 c. gourmet mixed greens

2 tbs. chopped scallions

1 tbs. chopped fresh parsley

2 tbs. chopped celery

½ cucumber, peeled and sliced

½ green bell pepper, sliced

½ zucchini, sliced

2 tbs. Homemade Vinaigrette (see p. 95)

1. Wash the lettuce well, then dry in a lettuce dryer or on paper towels. (If you're getting an early start, you can keep the lettuce refrigerated, wrapped in paper towels, until you are ready to make your salad.)

2. Tear the lettuce into bite-size pieces, place in a salad bowl, add the rest of the ingredients, and toss with the salad dressing.

•• *Serves 1–2*

—

SLICED TOMATO SALAD

Diet to Lose: Days 13, 20, 27, 29
Diet for Life: Sample Days 2, 4

2 or 3 tomatoes, sliced
½ head lettuce of your choice
2 tbs. chopped scallions
2 tbs. Homemade Vinaigrette (see p. 95)
Pinch fresh ground black pepper

1. Layer the tomatoes on a bed of lettuce.

2. Sprinkle chopped scallions on top, drizzle with the Homemade Vinaigrette, and add a pinch of freshly ground black pepper.

•• *Serves 2*

TOMATO DRESSING

Diet to Lose: Days 3, 10, 17, 22, 28

....

1 c. tomato juice

1 clove garlic, peeled and pressed

1 tbs. chopped fresh parsley

1 tbs. chopped fresh chives

½ tsp. Dijon mustard

Fresh ground black pepper to taste

Pinch raw sugar

1. Mix all the ingredients together in a small bowl with a wire whisk or in your food processor.

2. Refrigerate in a closed glass jar until ready to use.

•• *Makes 1 cup*

—

HOMEMADE VINAIGRETTE

Diet to Lose, Diet for Life, and Bikini Diet

....

½ c. olive oil or other vegetable oil

1¾ tsp. paprika

1 tsp. dry mustard

1½ cloves garlic, minced

½ tsp. dried basil

⅛ tsp. fresh ground black pepper

1 tbs. chopped onions or chives

3 tbs. cider or red wine vinegar

3 tbs. lemon juice

2 tsp. chopped fresh parsley

1. Combine all ingredients.

2. Let sit in a covered jar in the refrigerator at least 12 hours before serving.

Remember to always shake before using. (Sometimes I put the dressing in my food processor for a few seconds to give it a creamier texture.)

•• *Makes 1 cup or eight 2-tablespoon servings*

—

PASTA WITH VEGETABLES

Diet to Lose: Days 4, 15

SAUCE:

4 ripe tomatoes (Italian plum are best)

2 tsp. olive oil

¼ tsp. dried oregano

1 tbs. chopped fresh basil or ¼ tsp. dried

Fresh ground black pepper to taste

2 cloves garlic, peeled and mashed

1 small onion, diced

1 green bell pepper, diced

1 red bell pepper, diced

¼ lb. button mushrooms, sliced

Pasta of your choice
4 quarts water

1. Gently drop tomatoes into a medium saucepan of boiling water for 30 seconds. Remove with tongs. Peel and chop loosely.
2. Heat olive oil in a skillet over medium heat.
3. Add the tomatoes, oregano, basil, and black pepper and sauté until tender, about ten minutes.
4. Add the garlic, onion, and green and red bell peppers and simmer for about 15 minutes.
5. Add the mushrooms and simmer an additional 5–10 minutes.
6. While the sauce cooks, bring the 4 quarts of water to a boil and add the pasta. Cook according to package instructions or as long as you like. (Most pasta requires approximately 10 minutes of cooking, less if you love yours al dente.)
7. When done, drain and rinse the pasta with warm water (to remove excess starch) and put in a bowl.
8. Pour the sauce over the drained pasta and serve.

•• *Depending on how much pasta you've made, this recipe serves 2–4 people.*

Mini Omelette

Diet to Lose: Days 7, 14, 20, 29

2 egg whites
1 egg yolk
Dab unsalted butter
2 tbs. salsa for garnish (optional)

1. In a small mixing bowl, hand-beat the egg whites and yolk.

2. In a small frying pan over medium heat, melt the butter and pour in the egg mixture. You can scramble the eggs or make an omelette by turning it over once.

3. Garnish with salsa on the side or with pepper and salt (if you must).

•• *Serves 1*

—

Vegetable Omelette

Diet for Life: Sample Day 4

2 egg whites
1 egg yolk
1 tsp. olive oil or unsalted butter

Your choice vegetables: sliced mushrooms, chopped onions,
chopped tomatoes, sliced peppers
2 tbs. salsa for garnish (optional)

1. In a small mixing bowl, hand-beat the egg whites and yolk.
2. In a small nonstick frying pan over medium heat, heat oil or melt butter and quickly sauté the vegetables, about 1 minute.
3. Remove the vegetables from the pan and pour in the egg mixture.
4. When it sets, place vegetables in center and fold in half. Turn over carefully and lightly brown.
5. Garnish with salsa on the side, if desired.

•• *Serves 1*

—

SCRAMBLED EGG WHITE

Bikini Diet: Days 1, 4

Dab unsalted butter
1 egg white

1. Melt the butter in a small nonstick pan.
2. Add the egg white and cook over low flame until the white starts to set.
3. Flip and cook until done.

•• *Serves 1*

BANANA BREAD

Diet to Lose: Days 5, 26
Diet for Life: Sample Day 5

½ c. unsalted butter, softened, or lower-fat/cholesterol
    substitute such as I Can't Believe
    It's Not Butter! Light
¾ c. brown sugar
1 whole egg
1 cup unsifted whole wheat flour
½ c. unsifted unbleached white flour
1 tsp. baking soda
¼ tsp. cinnamon
3 ripe bananas, mashed
¼ c. nonfat plain yogurt
1 c. chopped walnuts (optional)

1. Preheat oven to 350 degrees.

2. In a blender or food processor, cream the butter or butter substitute and sugar until smooth and light brown in color, then blend in the egg and pour into a medium bowl.

3. In a small or medium bowl, sift together the flours, baking soda, and cinnamon.

4. In a separate small bowl, mix by hand the bananas and yogurt.

5. Alternately add portions of the flour mixture and the banana mixture into the bowl with the butter, mixing thoroughly after each addition. Stir in walnuts at the end, if using.

6. Pour the mixture into a nonstick or very lightly greased 9″ × 5″ loaf pan.

7. Bake for 45 minutes or until an inserted knife comes out of the bread clean.

8. After you remove the bread from the oven, let it stand for 15 minutes to cool. Then remove it from the pan and cool for an hour so that it won't crumble when sliced.

•• *Makes 9 one-inch slices (You can freeze extra slices individually)*

—

GOOD-FOR-YOU FRENCH TOAST
Diet for Life: Sample Day 3

2 slices whole-grain bread
1 whole egg, beaten
⅛ c. low-fat or nonfat milk
¼ c. raw sugar
½ tsp. vanilla extract
Nutmeg

1. Preheat oven to 450 degrees.

2. Remove crusts from bread slices.

3. Mix together the egg, milk, sugar, and vanilla.

4. Soak the bread in the mixture for 2 minutes.

5. Place the slices in a nonstick baking dish, sprayed with Pam or other cooking spray or very lightly oiled.

6. Bake for 7 minutes on one side, then turn and cook for 5 minutes on the other.

7. Sprinkle with nutmeg. Serve with all-fruit spread, honey, reduced-calorie syrup, or plain nonfat yogurt.

•• *Serves 1*

—

BANANA AND WALNUT BREAKFAST

Diet for Life: Sample Day 1

1 c. nonfat plain yogurt
1 banana, sliced
2 tbs. chopped walnuts

Mix together and enjoy!

•• *Serves 1*

—

FRUIT AND YOGURT BREAKFAST I

Diet to Lose: Days 3, 11, 17

½ apple, sliced
½ banana, sliced
1 c. nonfat plain yogurt
1 tsp. toasted wheat germ

1. In a parfait glass or bowl, alternate layers of the apple and banana slices with the yogurt.

2. Sprinkle a teaspoon of toasted wheat germ on top for added crunch.

•• *Serves 1*

—

FRUIT AND YOGURT BREAKFAST II

Diet to Lose: Days 21, 24, 30

½ *c. melon pieces*
½ *c. sliced strawberries*
½ *c. sliced banana*
½ *c. nonfat plain yogurt*
1 tsp. toasted wheat germ

1. In a parfait glass or bowl, alternate the melon pieces, berries, and banana slices with the yogurt.

2. Sprinkle a teaspoon of toasted wheat germ on top for added crunch.

•• *Serves 1*

Popovers

....

2 whole eggs
1 c. nonfat milk
1 c. sifted flour
½ tsp. salt

1. Preheat the oven to 375 degrees.

2. Lightly beat the eggs. Add the milk, sifted flour, and salt. Mix lightly, disregarding the lumps.

3. Grease a 6-cup muffin or popover pan (made of cast iron and deeper than muffin pans).

4. Fill each cup ¾ full and place in the oven.

5. Turn up the oven to 450 degrees and bake for 20 minutes.

6. Remove and eat immediately. These are my favorites!

•• *Serves 6–8 muffin-size, 4–6 popover-size*

HONEY APPLES

Diet for Life: Sample Day 3

4 medium cooking apples
1 tbs. chopped nuts, toasted
1 tbs. chopped dates
Juice of ½ lemon
2 tbs. clear honey
½ tsp. ground cinnamon

1. Preheat the oven to 350 degrees.
2. Wash and core the apples, then peel the top half.
3. Mix the remaining ingredients in a small bowl.
4. Place the apples in an ovenproof dish and fill the centers with the honey-nut mixture, topping any leftover mixture over the apples.
5. Cover with aluminum foil, bake for 45 minutes, and serve warm.

•• *Serves 4*

BANANA-BERRY DESSERT

. . . .

2 c. frozen unsweetened berries (your choice: strawberries,
   blueberries, boysenberries, raspberries, blackberries)
2 tsp. raw sugar or ½ tsp. liquid artificial sweetener
3 bananas
2 tbs. cognac or brandy
¼ c. unsweetened orange juice
2 tbs. chopped walnuts or slivered almonds (optional)

1. Preheat the oven to 350 degrees.

2. Put the frozen berries and sugar or sweetener into your blender or food processor and blend until smooth.

3. Slice the bananas diagonally, put in a saucepan, cover with the cognac and orange juice, and sauté for about 3 minutes.

4. Now put the bananas in a glass baking dish and pour the berry sauce over them.

5. Put in the oven and bake for 10 minutes.

6. When done, remove to a serving dish and garnish with the walnuts or almonds, if using.

•• *Serves 4–6*

Theoretically, a balanced diet should provide us with our required amounts of vitamins and minerals. Because of environmental and internal stresses, however, most medical experts agree that supplements of vitamins and minerals are needed. While many of these are found in most of the better multivitamin/mineral supplements, some research suggests that the amounts now labeled RDA (recommended daily allowance) should be revised, in some cases four to eight times the current RDA, and should be labeled ODR (optimum daily requirement). Nutrients among those to increase for health and anti-aging include a vital class of vitamins and supplements known as antioxidants, such as vitamins C and E, green tea extracts, and a natural antioxidant that can be supplemented called coenzyme Q-10. Together with a diet that has lots of fruits and vegetables—which are naturally rich in antioxidants—along with some topical skin creams that include antioxidants, use of these supplements has shown to help prevent or repair damage to the body and skin.

Antioxidants defend against oxidation from free radicals. While they may sound like freedom-loving revolutionaries, free radicals are not quite so illustrious. The simple explanation of the oxidation process is to imagine how metal rusts or corrodes when exposed to oxygen. The molecules of our cells can likewise become oxidized, a natural internal process, causing paired electrons to break away into single freewheeling entities or radicals. Our own stress can create free radicals, as can the environment. The book *Feel Fabulous Forever,* by British journalists Josephine Fairley and Sarah Stacey, explains:

> In the course of modern life, we encounter many more free radicals—
> in smoke, toxins, chemicals and other pollutants in the air and in our
> food. What they do is trigger peroxidation—in less than the blink of an
> eye. That peroxidation leads to oxidation—which in turn leads to cell
> breakdown. Cells, organs and tissues break down or decay, resulting in

skin aging and internal disease. . . . While the body manufactures some free radical neutralizers, science is still looking at ways of increasing the supply.

When it comes to regularly taking vitamins and minerals in supplement form, I've found that several patterns exist. There are those who were probably raised from childhood to take their daily multivitamin and continue to do so as adults. Then there are those who have studied the nutritional benefits of every vitamin, mineral, and nutritional substance found in nature or in the lab and who run their lives around their supplementing schedules. And finally, there are those who know they really should remember to take their daily multivitamin/mineral supplement, but somehow it's just one more task in their day they don't get around to accomplishing. Another pattern applies to the in-betweeners, those who take supplements on some days and not on others; who remember now and then, forgetting sometimes too; or who go on health kicks but then burn out.

I was one of those people who did not think of taking supplements until I was advised to do so at the age of twenty-eight. And since then, supplements have become a mainstay of my whole-health approach.

I'd like to offer some simple, helpful guidelines that might bridge the gap for all our patterns and make the process more user-friendly. Of course, the reason that we take nutritional supplements is to address deficiencies that aren't being met by what we eat or are created by the stress of our lives, along with pollutants in our environment. And because we all have individual lives with varied, individual needs, there are no one-size-fits-all supplemental plans. What we can discuss are some basics that should be on most plans, general information valuable to most of us, as well as some of the special concerns that many of us share.

How important is nutritional supplementing to our whole-health picture? For that answer, I was fortunate to speak to Dr. Soram Singh Khalsa, whose many-months-long waiting list for new patients attests to the benefits of his integrated approach in helping people get well and stay well. A board-certified internist, Dr. Khalsa uses his training in Eastern modalities, along with homeopathy, herbal therapies, and acupuncture, to complement his practice of Western medicine.

Though Dr. Khalsa is not a nutritionist, he saw early on in his medical training the importance of nutrition and nutritional supplementation when he helped resolve his own health issues with a change in his diet and a simple regimen of vitamins. He has continued to emphasize that importance in his practice. The following Q&A will give insight as to how our whole-health can be positively impacted by remembering to take our supplements.

Dr. Khalsa: It's important to say that I am first a physician and secondly a holistic physician, using these complementary modalities to assist my work as a physician. The difference is that often when you look at patients as a Western physician, they don't have anything wrong. And yet they have a list of ailments. In integrative medicine, we see health as being on a big spectrum. On one end, we have diseases like cancer, and at the other end, we have ideal well-being. But what they never told us in medical school is that there is a gray area in the middle. Someone who is in that area doesn't necessarily have heart disease, cancer, or lupus, but they aren't as healthy as they want to be. They may have digestive problems, migraines, backaches, recurring sinus infections. These are all signs of the middle zone. What's going on in the middle zone is that there are no organs that are sick, but there are organs that are weak, run-down, toxic, or stressed. And so if we can identify where organs are weak or not working up to their full capacity, we can then target the organs for these complementary modalities—and that includes giving herbs and nutritional supplements that help people move toward being more well. And if we can identify weak areas in the body before they manifest as dense disease, we can strengthen those areas.

Q: If I already take a multivitamin/mineral supplement to fortify myself, would I need to supplement additionally?

A: The only reason to supplement with additional things is to strengthen your weaknesses, the ones you are aware of now, as well as your genetic weaknesses. For example, if you have a family history of heart disease, you may want to take vitamins, to say nothing of herbal or homeopathic medicines or other nonvitamin dietary supplements to support the heart or any organ that may be genetically weak.

Q: Do you think that the current RDAs for vitamins are sufficient?

A: Most people in our society need more than the RDA to have optimal functioning. The question we have to ask is whether you want to function adequately or optimally. Patients that come to me want to function optimally.

Q: So we should take more of everything?

A: No, that's a fallacy, that more is better. If, for example, it's determined that 1,000 milligrams of calcium will help you, you might think 2,000 milligrams is twice as good, or 3,000 milligrams three times as good. It's actually the opposite. If you start taking these doses of calcium, you might start calcifying your arteries. The same thing for other nutrients—selenium, for instance—the upper limit is 200 micrograms a day. You wouldn't want more.

Q: Are there other misconceptions or fallacies about supplementation?

A: There's a group who call themselves "quack busters" and say if you take more than the RDA of a given vitamin, because the vitamins are water soluble, all you're doing is making expensive urine. What I say to those people is that if they believe the concept that nothing happens in between the time when you swallow something and the time when its products come out in the urine, then why bother to drink any water at all during the day? Doctors always tell their patients to drink a lot of water—because water does something in between the time you drink it and urinate it out. So it is with vitamins—they do their work and then the body excretes their by-products.

Q: What about all these new natural miracle cures?

A: I think that any miracle cure should be regarded with great suspicion and close evaluation. There is so much hype about these products from companies whose purpose is profit. But they need to be evaluated individually because there are also some wonderful new products. Many of these are specialty products, to address special needs. As an example, if you have a cholesterol problem, you may want to try red rice yeast, a phenomenal product from China that has been extraordinarily effective at lowering cholesterol. As opposed to taking cholesterol-lowering drugs that can be very costly, red rice yeast has been equally effective for many people in my practice, though not all, and is much less expensive. In some cases we've dropped LDL, the bad cholesterol, sixty points with this product. But if you don't need to lower your cholesterol or don't have heart disease in your family, it's not a miracle for you. What's also important is that with a product like this, you need to monitor your cholesterol, so you need a doctor.

Q: If you could recommend just three categories of supplementation that could improve health and well-being for most women, what would they be?

A: The first category is calcium and magnesium, especially as they pertain to women and osteoporosis. When it comes to calcium, I recommend opting for the higher-quality forms, calcium hydroxyapatite or calcium citrate. Calcium is in every cell of our body and is important for healthy bones, hair, and neurological tissue. Calcium should always be balanced with magnesium, which I consider the unrecognized mineral and is needed to interact with calcium to prevent osteoporosis. Combination calcium/magnesium products are available in health-food stores. It's also better to opt for higher-quality magnesium, such as magnesium glycinate, as opposed to the lower quality, which is magnesium oxide and is much harder to absorb. I usually recommend a two-to-one ratio of calcium to magnesium, or two parts calcium to one and a half magnesium, even one-to-one. The problem with taking too much magnesium is that it can serve as a laxative, leading to diarrhea and abdominal cramps. Milk of magnesia is, in fact, mainly magnesium citrate—which you wouldn't want to take unless you had constipation, and in that case, it can help your bowels.

Q: So it would depend on the individual woman?

A: Yes, every woman needs to individualize, because every individual has a unique biochemistry. And hopefully she has the help of a practitioner. It doesn't have to be a medical doctor; it could be an acupuncturist, a chiropractor, or a nutritionist—with the appropriate training. The second category that should be addressed by supplements is in the group known as antioxidants. A good multiple vitamin should be loaded with antioxidants, but if it's not, additional supplementing is in order. Oxidative stress is connected with almost every chronic degenerative disease, including the two leading killers of the majority of women and men in our country—cardiovascular disease (heart disease and stroke) and cancer. Antioxidants are essential in helping protect us against oxidative stress.

Q: What about antioxidants in our diet?

A: Fruits and vegetables, vitamins C and E, and green tea extracts with polyphenols (bioflavonoid family) are all loaded with thousands of antioxidants. In addition, there are antioxidants to consider that have different propensities for different organs. Alpha-lipoic acid, for example, is a very potent antioxidant targeted toward the liver. The question remains—are foods alone sufficient to compensate for the degree of oxidative stress that a given person is under? There are now blood tests to tell if a person needs more antioxidants.

Q: What's the third category that seems to be needed across the board?

A: Essential fatty acids (EFAs) have to be included. We hear doctors talking a lot about protein needs and about amino acids, yet I rarely see problems here. I have been a vegetarian for almost thirty years, and I see many people who are vegetarian—or are tending toward consuming more vegetable protein than animal protein—and I've almost never seen a protein deficiency in the blood tests. The concern that vegetarians don't get enough protein is another myth. On the other hand, every day, three to six times a day, I see people with essential-fatty-acid deficiencies. Since they are essential for the proper functioning of all our body, including the immune system and the neurological systems, an EFA deficiency may begin a weakening of the immune system or the neurological system, including the brain. EFAs are so important to brain function that we now use them as an effective holistic adjunct to treating children with attention deficit disorder (ADD).

Q: What are the sources?

A: Sources of Omega-3-family fatty acids include flaxseed oil and fish oil. Sources for the Omega-6 family would include evening primrose oil, black currant–seed oil, and borage seed oil. These Omega-6 fatty acids can pertain to PMS, menopause, and hormonal issues, as well as inflammation issues in the body.

In addition to these three areas, I spoke to Dr. Khalsa about needs particular to a lot of women. For energy and brain power, he emphasizes, "Multis should have all the B vitamins, because B's are for brain, they help you think."

About herbs, Dr. Khalsa cautions that many are not meant to be taken every day; for example, we would never want to take echinacea every day. Although we think we are strengthening our immune system, studies are now showing that chronic use may actually weaken it. However, for colds and flus, taking echinacea for a week or two would be helpful. On the other hand, a woman who is having trouble with memory can take an herb such as ginkgo biloba every day.

For stress and anxiety, he notes that Kava Kava is an excellent alternative to Valium, as is valerian. Another recommendation for improving mood is SAM-e, which Dr. Khalsa prefers over Saint-John's-wort. (In Europe, SAM-e requires a prescription, though here it is available in health-food and homeopathic stores. It is advisable to consult your doctor before taking SAM-e.) For very high stress—as long as you are under the care of a doctor—you may inquire about the use of adrenal tissue extracts from which all hormones have been removed, to be taken for no more than four to six weeks.

For intestinal function, Chlorella is a very good product to help digestion and soothe the stomach.

For insomnia, valerian can be helpful, and tryptophan (available by prescription) is very effective, besides its potential for improving mood. 5HT (5 hydroxytryptophan) is available over the counter and can also be used for sleep and mood.

In concluding, Dr. Khalsa underscores the fact that natural supplements cannot do all the things prescription drugs and other pharmaceuticals can do for some of our health concerns. These medical drugs cure diseases that can't otherwise be cured and help people who couldn't otherwise be helped. What we should not do, he says, is depend on the long-term chronic use of drugs that were intended for short-term acute use.

Instead, we should strive, through the different modalities, including nutritional supplements, to achieve optimal balance—physical, mental, emotional, and spiritual—all of which contribute to whole-health.

When references are made to the vitamins and minerals most often contained in significant amounts in vitamin/mineral combination supplements, we're usually talking about those listed in the following chart, which shows the natural food sources for these nutrients as well as what we need them for.

VITAMIN	SOURCE	NEEDED FOR
A	Fish-liver oils, liver and kidneys, green and yellow vegetables, yellow-fleshed fruits (peaches, apricots, cantaloupe, papayas, tangerines), tomatoes, butter and margarine, egg yolks, carrots	Growth Healthy eyes Structure and function of cells of skin Antioxidant
B_1 (Thiamine)	Seafood, meat, soybeans, nonfat milk, whole-grain products, fowl, pork, pasta, oatmeal, lima beans, oysters	Growth Carbohydrate metabolism Functioning of heart, nerves, and muscles

VITAMIN	SOURCE	NEEDED FOR
B_2 (Riboflavin)	Meat, soybeans, nonfat milk, green vegetables, eggs, fowl, yeast, whole-grain products, pasta, mushrooms, dried beans and peas	Growth Healthy skin Carbohydrate metabolism Functioning of pancreas Sugar control Functioning of eyes
B_3 (Niacin)	Meat, fowl, fish, peanut butter (low-fat), potatoes, tomatoes, leafy vegetables, tuna, eggs, whole-grain products, dried beans and peas	Carbohydrate metabolism Functioning of stomach, intestinal, and nervous system
B_{12}	Green vegetables, liver, meat, eggs, fish, nonfat milk, kidneys	Preventing anemia Feeling sensations
C	Citrus and other fruits, tomatoes, leafy vegetables, potatoes	Antioxidant Strength of blood vessels Teeth and gum development Growth
D	Liver, fortified milk (nonfat), eggs	Growth Calcium and phosphorus metabolism Bone and tooth maintenance

VITAMIN	SOURCE	NEEDED FOR
E	Wheat germ, butter and margarine, green leafy vegetables, whole-grain products, bread, dried beans, liver	Normal reproduction Energy Antioxidant
K	Green vegetables, tomatoes, soybean oil, cabbage, cauliflower, potatoes, cereals	Normal clotting of blood Normal liver functions Bone support

MINERAL	SOURCE	NEEDED FOR
Calcium	Parmesan cheese, nonfat or low-fat dairy products, cream, whole milk, cheese, green leafy vegetables, bonemeal, sardines, canned salmon (with bones), citrus fruits, dried beans	Bones and teeth Muscle contraction Blood clotting Cell membranes
Phosphorus	Parmesan cheese, nonfat or low-fat dairy products, fish, fowl, meat, cream, whole milk, cheese, eggs, nuts, bonemeal, dried beans	Bones and teeth Formation of cell membranes and enzymes
Magnesium	Nuts, whole grains, green leafy vegetables, fish	Bones Making proteins Nervous system

MINERAL	SOURCE	NEEDED FOR
Iron	Meat, eggs, green leafy vegetables, whole grains, dried fruit, dried beans	Supplies oxygen to cells Proteins and enzymes
Zinc	Meat, fish, eggs, fowl	Makes up enzymes
Iodine	Iodized salt, fish	Functioning of thyroid Reproduction
Potassium	Dried fruits, orange juice, bananas, meat, peanut butter, dried beans, potatoes	Muscle contraction Release of energy from proteins, fats, and carbohydrates Nervous system

These are some of the other important nutrients that may also be included in vitamin/mineral combinations but often get less attention:

NUTRIENT	SOURCE	NEEDED FOR
B-6	Yeast, wheat bran, wheat germ, liver, kidney, soybeans, eggs, oats	Proper absorption of protein and fat Antinausea Antistress Helps as a diuretic Prevents anemia, skin disorders
Choline (from B-complex family)	Yeast, liver, wheat germ, egg yolks, green leafy vegetables	Helps with memory Liver detox Works with inositol to prevent cholesterol buildup

Inositol (from B-complex family)	Yeast, liver, wheat germ, cantaloupe, grapefruit, cabbage	Helps lower cholesterol Helps healthy distribution of body fat Promotes healthy hair and skin
Folic acid (from B-complex family or vitamin M)	Beans, egg yolk, pumpkin, apricots, liver, rye flour, cantaloupe, carrots, green leafy vegetables	Prevents birth defects, supports lactation Promotes healthy skin
Chromium	Wheat germ, calves' liver, chicken, clams, corn oil, brewer's yeast	Growth Aids healthy blood pressure Helps deter high blood pressure
Copper	Legumes, whole wheat, prunes, shrimp, most fish	Helps iron absorption
Manganese	Whole grains, nuts, peas, beets, green leafy vegetables	Reduces fatigue Bone support Helps memory Calming
Selenium	Liver, seafood, wheat germ, bran, broccoli, onions, tomatoes	Antioxidant Helps fight cancer Offers hormonal support, helps reduce hot flashes

With this general knowledge, I then sought out one of the world's leading nutritionists, Dr. Carsten Smidt. German-born, educated in Europe and in the United States with a Ph.D. in nutrition science and physiological chemistry, Dr. Smidt has formulated many cutting-edge supplements for both women and men. Moving beyond the basic guidelines for supplementing, I asked Dr. Smidt to help me design a comprehensive but simple regimen. I also asked him to take into account the different vitamin, mineral, and herbal needs for the following three groups of women, whose ages and varying levels of hormonal activities raise distinct issues:

1. Women in reproductive peak years (teens, twenties, thirties, and beyond)
2. Women in transition between their reproductive peak and menopause, a process that can last more than ten years and is known as perimenopause (late thirties, forties, fifties)
3. Women who are menopausal, meaning they've reached and passed menopause (forties, fifties, sixties, seventies, and beyond)

Dr. Smidt's action plan begins with the youngest group of women, as we look at the question of what nutritional needs should be covered in a high-quality multivitamin/mineral supplement. Drawing from the latest government reports about common deficiencies in the average diet for this population of women, Dr. Smidt notes: Two thirds aren't getting the RDAs of vitamins A and E; more than half aren't getting enough B-6; 75 percent aren't getting enough magnesium or iron; and 80 percent aren't getting enough calcium or iron. Another critical area of deficiency is folic acid, falling below the daily 400 to 800 micrograms that are so important to this age group for reproductive health.

In selecting a multi, then, be on the lookout for those nutrients in particular. Also look for the following either in the multiple or in a separate supplement:

- All the B vitamins for energy, mental functioning, and antistress should be included in the multiple, as should antioxidants we've already covered, along with vitamins D and K, boron, and silica for healthy bones and tissues.
- Either in the multiple or in a separate supplement, look for Alphalipoic acid, helpful as an anti-aging nutrient; you can start early rather than later.

- For your essential fatty acid needs, which aren't usually included in multiple formulations, Dr. Smidt cites health data suggesting that emphasis be placed less on Omega-6 oils and more on increasing the Omega-3 sources. That can be accomplished by eating more fatty fish like salmon and sardines or by taking fish-oil capsules. Flaxseed oil, another rich source of Omega-3 oils, cannot be heated to cook but can be used in salads or health shakes. It must be refrigerated, and opened bottles should not be kept longer than a few weeks.

- Balancing your calcium/magnesium needs (calcium RDAs range from 1,000 to 1,300 milligrams a day) may require some conscious attention on your part. Many food products are calcium-fortified, and as most women get approximately 500 to 800 milligrams from their diet, you need only 200 to 500 milligrams to make up the deficits, either in your multiple or in your calcium/magnesium supplement.

- Your calcium intake is important for PMS; also helpful, says Dr. Smidt, would be an investigation of the natural soy isoflavones available at health-food stores.

In looking at women in the second group, with more hormonal fluctuations and the beginning of aging changes, Dr. Smidt observes many of the same deficiencies, with the exception of iron—due to diminished frequency of menstruation and the blood loss that goes along with it. So a multivitamin/mineral should cover the main nutrients we discussed for the previous group but should have less iron. Many multiples can contain as much as 18 milligrams, which is too much for this group and may serve as a pro-oxidant (the opposite of an antioxidant), negating the benefits of other antioxidants being used, such as vitamin C and E and green tea extracts. Follow the guidelines of the previous group, as well as those for further special needs often shared by this group, to address common issues:

- The herbal help that Dr. Smidt recommends for hormonal fluctuations is Black Cohosh (good for relieving hot flashes, night sweats, and water retention), as well as soy isoflavones. We should note that while some doctors suggest Dong Quai for hormonal balance, Dr. Smidt is less favorable about its use.

- Because the greatest amount of bone loss takes place within these years, do not shortchange your calcium/magnesium needs. (Later we'll look at natural hormone supplements that can make a huge difference.)

- In demand now are those essential fatty acids (especially EPA, GLA, and DHA), which can work as natural anti-inflammatories for allergies, irritable skin, and cardiovascular disease.

- If moodiness, stress and/or anxiety, or sleep difficulties increase during these years, Dr. Smidt notes that Kava Kava can work for all age groups. He doesn't recommend Saint-John's-wort for improving mood or sleep because of problems with drug interactions, including its potential for interfering with birth control pills.

Dr. Smidt indicates the most significant differences in needs among women in our third group. Because of the cessation of menses, even less iron is needed, as little as 3 to 5 milligrams, except for those few women in this age range who may have an iron deficiency. The other nutrients not being met by diet are similar to the two previous groups, with the exception of vitamin A. Therefore, says Dr. Smidt, for this age group it's important not to supplement with too much preformed vitamin A, something that aging enables us to retain more efficiently in our livers. Vitamin A in the form of beta-carotene is not the concern, which is fine to have in amounts up to 25,000 IU. It's the other, preformed vitamin-A forms that Dr. Smidt advises to reduce to 2,500 IU. Other particulars to note for this group:

- All those bone nutrients that you started in your earlier years continue to be of major importance. For the improvement of joint cartilage, a supplement to investigate is glucosamine capsules. Though glucosamine occurs naturally in our body and diet, supplementing can improve cartilage formation, which may be very helpful for osteoarthritis and other joint concerns.

- "There's more to ginkgo than just the usual memory story we've been hearing," says Dr. Smidt, who recommends it not only to address forgetfulness, but also to enhance circulation in our extremities, and for eye health.
- Different varieties of ginseng (Korean, American, Siberian) can be explored—preferably with professional guidance—for this group (and for women of all ages) if one is looking to improve sexual drive, sports endurance, stamina, energy, clarity of mind, or relieve stress. However, Dr. Smidt notes, "The scientific substantiation for ginseng is still weak, and Korean [Panax] ginseng may increase blood pressure in hypertensive people."
- Fiber is needed for all ages, particularly in the later years, when many women experience bowel irregularity. Fiber deficiencies affect our ability to fight off cancers and can impact our blood lipids, contributing to heart disease. The best fiber comes from vegetables, fruits, and whole-grain cereal sources. Supplements can be obtained in powders or mixes that would hopefully include a balance of soluble and nonsoluble fibers, along with both fermentable and nonfermentable fibers. If not, a heavy fiber supplement can be too rough on the gastrointestinal system.

And for all the age groups, particularly as it relates to this chapter, Dr. Smidt gives us his opinion of the many supplements being touted for help with weight loss. For starters, he reminds us, there is no magic pill for weight loss, no miracle drug, no dietary supplement that works overnight. Nor has Dr. Smidt found any benefits from two frequently mentioned supplements for weight loss—chromium picolinate, said to preserve muscle mass during dieting, and L-Carnitine, which is supposed to help us burn fat.

Using both the general guidelines provided by Dr. Khalsa and the age-specific information from Dr. Smidt, the following table gives you a range of options to create a supplementation plan that suits your needs. Because you know yourself better than anyone, you can be the best judge of whether you should try all five categories of supplementation or start by taking a multi and then adding the other categories gradually. For needs other than those addressed in the following chart—such as help for mood, sleep, improved digestion, control of cholesterol—you might want to review suggestions for supplementation from both doctors.

SUPPLEMENT	REPRODUCTIVE PEAK TWENTIES, THIRTIES +	TRANSITION FORTIES, FIFTIES	MENOPAUSE FORTIES TO EIGHTIES +	HOW TO TAKE
1. Multivitamin/ mineral combination Needed for complete health	Look for all major nutrients, especially B's, iron, folic acid	Look for all nutrients Limit iron to 8 mg Lower A	Look for all nutrients Limit iron to 3–5 mg, Limit A to 2,500 IU	Multis come as one or two a day, but can be more, capsules or tablets, take with meals
2. Anti-aging antioxidants Needed to prevent formation of free radicals and anti-aging help for memory and energy	C, E, selenium should be in multi; you can take additional C, E, green tea extracts, bioflavanoids	Antioxidants in multi; you can supplement C, E, green tea extracts, bioflavanoids, coenzyme Q-10	Antioxdiants in multi and take separate C, E, and green tea extracts, bioflavanoids, coenzyme Q-10, gingko biloba	Follow product dosage guidelines for individual supplements or combo antioxidants
3. Bone and tissue support Needed for healthy growth, prevention of bone loss	Combination or individual supplements of calcium, magnesium, boron, silica, vitamins D, K	Combo or individual supplements of calcium, magnesium, boron, silica, vitamins D, K	Combo or individual supplements of calcium, magnesium, boron, silica, vitamins D, K, glucosamine	Follow product dosage guidelines
4. Essential fatty acids (Omega-3 and Omega-6)	Supplement	Supplement	Supplement	Take individually or as a combo: fish and flaxseed

SUPPLEMENT	REPRODUCTIVE PEAK TWENTIES, THIRTIES +	TRANSITION FORTIES, FIFTIES	MENOPAUSE FORTIES TO EIGHTIES +	HOW TO TAKE
Needed for immune and neurological systems, anti-inflammatory for allergies, skin				oils, evening primrose, borage, and black currant–seed oils
5. Hormonal support	For PMS: soy isoflavones, calcium	For fluctuations: Soy isoflavones, Black Cohosh, Kava Kava for mood	Ginseng for sexual drive (avoid Korean)	Follow product guidelines

Finally, for all our nutritional supplementing needs, Dr. Smidt suggests opting for the higher-end products for better quality nutrients and better absorption and tolerability.

THE MIND-BODY LEARNING LINK

Because one of the fundamentals of *Living Principal* is that we be open to learning every day of our lives, I hope the nutritional basics covered here have given you a foundation of knowledge that will encourage you to learn more. There are many excellent nutritional guides currently on the market that can offer you even more insights.

In the meantime, learning about exercise, the other part of what your body absolutely needs, is our next chapter.

Practical Steps for Saying Yes
to Diet and Supplements

In recalling the major points from this chapter, I'd like to first reinforce the idea that you already have the secret to successful weight loss—you. Instead of assigning blame to outside causes or to yourself, congratulate yourself right now that you have the ability to responsibly confront your current weight and choose to change it, if that is what you desire and what you believe is healthiest for you. Now take action.

COMMIT TO A REALISTIC PLAN FOR YOURSELF AND YOUR LIFESTYLE

Take however many days you need to honestly assess your current eating habits and your health as they relate to weight, food, and supplements. How healthy are your choices for what you eat, when you eat, and how much you eat? Do you make a habit of drinking six to eight glasses of water a day? Do you take supplements on a consistent basis? Once you've made an honest, thorough evaluation, choose which habits and patterns you're ready to change, to which you can commit every fiber of your being for the next thirty days. This is the moment of truth. If you are not ready for the *30-Day Diet to Lose* or any structured weight-loss program, you may opt to start your own plan by committing to changing three habits and sticking with that resolve for thirty days. (Examples: drinking eight glasses of water a day; taking vitamins and minerals every day; cutting out foods that are on the list of what we don't need; cutting down your portions; eating at set times rather than chronic snacking; eliminating night eating; using positive alternatives for typical situations that trigger emotional eating.) Commitments to change these habits are just as vital if you're ready to follow the *30-Day Diet to Lose* or the seven-day *Bikini Diet,* or when you want to maintain your healthy weight with the *Diet for Life.*

GET STARTED!

. . . .

Now that you've committed to a realistic plan, go to it. Take this as an opportunity to focus on the journey rather than the destination. Do this one day at a time, cheering yourself with your internal voice.

ELICIT SUPPORT FROM PROFESSIONALS AND LOVED ONES

. . . .

Whether you're changing habits or embarking on one of the diets in this chapter, check in with your doctor. (Have your blood pressure and cholesterol levels taken while you're at it.) For added professional guidance, if you need it and can accommodate it in your budget, you may also want to consult with a nutritionist and/or a psychotherapist. Again, the secret to success lies within you. At the same time, reinforcing your commitment with professional guidance can help you make permanent changes. You may want to delegate a friend or family member to be your point person to offer support and encouragement for your weight-loss journey.

STOCK UP ON WHAT YOU NEED; RID YOURSELF OF TEMPTATION

. . . .

Rid your pantry and fridge of as many foods that we don't need as you can. Though family members may prefer that you not give away the brownie mix or the potato chips, you might ask them to have their snacks outside of the house or even to join you in eating healthier foods. Then, using the menu plan for the diet you are starting or the lists of foods we need most of the time and occasionally, stock up for the week ahead. If you have work or social obligations that require dining out, or you are unable to cook a particular meal, try to plan ahead so that you can order what's specified on the diet for that meal. It should be easy, as long you anticipate those moments and choose restaurants that offer salads, steamed vegetable plates, and grilled fish and chicken.

SUPPLEMENT

Whether this step is the only one you're ready to take at this time or whether you've opted to lose weight with one of the diets in this chapter, supplementing can make a major difference in how you feel and look. Follow the suggestions for getting started in the supplement section, and use those guidelines at the health-food or homeopathic store. If you'd like more information, ask the clerks at those stores for their input, along with any handouts the product manufacturers offer. Again, your doctor's guidance can be helpful, as can that of a nutritionist.

DOCUMENT YOUR PROGRESS

Select a type of measurement to gauge your success—weigh yourself; take measurements with a tape measure of your chest, waist, hips, and thighs; or use the doctor's test measurements. Recheck those measurements once a week. If you're making changes, expect improvements to show up soon. But don't be discouraged if you don't measure external improvements—remember that there are other internal improvements taking place.

You don't have to be great
to start,
but you have to start
to be great.

—JOE SABAH

CHAPTER FOUR

EXERCISE—ANYONE, ANYTIME, ANYPLACE

The Beauty of Getting Moving

COULDN'T LIVE WITHOUT IT. TO ME, IT IS ALMOST AS AUTO-MATIC AS BREATHING. A FUNDAMENTAL PART OF EVERY DAY, just as I eat, sleep, work, love—I exercise. Regular exercise is a critical factor in how I look: in the shape, strength, and suppleness of my body; the tone, color, and glow of my skin; the clarity and brightness of my eyes. Exercise greatly determines how I feel and raises my energy level, mood, mental alertness, and problem-solving abilities, not to mention benefitting my bones, muscles, heart, lungs, digestive organs, blood, nerves, and hormones. Oh yes, and my libido!

Of course, I'm not alone in holding the belief that exercise is a whole-health essential. At the cusp of this new millennium, the United States surgeon general, Dr. David Satcher, issued a list of health priorities for Americans, and the number-one priority was exercise. The report stated that engaging in some form of exercise that raises your heart rate for a sustained twenty minutes just three times a week is not only a prescription for better health, but the leading longevity practice.

Sadly, in spite of all that most of us know about the need for lifetime physical fitness, an alarming percentage of Americans lead increasingly sedentary lifestyles—unwilling, uninterested, or unable to bring themselves to stick to a regular exercise program. Perhaps it's because of our technological dependencies, or maybe due to attitudes we took from our families, friends, and culture; however it comes about, I don't think our resistance to exercise is something that happens to us naturally.

When we were very young, long before most of us became conscious of how our bodies looked to others, we learned how our bodies felt. Well before we were introduced to the idea that exercise was important, we learned how joyful it was to simply move; how exhilarating it felt to stretch, jump, skip, dance, play, run, tumble, splash, swim, slide, swing, skate, pedal, row, throw, catch; how energizing it felt to breathe deeply during and after exertion; and even how good our bodies felt inside, with our hearts beating and our bones and muscles supporting all of our joyous movement.

The idea of exercise for most children is never a "have-to"; rather, it's a "get-to." But, unfortunately, somewhere along the road to adulthood, that attitude shifts. First we get mixed messages: "Sit still" is a refrain we hear constantly when we're young. Though we might be encouraged to move our bodies freely, we're also told that there is a time and place when that is appropriate. In fact, for some kids, getting to move their bodies sometimes becomes a privilege to be earned. Remember begging for permission to go out to play? Remember having to clean up your room or clean your plate first?

For some of us, the pressure to compete and excel athletically may shut down our natural love of moving our bodies. The pressure to make our bodies look pleasing to others can also get in the way of a natural drive to be fit in order to please ourselves. Then there are those of us who as adults stay connected to that natural drive and want to exercise, but because of a variety of reasons—the demands of work or lifestyle, pregnancy, motherhood, illness, or injury—can't find the time or the means to regularly include it in a daily schedule.

That was me in my early thirties, when my workaholism was at its peak, around the same time that a friend talked me into going on a long-overdue vacation. Though I wasn't overweight (thanks to the nutritional changes I'd made seven years earlier that allowed me to lose those forty pounds and keep them off), I had not made regular exercise an intrinsic part of my life.

I did participate in outdoor activities whenever I could—tennis, swimming, target shooting, volleyball. I also knew from past experience about the rapid benefits that an exercise regimen could bring. When I seriously injured my leg and kneecap, as an alternative to surgery, I learned and practiced an easy but amazingly effective method of resistive exercise based on isometrics. Then, after accepting an offer to be a contestant on television's *Battle of the Network Stars,* in which celebrities from different TV networks competed in various challenging sporting events, I managed to train rigorously beforehand. When I was invited to compete on subsequent occasions, again I would binge on exercise—but only enough to get in shape to compete and then collapse afterward.

I knew exercise would be good for me, but I couldn't accommodate it in my schedule. Since my *Dallas* working days started at five-thirty in the morning and went as late as nine or ten at night, fitting in workout time seemed a mathematical impossibility. Besides, since I was so active at work, I assumed my body would sort of naturally stay as tight and firm as it had been through most of my twenties.

It didn't. That was underscored when my very dear, very blunt friend made a remark to me one day that I would never forget. Wearing jeans, I was standing in my kitchen at the stove when she walked in, looked at me from behind, and said, "What's that?"

"What?" I asked and turned around to see.

"That thing on top of your legs," she said.

I looked around and down, looked again. Then I realized that the thing she was talking about was my bottom. What had once been my toned and tight derriere was starting to head south. Another defining moment. Her comment jolted me into action. I had to come up with a way to exercise that I could incorporate into my schedule and lifestyle—anywhere, anytime. Whatever exercise plan I chose, I knew it would have to be fun, convenient, and flexible enough to keep me committed; it had to be safe, simple, effective, and individualized.

After getting input from a number of experts—doctors, chiropractors, fellow actors, dancers, bodybuilders, fitness trainers, aerobics instructors—I developed my own resistive exercise-based workout that not only lifted and tightened my bottom but helped me resculpt, strengthen, and tone the rest of my body. The results were so rapid and obvious that my exercises were soon being appropriated by friends, colleagues, and shortly after that by readers of my first book, *The Body Principal.*

Over the nearly two decades that have since passed, as new information has emerged about exercise and as my body's needs have changed, I have updated and improved my basic workout into twenty minutes of total body toning—adding stretching and breathing elements from yoga, along with strengthening elements from Pilates and dance movements. Yet the principles that guided me in my thirties have remained effective to this day.

Maybe you've exercised in fits and starts in the past but have never found the time for it on a regular basis. Maybe circumstances have prevented you from participating in physical activity, and starting back has become too daunting. Maybe you've never liked exercise. Maybe you'd love to exercise but have spent so long being inactive that you believe you'll fail.

Very often, the reasons we use to justify not exercising are the excuses we use to mask other, deeper feelings. The following examples may sound familiar:

- "I joined a gym, but I don't have the discipline to work out on my own, and I can't afford a trainer." I'll bet this woman's internal voice has been calling her names, blaming her for lacking discipline and money. If she can get past the blame and commit to the desire to exercise, she has several options that don't involve the gym or money.
- "I hate exercise. I'm uncoordinated and find it boring, uncomfortable, stressful, and painful." Sometimes women who have been in

denial about their weight or age may use this excuse to express their hopelessness about improving themselves. The good news is that with a small amount of effort, women are finding plenty of exercise options that aren't boring, uncomfortable, stressful, or painful and don't require coordination. Medical studies have proven overwhelmingly that it's never too late to start exercising.

- "Whenever I put on sweats to go exercise, I feel too self-conscious and don't make it out the door." For lots of women who are just getting started with exercise or returning after a long period of inactivity, this is an honest expression of the fear of being judged by others. It might help to start exercising in the comfort and privacy of your own home or backyard—which goes along with the principle of anyone, anytime, anyplace. Your internal voice can also provide you support and encouragement. For all of us, too much energy is wasted in worrying about how others might judge us. Usually those people are too concerned with themselves to make judgments about us!

- "I'm not overweight, I'm thin. My problem is cellulite, and since I've read that exercise doesn't get rid of it, why bother?" Many women, regardless of weight—even those who exercise—are prone to retaining pockets of fat, usually on legs and buttocks, which dimple the skin. Genetics play an important factor in whether and to what degree you develop cellulite. Theories also suggest that as long as women have childbearing potential, the body stores fat in this way to support a healthy pregnancy. And it's true that there are no miracle cures to ridding oneself of cellulite, including liposuction. What can be effective—in slowing its development or even lessening it—is a disciplined regimen involving regular high-intensity aerobic exercise, a very low-fat diet without any dairy or meat, and frequent, intense massage of the affected areas. But if that routine isn't realistic for you, don't miss out on the other benefits that exercise can bring to your whole-health—including toning and shaping the rest of your body, making cellulite that much less noticeable.

- "Injuries prevent me from working out." With care and thoughtful planning, gentle, nonintrusive forms of exercise—such as resistive training and Pilates instruction—will still give you the health benefits you need without stress or further injury to your body.

Probably the most common reason for not exercising regularly is the same excuse I used: "I don't have time." As my story and the principles I employed to design my exercise plan will illustrate, the simple process of consciously choosing to find and make the time in your day will result in an attitude switch that will save you time with all sorts of activities. A term of our times, this is known as multitasking.

Did you know that you can do exercises to firm your bottom while standing in line at the grocery store? And on your way into the house, you can work your biceps by carrying a bag of groceries in each arm. Or if you're following a skin-care regimen and you have to wait twenty minutes after applying a facial mask, use that time to stretch and breathe instead of reading a magazine.

If you can make peace with time, not only to make room for exercise but for doing all the things you truly want to do, you'll have discovered a longevity secret that will enormously enhance your quality of life—if not the duration of your life. The first step is to declare exercise one of those things you truly want to do. As you do that, let go of the old excuses and whatever resistance you've had to making exercise a way of life. You are free to throw out the backlog of efforts that didn't pay off in the past. Let this be a new beginning, a new experience of the beauty and joy of getting moving.

BODY PRINCIPLES

Now that you've made the choice to embrace exercise, anytime, anyplace, the following steps will get you started, as well as offer general guidance along the way.

Renew your sense of fun in being active. Just because you've decided to incorporate an exercise plan into your day doesn't mean that other activities don't count. Whatever you do—walking the dog, doing housework and yardwork, walking to the store, or getting up from the chair at work to move to a different location—you can make it count and make that motion enjoyable. By consciously deciding to be more active in general, you might rediscover physical leisure activities that you loved in the past but haven't made time for—like golf, bowling, tennis, swimming, biking, hiking—and reincorporate those activities.

Bring your body awareness into daily activities. As you practice the art of enjoying daily activity, four factors can make the added motion count as exercise:

- *Posture.* The basics of good posture will serve you in formal exercise as they will throughout your day. Stand tall, chest up, stomach in, shoulders down, arms relaxed at your sides. A mental cue for proper alignment is to imagine a rope in a straight line from the back of your lower pelvis bone, up through your spine and out through the middle of the top of your head. In your effort to reach tall, be careful not to arch or sway your back and, above all, never lock the joints of your arms and legs.
- *Go all out when you move.* When you're using the steps instead of the elevator—good for you!—pick up your knees and take advantage of a full range of motion. If you're walking to the bus or to the store or into a different room at home, try taking longer strides and swing your arms. Weeding in the garden? Challenge yourself to dig and pull with more exertion, feeling your muscles tightening and strengthening as you do.
- *Pace.* By picking up the pace when you perform menial chores, walking faster and moving through your day at even a slightly quicker tempo, you not only receive the physical fitness benefits but, again, you may find more time in your schedule to do what you want.
- *Balance.* If you're exercising the muscles of your arm while scrubbing the kitchen—great for you!—remember to balance your body

by doing the same activity with your other arm too. Pay attention to the parts of your body that are getting more exercise than others and find ways to balance. Doing a lot of bending over to pick things up? Try stretching up to high shelves to put them away.

Learn the basics of body-resistive exercises. There is nothing new about the use of body-resistive exercises—also called isometrics—although with all the various workout fads that have come along in recent decades, this natural, nonstressful, and easy approach to exercise often gets lost in the shuffle. Very simply, isometrics are based on the understanding that the contraction and stretching of muscles are important, and that regularly using your muscles' resistance will result in toned and firmer muscles. By working an individual muscle in a static position—slowly, in isolation—it will be strengthened and tightened naturally.

You may be aware that as a result of inactivity, muscles waste away, and as bones lose calcium and become brittle, osteoporosis can develop. For individuals with injuries or illness requiring periods of bed rest, the atrophying of muscles can pose a real threat. That is why injured patients and those with bone diseases are encouraged to do resistive exercises, which strengthen dormant muscle tissues without undue strain or movement through the rest of the body. As our muscles become less resilient in the aging process, resistive exercises offer a sensible, effective way to maintain elasticity.

Try it for yourself. Take one hand and place it against your other hand, pressing them together. That's resistance. As you press, feel the muscles in your arms contracting and tightening. It's as simple as that. When you intensify how hard you're pressing and sustain it continuously for several counts, you're reaching total resistance; if you expend maximum energy, you get maximum results.

Let me emphasize that resistive exercises differ from most exercises used in weight training. The aim of resistance training is to redefine and tone your muscles so that they are longer and leaner, while training with weights—especially heavier ones—often results in building up or bulking up your muscles. Because working out with weights usually involves faster, higher repetitions of muscles' contractions, it's more likely to raise your heart rate and burn more fat. At the same time, if you don't really know what you're doing or don't have expert guidance, you can run a high risk of injury.

Set your own goals, design your own plan. In keeping with anyone, anytime, anyplace, create an exercise program by picking an activity or sport that appeals to you enough to sustain your interest—whether it's an isometrics workout; weight training with professional help; joining a local gym; toning with cords at home; doing a Pilates, dance, or yoga class; working out to a Pilates, dance, or yoga video; or any safe, regular exercise outlet that emphasizes muscle toning and strengthening. If you can commit to that activity three times a week, then incorporate an additional twenty minutes, three days a week, of basic aerobic exercise (see Heart Options, page 140, for ideas), that would be ideal. However, if you're beginning a plan of exercise for the first time, or starting back after a long hiatus, allow yourself to work slowly toward the ideal. For the first week, you might want to focus on stretching and warming up every day, then the following week add in three days of whatever strengthening and toning exercises you've chosen. By the third week, you'll hopefully have a varied schedule that you can adapt anytime, anyplace, which allows you to move your body six to seven days a week.

Whatever your level of fitness, be flexible and creative with designing a program and setting your daily and long-term goals. We tend to be more successful with regular exercise when we do it at the same time every day. That way it becomes a ritual or ceremony, a routine that you would miss if you didn't experience it daily. Many fitness experts recommend exercising in the morning—in part because we're physically and mentally rested, in part because early exercise can boost our energy and metabolism throughout the rest of the day. Also, if you skip your regular morning time to exercise, you still have the afternoon or evening in which to include it. That said, you may prefer exercising at midday, in the early or late afternoon, or at night.

Even with fervent commitment, there are days when we all resist an exercise plan, like those times when my internal voice loves to argue: *Are you kidding me? I'm not getting down on the floor and exerting effort! I'm going to the kitchen for something really good to eat!* Usually, I'm able to remind myself that even if I don't feel like it before I exercise, I know I'll feel good after I do.

Then there are those days when you're stuck in traffic or events come up that throw you off schedule. You can give yourself a break that day or make the most of the situation and do some "extras"—such as the sample body-resistive exercises included in this chapter. These use no obvious motion and can be done while driving a car; sitting in your chair at work; waiting in lines; or on a bus, subway, or airplane.

As I've said before, you are the best judge of yourself and your body. You know what your body's needs are now, how to best gauge the pace at which you move toward goals, and what will continue to motivate you over time. Don't set overly rigid rules. When you've established a routine, vary it so you don't get bored. If you feel like going longer one day, go for it. But do remember that moderation is best. If you find that you're overdoing it and your body is tired, slow down and take it easy, or shorten your exercise time. Most of all, enjoy the great feeling of rejuvenating your body.

Practice safe exercise. Just as a visit to your doctor is advisable before embarking on a diet, a checkup before starting an exercise plan—even a safe, slow-paced one—is always recommended. Again, keep safety in mind for your joints. You should never lock your knees or elbows when exercising. We want to exercise our joints, not wear them out.

Breathe noisily. By audibly releasing the air through slightly parted lips, you'll set an easily sustainable rhythm, and the sound will fuel the level at which you're working. Remember that your lungs don't fill up from bottom to top. Shaped like bellows, they fill from side to side, bottom to top. You can feel them expanding your rib cage, filling you with air and your blood with oxygen.

EXTRAS

These three resistive exercises are oldies but goodies that have accompanied me around the world:

Shoulder shrug: For on-the-spot relief from tension and for helping shape lovely shoulders. Start by shrugging your shoulders up, holding for a count of "one thousand and one," then releasing. Next, curl them forward, holding for a count, then release. Third, pull them back, squeezing your shoulder blades together, hold for a count, then release. Repeat eight times. You can also do this in the shower.

Counter push-ups: For firming chest and arms and stretching calves, these work as extras for anytime, anyplace, or as part of an exercise plan.

At a kitchen or bathroom counter, at your desk or ladies' room at the office, or using any piece of furniture that will offer you resistance, stand about two feet away with your feet flat on the floor, twelve inches apart. With your knees loose, lean forward and place your hands flat on the counter at the same width as your feet. Hold your back straight and tighten your abs; be careful not to clench your buttocks. Bending your elbows, drop your body slowly toward the counter, until your chest almost touches. Then straighten your arms and return to your original position. Keep moving, breathing, and repeat ten times, working up to twenty later on.

At the counter or desktop, turn around and face the opposite direction. Stand about two feet from the edge, leaning back at an angle with your buttocks just in front of the counter edge and your hands resting palm-down on the counter, your arms straight without locking your elbows. Now, bending your elbows farther, use your arms to drop your body into a leaning position, then push back up into your original stance. Keep moving, breathing, and repeat ten times, working up to twenty later on.

Turn to the side, with the counter or desktop at your right. Standing about two feet away, place your hand on top of the counter at the edge. If you splay your fingers for support, make sure you don't wrap your thumb under the edge; keep it close on the top edge. With your body and arm straight, bend your elbow as you slowly lean in to the counter at as close an angle as you can; without pausing, use your arm to push back to your original position. Keep moving, breathing, and repeat five times, working up to ten later on. When you're finished, turn and repeat on your left.

Bottoms Up: This is the very exercise that helped me redeem my derriere after my friend made her remark. You can do it in public or in private, standing or sitting. You might try these while checking your e-mail, putting on your makeup, having your nails done, vacuuming, taking a shower, driving a car, sitting on an airplane, reading, or talking on the telephone. I recommend that you learn it by standing with your feet twelve inches apart, knees slightly bent so you can isolate the contractions. Very simply, tighten the buttocks and the fronts and backs of your thighs as you pull in your stomach and hold for a count of "one thousand and one." Then release. Keep going for thirty seconds, at a pace that feels right for you. Rest for a moment, then go for another thirty seconds. Remember to keep your movements subtle. If you're standing in line at the supermarket checkout counter and others start to move away from you, it may be a sign that your contractions have turned into gyrations. That's a great exercise, but one you may prefer to do in private!

HEART OPTIONS

In addition to practicing body principles; doing extras anywhere, anyplace; and engaging in a regular form of fitness activity aimed at stretching, toning, and strengthening, the ideal fitness plans include at least twenty minutes of aerobics three times a week. Aerobic, of course, means "with air," and there are plenty of exercises to choose from.

Ten Minutes of Joy (yes, I am hugging my rosemary;
I planted it ten years ago!).

Make time
for yourself.

A natural
daytime makeup.

Use a cleanser that
safely and effectively
removes dirt and
eye and facial
makeup in one step.

Step 1: Gently cleanse
your face and neck,
then rinse and pat dry.

Step 2: Using your ring finger, gently pat a small amount of your eye product around your eye area.

Step 3: Apply moisturizer to face and neck with gentle upward and outward stroking motions.

Properly cleansed and moisturized skin is the smart way
to start and finish every day!

Shoulder shrug position number one.

Shoulder shrug up position number two.
Resume original position. Repeat until you reach desired number.

Shoulder roll
forward position
number one.

Shoulder roll
forward position
number two.
Resume original
position. Repeat
until you reach
desired number.

Shoulder roll
back position
number one.

Shoulder roll back
position number
two. Resume
original position.
Repeat until
you reach
desired number.

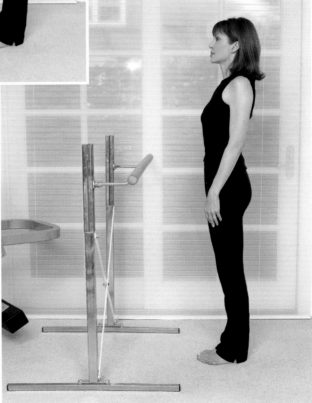

Push-up first position.

Push-up second position.
Resume original
position. Repeat until you
reach desired number.

Backward push-up
first position.

Backward push-up
second position.
Resume original
position. Repeat until
you reach desired
number.

Sideways push-up first position.

Sideways push-up second position. Resume original position.
Repeat until you reach desired number,
then change sides and repeat exercise.

Sample breakfast for the
30-Day Diet to Lose.

Sample snack for the
30-Day Diet to Lose.

Sample lunch for the
30-Day Diet to Lose.

Sample dinner for the *30-Day Diet to Lose*.

Ten Minutes of Joy can be as simple as taking your dogs for a walk.

For most of my life, I've loved fast motion—whether in sports or cars. It was natural for me, therefore, to include running as my preferred form of aerobic exercise. Over the years, however, I discovered that the jarring of my joints on hard surfaces had begun to take its toll. For that reason, I switched to fast walking, which I find gives me all the aerobic benefits of running, without the strain on my feet, ankles, knees, and hips.

When it comes to choosing your aerobic activity, base your whole-health choice on what will motivate you. You might choose the one activity that you're most likely to do three times a week. Or you might opt for variety: say, with a power-walk one day, twenty to thirty minutes of swimming laps two days later, and a low-impact aerobic class two days after that. Other choices include biking, hiking, tennis, skating, snow skiing and waterskiing, working out in your living room to twenty minutes of an aerobic dance video or other aerobic exercise tape, dancing continuously to music at home for twenty minutes, or taking a dance class. For not too high a cost, you can invest in a home or backyard-size trampoline and bounce for twenty exuberant minutes. Yoga has become more popular than ever, and some classes offer stretching combined with an aerobic workout. If you belong to a gym or health club, there are several machines, such as stationary bikes, stair climbers, and treadmills, that have programs for all levels of fitness. And if running gives you the endorphin-releasing boost that nothing else does, you should stick with it.

Before you throw on an old pair of sneakers and head out for the twenty-minute power-walk you plan on taking three times a week—congratulations for making the commitment!—make sure your shoes and bra are in good working order. Your shoes should provide ample arch support and good traction. Your bra or sports top should limit the movement of your breasts without cutting off your circulation.

Another essential before stepping out is to take a few minutes to warm up, doing any gentle stretches that can warm up your muscles. These basics apply to all vigorous exercise. Some other suggestions for healthy, happy walking:

- **Posture counts.** Stand tall, chest up, stomach in, pelvis forward, swinging your arms at your sides or pumping them for an added aerobic boost.

- At home on a treadmill, turn on music that gets your heart pumping. Outdoors, you can bring along headphones and a sports radio, cassette, or CD player.
- As you get started, if the awareness that you *have* to exercise burdens you, shift your mental focus elsewhere and let your body do what comes naturally. Use those twenty minutes to fly off in your imagination. Create stories and entertaining fantasies as you walk along briskly. Mentally sort through dreams and goals, or do some problem solving about matters that are pressing you in your work or personal life. Before you know it, the time will be over and the prospect of continuing will be a *want* to.
- As always, breathe.

Practical Steps to Getting Moving

As we recap the principles of exercise that apply to anyone, anytime, and anyplace, I want to mention again that it's better to take these practical steps at a slow and steady pace. Instead of feeling defeated that you can't do everything at once, feel euphoric that you've chosen one or two things that you've made a regular part of your lifestyle.

RECONNECT TO THE PLEASURE OF YOUR BODY IN MOTION

If the thought of exercise has come to trigger feelings of discomfort, let this be an opportunity to think back to times in your life when physical activity was a joyful experience. From that positive mind-set, make a commitment to having that pleasure in your life now by declaring exercise something you truly want to do. Just as you may have chosen to get rid of old attitudes about aging that weren't working for you, allow yourself now to let go of the old excuses for not exercising. Now stop thinking and start moving!

MOVE MORE THROUGHOUT THE DAY

Review the body principles in this chapter on the importance of posture, balance, pace, resistive exercise, and breathing, which you can practice as you go about your day, running errands, doing housework, gardening, office work, or commuting. Over the next few days, make a conscious effort to use better posture, to balance exertion on both sides of your body, to stretch up after you bend down, to pick up your pace, to contract your muscles (see Extras, page 138) to tone and strengthen, and to breathe.

DETERMINE YOUR CURRENT FITNESS LEVEL AND INTERESTS

If you have been relatively inactive for a substantial length of time, get your doctor's assessment on how much exercise (intensity, duration, and frequency) you can handle. If you are fairly active but have been inconsistent with regular exercise, make a prudent judgment about your fitness level and what amount, intensity, and frequency of exercise you're ready for. Next, review your options for toning, strengthening, and aerobic exercise. Explore those that interest you. If you need instruction, seek out fitness professionals. If costs are a concern, take advantage of community classes offered at modest prices. Remember to observe all safety practices when you exercise.

DESIGN A FLEXIBLE PERSONAL EXERCISE PLAN THAT INCLUDES STRETCHING/TONING/ STRENGTHENING AND AEROBICS

Take out your calendar and commit in writing to a realistic (yet flexible) exercise plan for the next thirty days. Flexibility means that if you plan to go to an aerobics class on Monday morning but have to handle a crisis at home and can't make it, you can then go to plan B—a power-walk outside on Monday afternoon. You might start out with three days of exercise the first week and increase that to four days of exercise the second week. Portable methods of exercise are wonderful—cords or videos that you can take along when you're not at home. An optimum balanced exercise plan should include some form of physical activity six to seven days a week— try devoting three days a week to stretching/toning/strengthening and three days a week to at least twenty minutes of aerobics. If you can add a seventh day that involves some form of outdoor physical activity you can share with loved ones, it will make the day's exercise that much more pleasurable.

CHALLENGE AND REINSPIRE YOURSELF DAILY

As your fitness level improves and you begin to see and feel positive results, add elements of challenge and variety. If you find yourself losing steam or growing bored, reinvigorate yourself by making a significant change in your personal program. Dare to dream: Train for a marathon. Climb a mountain. Enter a dance contest.

Prepare. *It wasn't raining when Noah built the ark.*

— HOWARD RUFF

CHAPTER FIVE

A LIFETIME OF BEAUTY—CARING
FOR SKIN, HAIR, TEETH, EYES

The Beauty Zone

NATURAL BEAUTY IS A GIFT TO BE TREASURED AND PROTECTED THROUGH THE YEARS. BEAUTY SHOULD never be simply taken for granted. Maybe you know someone who is so effortlessly beautiful she can look stunning day or night without a stitch of makeup, has never had a bad-hair day, a blemish, a hangnail, or a piece of unsightly lint. Maybe she's the same friend who eats fast food, tans, smokes and drinks to excess, who doesn't ever need to sleep, diet, exercise, take vitamins, drink at least eight glasses of water a day, or wash her face before she goes to bed at night. Either your friend is too young for such habits to take their visible toll, or she is a fluke of nature.

For the rest of us mortals, beauty takes work. But the effort we invest in taking care of ourselves doesn't have to be burdensome. In fact, like all the simple life-affirming daily ceremonies that can add meaning to our lives, beauty rituals can be fun and fulfilling, without becoming a central preoccupation. What's needed for that, I've found, is a practical plan that paves the way for a lifetime of beauty.

Preparing ourselves to weather the elements as we pass from one life stage to another is not unlike Noah building his ark before the rains. When it comes to beauty, preparation and protection can be as basic as wearing sunscreen and developing healthy sleep habits. A beauty plan means recognizing that how you treat yourself now will impact not only how you look today, but tomorrow, next week, and next year. Such a plan is possible with just a modest amount of time, a bit of organizational know-how, and the self-awareness to make choices that are right for you—along with a general knowledge of the tools, products, and techniques currently available.

It's my heartfelt belief that how you look is a reflection of how you feel about yourself. As we've been discussing, how you feel about yourself has to do with your whole-health, your connection to your senses, your primitive guide, and a positive internal voice. In this respect, beauty is very much a state of mind.

At one time or another, most of us have had those moments I like to call being in the Beauty Zone—when, for reasons we may not even know, we feel and look our most beautiful. Just as athletes and high-powered professionals use the notion of the Zone to explain peak performance, we, too, can experience feeling and looking our best in the course of our daily lives.

Those are the times when you look in the mirror and say, "*Yes.*" That feeling is contagious, because when you feel that you look beautiful, you radiate beauty. It's as if you've got fairy dust. People may even ask if you've changed your hairstyle or are wearing a new perfume when neither are the case. Or maybe you *have* been making some changes. Maybe your circulation has improved from starting exercise, your skin is glowing from a recent facial, you've been catching up on lost sleep lately, or maybe it's the soft flush on your cheeks from the fabulous blush you've begun wearing.

Most likely, it's not thanks to just one of those things. Instead, getting into the Beauty Zone most often occurs because of a combination of external and internal factors. Usually, feeling beautiful is the result of feeling good about yourself and how you're choosing to live your life, feeling good about your work, your family and friends, feeling good about your mind and body . . . *and* the way your hair looks.

Getting into the Beauty Zone doesn't happen only when all aspects of your life are running smoothly. Sometimes it comes from handling a difficult challenge or holding your head up through a stressful period. When you draw upon your inner resources of strength, resilience, and grace under fire to rise to the occasion, the physical expression of those qualities is indeed beautiful to behold.

Regardless of the particulars of our lives, beauty flourishes when we take pride in ourselves as human beings, thereby allowing our individual qualities of warmth, spirit, humor, confidence, and poise to shine forth. Here are some other principles that may be helpful:

- *Take pleasure in your face.* A mirror of your soul, your face, eyes, smile, and expressions speak for you, telling your emotions, passions, and experiences. If there are bumps, lines, wrinkles, or aspects of your features or skin that don't please you, you can change or improve them. But don't get mad at your face or become at odds with yourself. Minimize what you don't like and maximize what you do.

- *Be the one you love.* If you've been comparing yourself to the images of women you see in magazines, movies, or other media, I urge you to forgo efforts to conform to those unrealistic (often airbrushed and photographically enhanced) standards. Being yourself is attractive; embracing what is uniquely, originally you is gorgeous.

- *Commit to authentic beauty.* Use an awareness of who you are—your likes, loves, and passions—to develop your own distinctive style. Consult professionals, get ideas from magazines, investigate your options about what's most flattering for you, what techniques and products will enhance your best features. Women who have a sense of style—whether they have visible wrinkles, are overweight, or have a couple of crooked teeth—can be much more beautiful than women whose appearance may better comply with conventional beauty standards but who lack style. A sense of style, like grace, is about energy. It's how you present yourself, how you wear your hair, makeup, and clothes. It's how you carry yourself, how you communicate. It's the attention you show to others as well as to the details of your own presentation.

- *Practice beauty as you practice whole-health.* To me, healthy is beautiful. And because I believe whole-health is about being connected to my senses, I think the most "in-touch" individuals are the most beautiful.

Ironically, in our search for the newest beauty secrets, we often forget what we know from common sense—the old-fashioned beauty basics taught to many of us by our mothers and grandmothers. Add to those what we've learned in more recent years about the effects of ultraviolet rays, smoking, and pollution, and we get a beauty and health Rx all in one. At the top of that list is the age-old piece of advice "Get your beauty sleep," which I endorse emphatically. It turns out that not everyone needs exactly eight hours of uninterrupted sleep each night, but when I'm able to sleep for that length of time, it feels just about perfect to me. When I don't get enough sleep because of work or stress, I try to take a few minibreaks during the day to breathe deeply and surround myself with a feeling of calm. That way, even though I may be tired, I can still go about my daily activities without feeling too cranky or stressed. (In the anti-aging chapter, we'll hear from medical experts about the link between aging and diminished sleep.)

Another beauty basic we all know but which bears repeating: If you smoke as much as one cigarette a day, it's time to quit. If protecting your health and that of your loved ones isn't motivation enough, let vanity come into play. Smoking is a leading factor in accelerated wrinkling of skin; in tooth and gum disease and bad breath; a contributor to dry, brittle hair and nails; and it plays a role in weakening your eyesight. It's not easy to let go of any deeply ingrained habit, but there are effective ways to do it without feeling totally miserable. Classes, programs, books, nicotine gum and patches, and other medically safe approaches abound. The health, beauty, and anti-aging rewards to quitting are even more bountiful.

Some other commonsense practices include wearing sunscreen and hats outdoors. Shortly, I'll talk more about how ultraviolet rays hurt our skin and about options for self-tanning products. For the moment, I'll note that "wear your sunscreen" is considered by many women to be the single most important piece of beauty advice.

A woman I met while traveling—in yet another ladies' room!—approached me to say that though she had tried my skin-care products, they hadn't produced any marked improvement. I reviewed the easy 1-2-3 steps of the skin-care regimen, which she said she was following. "You do the three steps in the morning and at night?" I asked.

"At night?" she echoed. "Oh, no, just the morning. I'm too tired to wash my face at night." Which brings me back to where I began this topic—with the need we all have for a beauty plan. And what better place to start than with a subject about which I'm passionate.

SKIN

Two perspectives have long fueled my interest in skin care and the science that studies it. As I mentioned before, my concerns were originally personal as I sought to find products and treatments that were beneficial to me. This started even in my preteens, when I used to concoct my own facials in our kitchen, continuing into my twenties, when I had problems with serious breakouts, and on into the years when my skin began to show the initial signs of aging. Since I've been a professional in the business of developing and marketing products that are beneficial to women of all ages, another perspective has emerged over the past ten years that has definitely expanded my knowledge. From both perspectives, I can report that there's good news and bad news.

On an up note, science has made some important skin-care discoveries, particularly in its understanding of how skin can become damaged and how to prevent, defer, and repair those processes. From homeopathy, we've learned how to return to older, even primitive, treatments that use natural substances and to combine them with cutting-edge technologies based on findings about the ways our cells grow. But in spite of all that we're learning, the unfortunate news is that between the new hype about miracle cures and the old skin-care myths, many of us are left misinformed, confused, or both. If that weren't the case, a lot of women wouldn't have an array of almost full skin-care-product containers (which cost more than anyone wants to admit) collecting dust in bathrooms.

Before we tackle the myths and the hype, let's look at the facts about skin. You probably know that the skin is the largest organ of our body. You may also be aware that it has several functions. Skin regulates our body temperature and helps in the body's self-cleansing process by absorbing unwanted toxins into cells which are then sloughed off in our own ongoing, built-in skin-cell renewal system. As our protective outer covering, skin shields our body's insides from harmful chemicals and bacteria, and from environmental stresses such as the rays of the sun (here, skin can also use extra shielding).

Skin is also "the largest and most visible sex organ of the body," points out Dr. Peter T. Pugliese, author of *Skin, Sex and Longevity,* one of our country's foremost authorities in skin care, women's reproductive health, and anti-aging. Dr. Pugliese asserts that skin is where we first register our tactile sense, and that through touching, caressing, and hugging, we experience sexual sensations. Moreover, he writes, "It is the overall attractive appearance of skin that conveys the come-hither message."

Following that line of thinking, it's fair to say that our skin plays a central role in our beauty. This is just another reason that the care of our skin should play a central role in our beauty plan.

Most skin-care products and treatments are developed with a basis in long-standing scientific knowledge about the anatomy of skin. Starting from the outside, at the top of our skin, is our epidermis, which is made up of dead cells (that protect the live cells underneath), pigmentation cells, pores, and sebaceous glands, where we make our skin's natural oils. As those outer cells die, the skin manufactures new cells to take their place—a process that takes about a month or longer depending on age, hormones, skin care, and special treatments that can be used to speed up cellular replenishment. Below the epidermis lies the dermis, the lower, tougher layer which is made up of blood vessels, nerves, hair follicles, sweat glands, and fat cells, along with elastin and collagen fibers—the proteins that make up the connective tissue that gives our skin its plumpness and tone.

Experts tend to agree on how our skin changes as we age—hormonal shifts decrease estrogen levels, leading to diminished collagen and elastin and in turn to thinner, looser skin; to fine lines and wrinkles; and potentially to deep lines and folds. Compounding the hormonal influence is the accumulated damage from exposure to pollutants in our environment, through oxidation and the development of free radicals, plus the emotional and psychological stress of our modern lifestyles. These factors can lead to a further breakdown in collagen and elastin, rougher, drier skin, age spots and moles, broken veins, and irregular pigmentation.

We know what we *don't* need for healthy, beautiful skin. Although, let's be honest, the media still tends to represent the beauty image with young, tanned bodies, male or female. Not so long ago, sunbathing wasn't merely a fun pastime but part of a beauty regimen for many. We know now that because of human-made environmental changes in our atmosphere and the subsequent damage to the ozone layer, exposure to ultraviolet rays has become more dangerous than ever. This doesn't mean that tanning beds are better for you. As a matter of fact, they're worse, because there's only a thin layer of Plexiglas offering protection between you and high-powered, concentrated ultraviolet light. Don't be fooled by tanning salons telling you that the bad rays are filtered, leaving only the good rays. A tan is a tan—a form of skin aging.

You may be aware that there are two types of ultraviolet rays—UVA, which causes cells to age and results in wrinkles, and UVB, which causes burning, blotchy skin, and can cause basal-cell skin cancer. In selecting sunscreen, look for protection from both. How much SPF (sun protection factor) you need is determined by how long you plan to be in the sun (the longer you plan to be outside, the higher the amount needed) and the amount of melanin in your skin. If you are fair, and especially with red hair and green eyes, and/or have a complexion that always burns and never tans, you need the greatest amount of SPF. If you are dark, tan easily, and never burn, you can get by with less SPF. If you're in between, you should use amounts in between.

The middle-of-the-road safe approach for most of us is to wear sunscreen with at least SPF 8 on days when we're not outdoors much, and SPF 15 to SPF 20 on days when we anticipate being outdoors for any significant length of time. For the fairer-skinned and those who always burn and never tan, SPF 30 is recommended. The number of the SPF relates to how many hours the protection should last, but because sunscreens require reapplication after two to three hours, those higher SPFs are not necessary. Dr. Pugliese also cites recent studies that indicate the ingredients used to make the SPF in higher concentrations may irritate the skin.

Dr. Pugliese affirms that the good news for women of color—because of higher levels of melanin—is that the risk of damage and aging due to sun exposure is much lower than women who don't have as much melanin. Nonetheless, you will get darker in the sun, and some protection with lower SPFs, a moisturizer, and an antioxidant is still advised.

For all of us, sun protection for lips is required. The lips are a mucous membrane, different from the rest of our skin. With lower melanin and no oil or sweat glands, the thin skin layers of our lips don't absorb moisture very well, so regular remoisturizing is important. While conventional lipsticks do a basic job of protection, better bets include special sunscreens designed for lips, lipsticks with an SPF of 15, or vitamin-E sticks for lips with an SPF of 15, any of which need to be reapplied throughout the day.

When putting on sunscreen, don't overlook your hands, a common oversight, or your ankles and feet—especially if you're going bare-legged or wearing sandals, slip-ons, or mules. Reapplication of sunscreen is important if you've been exercising or swimming outdoors. Incidentally, you don't need to wipe off your perspiration when you're outdoors; sweat not only cools your body but can help as a natural sunscreen.

Even with regular use of sunscreens, you can still get a light tan. Ironically, many of us feel our complexions bloom with a little color from the sun. Nonetheless, those sun-kissed hues are evidence of skin damage and skin aging. Since full-force sunblock (the white, pasty type) is advisable only for those with sun allergies or autoimmune deficiencies and higher sun sensitivity, the more practical option is to help your sunscreen by wearing hats and sunglasses, plus more diligent moisturizing and antioxidant protection.

There is a range of quality in the many self-tanning products available, from inexpensive and ineffective to expensive and unimpressive to moderately priced and pretty good. This latter category works best from the neck down, provided you apply it evenly. Even when a self-tanner is designed specifically for use on your face, it's a good idea to test it on your arm or leg first. Though most of these products say that they provide sun protection, you should still wear sunscreen in addition to the self-tanning lotion.

Besides smoking, exposure to sun, and pollution, another substance believed to be unfriendly to skin is alcohol. In addition to dehydrating and depleting nutrients in your system, alcohol can deter circulation and cause broken veins or splotches on the nose and cheeks. Short of abstaining from alcohol, you can combat these effects by sticking to one drink a day and/or increasing your water intake when you do drink. My rule of thumb is that for each no-salt margarita I drink (one cocktail a week is usually my max), I'll sip two glasses of water. The diuretic effects of caffeine in coffee and cola drinks can also dry your skin. Another plug for herbal tea! But for you hard-core latté drinkers, increasing your water intake—two glasses for each coffee drink—can help.

Tugging, picking, or pulling at your skin isn't good; even frequently touching your face absentmindedly isn't good, especially since hands are magnets for dirt, oils, and bacteria. Sleeping on your face is also thought to stretch or crunch your skin to its detriment.

It's worth mentioning one more culprit in the list of what your skin doesn't need: rapid weight loss. Besides other concerns about what crash dieting can do to your health, it can wreak havoc with your skin, causing baggy wrinkles all over your body and a droopy face. This is yet one more reason to remember, no matter how rapidly you might wish to lose weight, that the best way to do it is slowly and steadily, with a nutritionally sound eating plan and regular exercise.

While medical and beauty experts generally concur about what can harm our skin, disagreement often begins once the discussion turns to how and what will best help us to attain and maintain healthy, beautiful skin.

For instance, some believe that there are just three types of skin—normal, oily, or dry. Very reputable product lines have been developed and sold based on those distinctions. If you ask a dermatologist or an aesthetician about that approach, most will tell you that as many as 90 percent of women they treat have combinations thereof—usually drier around the eyes and cheeks and oilier around the nose, chin, and forehead (the T-zone). As for so-called normal skin—the smooth, silky, lineless, poreless, creamy skin we all yearn for—the only people who have it are under the age of two.

And furthermore, says Dr. Pugliese, the problem with identifying your skin as dry, oily, or combination is that it doesn't take into account the other factors that determine what kind of skin you have. These include your genetic and ethnic heritage, blood type, pigmentation, weight, hair type, age, environment, lifestyle, and individual skin history.

We know that there are women who have *basically* dry skin—characterized by flaking and thinness and a tendency to become dehydrated and wrinkle more easily—and we know that for them, moisturizing is going to be an important part of any skin-care regimen. But that doesn't mean that women who have a history of generally oily skin don't risk becoming dehydrated. In fact, because women with oily skin—characterized by a shiny appearance, large pores, pimples, and blackheads or whiteheads—usually follow a regimen to dry their skin, it may be even more likely to become dehydrated.

Rather than pigeonholing our skin into one type or another, the solution I offer is twofold. First, get to know your own skin. If you don't have a sense of when it looks and feels more or less healthy, make a point of paying more attention to its texture, tone, and appearance—not just on your face but all over your body. Get input from professionals such as your doctor, aesthetician, or retail beauty consultant about what kind of skin you have. My other piece of advice is to select high-quality products that are designed to work for all skin types. Otherwise, you run the risk of either drying or oiling your skin to excess.

There are a few points of ongoing debate within medical, health, and beauty circles about the relative importance of nutrition as it relates to skin care. On one side are the dermatologists, who play down the role of nutrition in attaining healthy skin and treat skin disorders primarily with chemical medications that are ingested internally or applied topically.

Then there are the skin-care experts, who emphasize the procedures and products only they provide, again talking about caring for the skin externally. I'm of the whole-health school that believes skin is cared for externally and internally, and that there is a direct relationship between what we feed our bodies and what shows up on our skin.

Generally speaking, the nutritional guidelines for whole-health and for weight management are the same nutritional guidelines for healthy, beautiful skin. Specifically, if you have a propensity for oily breakouts, you have added reasons to stay away from foods with high oil content—all fried foods, creamy salad dressings, heavy sauces, avocados, olives, fatty fish, and fatty dairy products. Eating fiber in the form of fresh vegetables, fruits, and grains will assist your metabolism in flushing toxins from your body and clearing your skin.

If your skin is dehydrated, vegetables, fruits, and grains will help. You may want to eat small portions of healthy foods with higher oil content—avocados, almonds, or fatty fish. A tablespoon a day of mineral oil can be helpful for dry skin (and for regular elimination). Instead of using bottled dressings, dress your salad with a splash of flavored vinegar, a teaspoon or two of olive oil, and some fresh herbs. As you recall from our discussion of supplements, vitamin E, evening primrose, and other essential oils are excellent for improving the texture and tone of dry skin.

For everyone, following nutritional and supplement plans rich in the antioxidant vitamins A, C, and E is always a plus for the longevity of your skin. Vitamin D is also a boon for cell growth, and vitamin K keeps blood vessels strong. Green tea leaves that contain antioxidant properties can be brewed for hot or iced tea; if you use tea bags, let them cool after you make your beverage, then use them as a refreshing compress on your eyes.

You probably know that those eight glasses of water so good for you to drink each day are the ultimate nourishment for the skin. Indeed, replenishing the water that is lost in the course of each day is a fundamental step for hydrating your skin.

Another point of contention has arisen in regard to the strict beauty advice that you avoid excessive facial expressions—a bit extreme, in my opinion. Now, if you knit your brow in perpetual worry or purse your lips in a regular pout or routinely squint your eyes, those are habits you can work to correct or minimize—as much for your emotional health as well as for preventing wrinkles. Otherwise, I find an expressionless mask to be lifeless, and the prospect of stopping the flow of your feelings to be unhealthy and unattractive.

Myths and controversy continue to exist about what you put on your face. Given the hype of some products' marketing promises, it's little wonder that skepticism abounds. But the counterargument—that you need not waste your money on expensive products when household substances like Crisco work just as well—merits equal skepticism. Then there's the old-fashioned claim that the girl next door achieved her clean-scrubbed, healthy-looking skin with soap and water. Some dermatologists recommend using antibacterial soaps for cleansing your skin if you have acne, but experts like Dr. Pugliese have found that using soap on your face is nontherapeutic and dehydrating, at the least, and damaging at the most. Dr. Pugliese's research also suggests that the use of soap is the main cause for developing sensitive skin; part of that has to do with the skin's pH balance. Simply stated, pH balance uses a scale of 0 to 14 to measure the balance between the acid (at zero) and alkali (at fourteen) levels of various substances. Skin has a pH balance of 5.5 (more on the acidic side) and soap has a pH of 10 (more alkaline). For the best care of your skin, products should have compatible pH levels ranging from 5.0 to 6.0.

Needless to say, I believe that the products you choose do make a difference. Will they clean your house, balance your bank account, help you deal with childhood issues, improve your love life, get you a new job, and enable you to be more active on important social issues? No. But the right products for you, used properly, will absolutely give you more beautiful, lovingly cared-for skin.

On a personal note, let me mention that you can take a positive stand on the issue of animal rights by making sure that your cosmetic products aren't made from substances or processes that involve animal testing or by-products from the harm of animals.

To answer the questions about the right products for you and what's entailed in their proper use, it may be helpful to look at the basics of skin care for your face. Simple as 1-2-3, the three steps of cleansing, applying eye cream, and moisturizing should take no more than six minutes out of your day, three minutes in the morning and three minutes at night. You may have other skin-care treatments you use as "support systems" on occasion, but the basics should not be time-consuming.

1. The purpose of cleansing, as you may know, is to remove the dirt, makeup, dead cells, and unwanted oils that have accumulated over the course of the day, or during sleep when your skin's work in cleaning itself has been performed.

In the morning and the night, the first step is to begin by washing your hands—an antibacterial soap for hand washing, bar or liquid, is a good choice not just for you but for the whole family. For your face, the best cleanser to use is one that is water-soluble and nondrying—in either lotion or gel form. If you prefer soap in a bar, select one that is mild and nonalkaline. Your skin cleanser may serve double duty as a makeup remover. If not, be sure to get a gentle, nonoily makeup remover to use before cleansing.

After you wash your hands, spread facial cleanser on your face and neck, gently stroking with your fingertips in an upward, circular motion. Then with your hands or a soft, wet washcloth, rinse off your cleanser with warm water, then cool. Now pat your skin dry with a clean, soft towel.

2. Now apply an eye cream or gel to the skin under, above, and around your eyes. If you use a good moisturizer, you might wonder why we need a separate product for the skin around the eyes. It's because that skin is much more delicate than the rest of the face and can benefit from special emollients prepared specifically for the area.

Many top-of-the-line cosmetic companies make trustworthy eye creams. Some of the newer ones can do wonders not only to nourish and protect the skin but also to reduce the appearance of swelling, puffy undereyes, even fine lines and wrinkles.

When you apply your eye cream or gel, place a small amount on one or two fingers and very gently spread over, under, and around your eyes, being careful not to get it in your eyes. If you do, a wet Q-tip placed lightly in the corners of your eyes should absorb it easily.

3. The final step, moisturizing, serves the obvious purpose of returning the moisture (not necessarily the oil) that the skin has lost in the preceding hours, or to fortify its moisture capacity that may be depleted in the hours ahead. The better, enriched moisturizers also repair and protect the facial skin cells from environmental damage. Some of the newer moisturizers for women wanting help with fine lines and wrinkles include lifting agents that softly give the skin a tightened appearance.

What kind of moisturizer you choose will depend on your skin's particular needs. If you have very oily skin, choose a light nonoil-based moisturizer and apply it lightly; if you have very dry skin, use a good moisturizer for all skin types or a heavier moisturizer. But even when you're looking for all the moisture you can get, avoid greasier creams that can clog your pores. You can purchase moisturizers that are prepared as either day creams or night creams, or one moisturizer that can be applied morning and night.

For many of us with histories of oily breakouts in our T-zones or during hormonally active times of the month, it may be helpful to skip applying moisturizer to the forehead, nose, and chin on those particular days.

I recommend avoiding any moisturizer that lists mineral oil, wax, lanolin, or perfume as an ingredient. This goes for almost all types of skin-care formulations. There are several good moisturizers on the market with enrichment from vitamins A, B, C, E, and sometimes K. Natural enzymes can also be beneficial in moisturizers, as can protein enrichment of collagen and elastin. A high-quality daytime moisturizer may sometimes include sunscreen, thus eliminating the need to apply it separately.

Place a small amount of moisturizer on your fingertips and gently pat it onto your face, neck, and décolleté just after cleansing. Don't pull or stretch the skin; just smooth the moisturizer on softly and carefully.

If all you ever do for your skin is follow this simple 1-2-3 regimen, three minutes each morning and evening, you'll have achieved the most important part of a successful practical beauty plan—for life.

Of course, anywhere from once to three times a week, or a couple of times a month, you might want to consider some of the following other treatments for your skin, which will enhance your basic daily care:

Facial Masks. Masks come in a variety of deep cleansing and toning preparations with ingredients that range from clay to mint to cucumber and beyond. Before you apply the mask (according to the directions provided with the product), use your regular cleanser and apply your eye cream. Then, using your fingers, carefully spread the mask around your face, avoiding the eye area. After the mask dries for twenty or thirty minutes, remove with warm water and a wet, soft washcloth, then rinse with cool water and moisturize for the finishing touch.

Facial scrubs and other exfoliants. Like masks, facial scrubs deeply cleanse the skin, with an added feature of grainy or gritty ingredients that work to remove dead skin cells. A process known as exfoliating, getting rid of the older cells to make way for the newer ones is a way to promote "younger" skin—both in terms of the age of the cells and toward a smoother, brighter appearance. These products mustn't be too harsh. If the facial scrub you select is gentle enough, it shouldn't irritate your skin; and the massage you give your face when you apply the scrub is also beneficial for circulation.

How often you use a scrub will depend on how sensitive your skin is. If you are mildly sensitive, a gentle scrub once a week may be your maximum; if you have oil-rich skin, you may be able to use the same gentle scrub up to three or four times a week.

In case you're wondering, the shower is a fine place for cleansing your face—whether you're using a scrub, removing a mask, or as the first step of your daily skin-care regimen.

Alpha-hydroxy acids, enzyme treatments. Named after their type of molecular structure, alpha-hydroxy acids (AHAs) and their relatives, beta-hydroxy and poly-hydroxy acids, can be derived in such acid forms as citric, glycolic, and malic, from such natural sources as fruits, plants, and trees. Found now in products that range from scrubs and daytime moisturizers to makeup foundations, the acids exfoliate through a chemical reaction that dissolves the top dead layer of skin cells, plumping up the newer, younger cells underneath and boosting a rosier, brighter complexion. The watchword with any product containing AHAs has to be "gentle." Otherwise, any subtle inflammation of the skin will become an aggravation. For sensitive skin, this may mean avoiding products with AHAs altogether, or using them only occasionally.

The solution that works for me is to make the most of AHAs in a daily serum under my moisturizer, which mixes the fruit acids with the protection of antioxidating, moisturizing ingredients. Remember, the purer the acid formulation, the greater the difference between its low pH and the pH of your skin.

Again, unless AHAs are prepared in a gentle complex, Dr. Pugliese does not advocate their use. On the other hand, he does recommend products made from natural enzyme preparations. Derived from fruits and plants, many of these are also used for exfoliation. Additionally, there are some exciting new enzyme products on the market that are designed to be absorbed into the skin, to assist our own enzymes in enhancing collagen and elastin, and to fend off attack by the proteins that damage those fibers. The result is a plumper, firmer appearance to the skin. These newer enzyme products are available in special masks and in nighttime treatments that work well under a moisturizer.

A cream is recommended at night because our skin does much of its internal repair while we sleep; research on natural circadian rhythms suggests that those particular cells seem to prefer the dark.

Retin-A and other vitamin A–based skin treatments. For some women, the regular use of a gel or cream containing the vitamin A–based Retin-A or

Renova (both available only by prescription) has proven immensely successful in combating acne (for which it was formulated) and in minimizing fine lines and wrinkles. As wondrous as these achievements may be, the process is basically straightforward—peeling away the top layer of skin, which eliminates the visibility of the blemish or fine line. The downside is thinning of skin and extra vulnerability to sun and dehydration. Bearing that in mind, if you are on Retin-A, make sure you follow your doctor's directions for its use, moisturize, and wear sunscreen.

Chemical cousins are available in nonprescription strengths such as retinol or retinyl. You may see those ingredients featured in some higher-end antiwrinkle creams. I haven't incorporated them into my regimen because of skin sensitivity and my concerns about the long-term effects.

Since many of our discussions involve selecting professionals for help with our beauty and whole-health planning, we should briefly interrupt the subject of skin care to talk about these choices. Whatever professional you are choosing—dermatologist, aesthetician, hairdresser, tattoo artist, manicurist, personal stylist, massage therapist, personal trainer, teacher of dance, yoga, or Pilates, nutritionist, general practitioner, dentist, optometrist, podiatrist, gynecologist, plastic surgeon, psychologist, psychiatrist, or any other professional to whom you wish to entrust your well-being—your primitive guide may be your best asset to help steer you away from someone who isn't right for you and toward a person who is. Here are some other practical and philosophical pointers to guide you in a successful search:

- Start the process by getting referrals from professionals you know you can trust. If your hairdresser has an ability and personal touch you value, chances are that she or he may know other beauty experts of like talents. If you're looking for a dermatologist or cosmetic surgeon, your GP or internist will usually have top names to whom you can be referred (and possibly even their business cards).

- Get suggestions from friends and colleagues. We all have our own preferences, but usually, if you hear the same name recommended more than once or twice, you can safely conclude that professional has an excellent reputation.

- When you call to make an appointment, don't be shy about asking for that professional's credentials—level of education, licensing, and board certification. You can contact that board (phone numbers of most professional and medical associations are listed in the front of your phone book) to make sure the professional is in good standing. Unfortunately, they do not differentiate an A-caliber professional from a C-caliber, but they will weed out the F's, or those who've had serious complaints lodged against them.

- When you have your first appointment or decide to receive services, intelligently assess both the professional's abilities and personal demeanor. Does she take time to find out what you're looking for? Is he open to questions about new techniques you may have read about? Do you feel that you're important, even when a heavy client or patient load may be keeping that professional very busy? In making your assessment, know your own boundaries. Some of us want top-notch technical skills, and a lack of certain people skills may not bother us; for others of us, the best technical abilities in the world won't compensate for a brusque, impatient, or thoughtless way of communicating. And for all of us, I don't care how nice a professional is, when it comes to cutting your hair, touching your body, evaluating your health, or giving you surgery, a lack of technical expertise isn't acceptable.

- If you aren't sure whether a professional is right for you, get a second opinion. This is especially true for medical experts but can also apply, say, if you're choosing a yoga studio or spa. Try a class in a couple of different studios before sticking with one teacher or one place.

- Before you receive services, make sure you know what all the costs will be. If you're going to a medical office for a procedure that may be covered by your insurance, you should understand how much your policy covers, whether you should pay in the office and then submit your own claim for reimbursement, or have the office do it for you. No matter where you are, if you ask ahead of time for an estimate of costs and that business throws in hidden costs or last-minute extras you weren't forewarned about, consider raising a complaint with a manager or calling your better-business bureau. Nor should you be bullied into buying additional products or services you didn't come for.

- Though shopping around for the best professional for you is a positive thing to do, guard yourself against putting too much power in the hands of these professionals. Many of us have a friend who makes a full-time job of professional shopping—going from doctor to doctor, beauty expert to beauty expert. Maybe she's craving attention, and this practice gives her a sense of importance, but sadly, it also robs her of her own ability to know what she needs. Before long, she may start hearing so much conflicting information— often subjective—that she's worse off. Even more dangerous is when she starts taking medications or treatments prescribed by different professionals that may not be healthy to take together or in such quantity.

- The bottom line on making changes: To maintain the most productive ongoing relationships with professionals who provide your care, stay tuned to all your senses. If you feel that a new provider may be good for you and your whole-health, that is your prerogative. Or open a channel of communication and see if your current provider can adapt to some of the changes you feel you need.

Even though my work in the skin-care industry has given me a great education, I learn something new whenever I have the opportunity to take advantage of facials provided by professionals who are trained in what is truly an art form.

Aestheticians are trained and licensed to spend an hour or more on the utmost care for your skin. The process includes a special deep cleansing of the pores. Your aesthetician will first steam your face and open your pores, then remove dirt and blackheads through precise extraction methods and exfoliate dead cells by means of an electric brush or scrub. Expert facial massage, wonderful for your circulation—which impacts your vascular and lymphatic systems—can spur the skin's self-cleansing mechanisms. Massage stimulates the release of EGF (epidermal growth factor), a hormone that reacts to pressure on the skin by signaling the cells to promote collagen and elastin while spurring new cell production. Facials usually include special masks, moisturizing methods, and sometimes enzyme treatments and acid peels. Some salons use specialized equipment that sends high-frequency electric pulses into the skin which help kill bacteria and accelerate healing.

A talented aesthetician will not only perform these procedures gently and adroitly, she will also create a comfortable, peaceful, enjoyable experience that makes you feel great. By letting you know what the procedures are and giving you input about your skin, the best aestheticians empower you to become your own beauty expert. Having a facial once a month is ideal.

When having periodic facials isn't a practical option, giving yourself a home facial is much easier than you may think and, because you enjoy it in the comfort of your own home, sometimes just as rewarding. A home facial is one of my favorite occasional ceremonies when I find myself with a free weeknight or weekend afternoon. Or it can be a fallback routine if a day's events haven't gone according to plan and I'm coping with stress, frustration, disappointment, or boredom. Yes, those are also the times I'm tempted to reach for a bag of cookies and a carton of milk . . . or a stiff drink! But most of the time, instead of eating or drinking as forms of comfort, I perk myself up with a home facial and a long soak in the tub.

Ingredients and tools you'll need: 1) A device for steaming your face, such as a portable steamer (available in most drugstores), an enclosed shower, or a large bowl filled with steaming water. 2) Facial scrub. 3) Your daily facial cleanser. 4) Facial mask for deep moisturizing. 4) Your daily light moisturizer and eye cream. 5) Magnifying mirror.

- Apply cleanser to your wet face in a circular motion, even around the eye area, thoroughly removing all traces of dirt and makeup.
- After you steam for five to ten minutes—either with your portable steamer, by stepping into a steamy shower, or over a bowl of water—gently apply facial scrub and massage for one to two minutes to unclog pores and slough off the dead skin cells. Gently remove with a wet washcloth and rinse thoroughly with tepid water.
- As you look over your face in the magnifying mirror, examine your pores to make sure they're clean and unblocked. If you press lightly with your fingertips and can see blackheads or whiteheads pushing easily to the surface, release them by placing a fingertip on each side of the blemish and applying gentle pressure; then release from the bottom and top. No squeezing, please.
- Use your cleanser to remove any debris that surfaced in the steaming process. Rinse with cool water.
- Next put on a moisturizing mask of your choice. Remove with warm water, then splash on cold water to close your pores.
- Finish with light moisturizer and eye cream. If you can avoid putting on makeup for the rest of the day or evening, you and your skin will reap the greatest benefits.

If you have any chronic skin eruptions, adult acne, irregularly colored or shaped moles, or anything that concerns you about your skin, see a dermatologist. For occasional pimples, as long as they are not embedded cysts that require medical attention, clean with a nonalcohol astringent and apply a topical medicated acne cream to dry the area. But extra abrasion is not going to get rid of a breakout; it may exacerbate the problem. If you have regular breakouts around your period or when you ovulate, it might work to dab on a light drying solution or a medicated mask before you expect a breakout.

Some so-called skin tags—little extra strands of tissue that crop up—and some sunspots can be removed or bleached by a dermatologist. If you're prone to getting them, you have further reason to protect yourself from the sun. Remember to follow your doctor's warnings about avoiding sun exposure while taking medications such as antibiotics or sulfa drugs. Wearing perfume on your neck and face can also cause a photosensitive reaction that may result in sunspots.

Dr. Pugliese has observed that because our skin plays a prominent role in ridding the body of what isn't good for it, the condition of our skin is often a barometer for how well we are doing internally. After all, many illnesses trigger rashes and bumps. Such external manifestations are important messages that there may be internal issues that need more attention.

Certain skin outbreaks can be caused by allergies. Some years ago a friend of mine, then in her thirties, came down with what the doctors determined was adult acne—something she hadn't gone through in her teens or her twenties. While her doctors couldn't explain what triggered her outbreak, my friend used her own instincts to pinpoint an allergy she had developed to the new pillows she was using. When she replaced them, her skin cleared up. I've heard stories of similar reactions to fragrances, detergents, fabrics, foods, cosmetics, even contact with animals, plants, and water.

As for the stress that we know isn't good for our health or our skin—causing everything from acne to hives to cold sores—it's as important to take steps to treat the stress as it is to find topical and medical solutions for the outbreak. Antihistamines can soothe hives, and the natural supplement lysine can help prevent or abate onsets of the herpes virus that causes cold sores, but those remedies are only part of the equation. More on antistress measures later, when we talk about anti-aging. Also coming up later, in our discussion of cosmetic surgery and its alternatives, will be various procedures for removing or reducing marks and moles, along with other skin treatments, such as chemical peels, dermabrasion, laser resurfacing, collagen and Botox injections, and more.

Most of the principles for taking care of the skin of your face and neck apply equally for your skin from the neck down. Unfortunately, even those of us who have adopted the kindest, most gentle care of our skin from the neck up can sometimes treat the skin of the rest of our body either too roughly or with neglect: not fair. Again, make sure your daily routine incorporates the three basic steps of gentle cleansing, moisturizing, and protecting your skin.

A great shower is really one of life's true pleasures. Anytime works for me—early in the morning as a wake-up start for the day, after exercise, after work, before going out to a party or a special event, or as part of the ritual of getting ready for bed.

For those of us who love a roaring-hot shower, Dr. Pugliese warns that your skin may not approve. Very warm water is fine, he says, but if the temperature is so hot that you wince in pain or your skin turns bright red, it can irritate your skin in the short and long run.

Just as you would for your face, choose a gentle body cleanser in a lotion, gel, or bar. A soft natural sponge is safe for both your body and your face. For scrubbing power, Dr. Pugliese recommends a washcloth—not a loofah or scrubbing net, except for your elbows and knees. For your feet, use a pumice stone in the shower.

Common sense dictates that you cleanse the skin of your breasts gently. While you're at it, the shower is one of three places recommended for doing a monthly breast self-examination:

1. *In the shower.* Raise your right arm and, with the finger pads of your left hand, check your entire right breast. Look for a lump, hard knot, or skin that feels thicker or more dimpled than the rest of your breast. Move your finger pads up and down in small circles, varying your pressure from light to medium to firm. Repeat for your left breast.

2. *Before a mirror.* Visually check your breasts for any changes in their shape or appearance. In four different positions, look for any dimpling, lumps, or nipple discharge; start with hands at your side; then arms overhead; then flex your chest muscles with your hands on your hips; then bend forward.

3. *Lying down.* This is considered the best way to check your breasts. With a pillow under your right shoulder and your right hand under

your head, check your entire right breast, using the same technique described for the shower. Repeat for your left breast.

Be thorough, and make sure not to exclude your nipples. Report any changes or anything you're not sure about to your doctor. Regular breast and pelvic exams with pap tests are vital. Check with your doctor about when and how often you should have mammograms.

Water and a washcloth are sufficient, says Dr. Pugliese, for cleansing the external skin of your vagina and the crease at the tops of your legs. Ever mindful of ways to maintain the youngest skin possible, he points out that wearing tight bikini underwear contributes to rough skin in that area, in addition to the formation of spider and varicose veins; it also exacerbates cellulite. His recommendation? Wear loose underwear during the day, and sleep without any undergarments at night.

If you get regular bikini waxes, your skin may react with chafing—this can be soothed with natural aloe vera in gel or lotion; or, if you live in a desert or tropical climate, you can grow and squeeze fluid from the actual aloe plants.

Since we're on the subject of hair removal: Most of the techniques currently used are safe and effective. Dr. Pugliese has scientifically refuted the myth that shaving causes hair to grow back thicker and coarser. After all, he argues, if shaving caused hair to grow, bald men would shave their heads to restore their hair. This goes not only for shaving our legs and underarms but, if we so choose, around our bikini line. You may be surprised to hear that he even advocates facial shaving for some women—once a month—to get rid of unwanted facial hair. The options I prefer are waxing, gentle cream depilatories, and electrolysis. These methods will work for eyebrows, along with tweezers. For unwanted hair on your breasts, stick to the gentle use of your tweezers and pluck the hair close to the root without pinching the skin.

Back to my regular shower routine, which usually includes shaving my legs and underarms, smoothing calluses on my feet with a pumice stone, using a loofah on my elbows and knees, then finishing up with facial cleanser, and, if it's a shampoo day, cleansing and conditioning my hair. I always complete my shower with a cool rinse. After stepping out of the shower and while I'm still damp, I smooth on a body moisturizer that's rich in antioxidants and contains sunscreen.

While I prefer showers for cleansing, I love the ceremony of bathing as a way to relax and meditate or to rejuvenate, refresh, and transform. With a little creativity and some of the following items, any bathroom can be turned into a luxurious spa:

An inflatable bath pillow, soothing eye mask, moisturizing bubble bath or foaming bath beads, aromatherapy bath oils, natural bath gel, gentle bath salts, scented candles, a bathroom-safe CD player, a good body scrub, and a bath tray with a plastic wine goblet for sipping bottled water (why not, you deserve it!). Don't forget your body moisture lotion after your bath.

If you love showering and bathing as much as I do, it's that much more important not to skip moisturizing and protection of your skin after cleansing, morning and night, if and when possible. Take the example of hands that spend so much of the day immersed in water. Dr. Pugliese reports a recent study that revealed most women have their hands in water no fewer than an average of twenty-eight times a day. Some of us know all too well the red, cracked, chapped skin of "dishwater hands." To avoid such hand abuse, rubber gloves for kitchen and laundry work are indispensable, as is frequent reapplication of hand lotion—five or more times a day.

In order to make hand lotion a habit, I keep containers in as many visible places as I can—the bathrooms, kitchen, bedroom, den, at my desk, in my purse, even in my car's glove compartment. In selecting what I put on my hands, I look for vitamin enrichment, built-in sunscreen, and enough moisture to soften my hands without making them too slippery.

And then there are our feet, those two incredibly important and often overworked body parts—marvels of nature, actually, when you consider their difficult job of supporting us throughout the day. To give them their due, the following guidelines may help:

- Wear comfortable shoes with adequate arch support and cushioning of the insoles. If you love how you look in four-inch-high heels, don't give them up; opt to wear them when you know you won't be walking or standing for long periods of time.

- Have your feet measured every now and then to make sure you're wearing your correct size. Feet can grow or spread, just as they can thin out.

- Whenever you remove your shoes, give yourself a quickie foot massage—good for your whole body.

- If you are prone to the dry, itchy, or painful effects of fungus such as athlete's foot, try the higher strengths of over-the-counter antifungal creams, along with a medicated antifungal foot powder. Because fungus thrives in wet environments, make sure your feet are dry and that you air them out frequently.

- For prolonged infections, infected or ingrown toenails, or stubborn corns and bunions, don't hesitate to see a good podiatrist.

Manicures and pedicures have long been staples in many women's beauty plans. As with facials, I welcome professional care, although there are times I'd rather give myself the home version. In the past, I liked wearing my fingernails longer and more brightly painted, with matching or complementary polish on my toenails. Recently, in part because of my own changing aesthetic and in part because I love gardening, I have opted for a shorter, more natural manicure—with either a light beige or clear polish. Since I wear open-toed shoes a lot, I continue to use a colored polish on my toenails.

Whether you regularly have professional or do-it-yourself manicures and pedicures, it's very healthy to take breaks from wearing polish. Otherwise, the polish's perpetual seal may be trapping unwanted bacteria and fungus. Does this mean we should never wear nail polish? Yes, according to some medical experts who rank polish on the same level as high heels—potential hazards that serve no therapeutic role. Then again, if having lovingly lacquered nails is how you get into the Beauty Zone and is part of your personal style, polish away—giving yourself a polish-free day or two every couple of weeks.

What about those of us whose beauty plans are so chock-full of other priorities that we opt for the just-can't-be-bothered approach to nail care? If you need an on-the-run, low-maintenance routine, here's a hardly-any-bother-at-all once-a-week nail regimen that may help:

Tools to have on hand: toenail clippers, fingernail clippers, emery board, nail file, orange stick, and cuticle cream. After a bath or shower, so that your nails are soft, massage cuticle cream around your fingernails and toenails. Clip your toenails short. Clip your fingernails only if you need to establish an even line. Follow by filing with a soft nail file to give them shape (rounded or squared, your choice) and to smooth any rough edges. The rule for filing is to hold the file sideways to the nail, moving in one direction, being especially gentle for thin, dry, or brittle nails. Then use your orange stick to push back cuticles and slide underneath nails to remove any dirt or dead skin.

This weekly routine will give you healthy, lovely nails. Or you may choose to take a few more steps to buff your nails for a natural shine, or paint fragile nails with a strengthening base coat, or finish up with two layers of colored polish and a clear gloss on top.

The bonus of simple, streamlined routines for the healthy care of skin and nails is that you'll have enough time left over to care for a major factor in how we look and feel.

HAIR

To stay beautifully consistent (the routine and ritual lover in me likes that), the basic principles of hair care follow the same easy 1-2-3 steps of skin care—cleansing, moisturizing, and protection. Generally, that translates into shampooing, conditioning, and protecting hair from the elements with basics like hats, conditioning lotion under bathing caps for swimming in chlorine, and leave-in conditioners with sunscreen; and avoiding the kinds of brushes, combs, and elastics that can damage hair.

Hair protection also means that the food and supplements we consume will make a difference. *Feel Fabulous Forever* cites the following as good "hair food": fresh vegetables and fruit, legumes, yogurts with live cultures, cold-pressed oils (flaxseed, olive), seeds such as pumpkin and sunflower, almonds, fresh fatty fish, lots of water (you really do get great mileage from those eight glasses of water!), plus cutting down on dairy, caffeine, sugar, and salt. In addition to the multivitamin/mineral with iron and antioxidant supplements that you're already taking for whole-health, and those B-complex vitamins for antistress and better metabolism, lysine can be helpful to hair.

Because stress can have a dire effect on your hair—shock, trauma, or anxiety can even cause a young person's hair to suddenly turn gray—reducing your stress is very important for hair wellness. To that end, exercise is beneficial, as is remembering to breathe. (And you thought I was going to forget.) If you are a smoker, another of the many health and beauty bonuses of quitting will be an improvement in the texture and shine of your hair. To protect against pollution and UV rays, try a leave-in conditioning sunscreen. It may also be helpful to know that prescription drugs—everything from chemotherapy and radiation, antibiotics and antidepressants, to sleeping pills and diet pills—have been found to cause hair loss.

A protective measure for keeping healthy hair is to have it cut periodically, every six to eight weeks, but not for the reason many of us assume from the ever-popular myth that cutting your hair more often spurs more rapid growth. On the contrary, Dr. Pugliese says that cutting hair does not make it grow. Cutting hair does, however, remove dry and split ends. A good haircut that rids you of top-heavy broken hairs and dead, frayed, and frazzled ends can give you the appearance of having longer, healthier hair.

Some beauty experts espouse certain styles for certain face shapes and ages. I disagree. After all, the shape of a face is not uniform. There are other factors to consider: the size of your eyes, the shape of your nose and mouth, the lines of your jaw and appearance of your neck, the color and texture of your hair, your body shape, your lifestyle, and, probably most important, your unique beauty personality.

A good haircut, then, will be determined by what kind of hair you have. The cut should flatter your face and body, be appropriate to your personal style and the demands of your life and work, and still allow you to change the style to suit your changing needs and moods.

Do I think that certain youthful or currently trendy hairstyles are inappropriate for older women? Absolutely not—as long as the style is a true expression of a woman's persona and is consistent with the rest of her beauty aesthetic. Frankly, a hip hairdo on a woman dressed in a seriously dated article of clothing *does* detract from a "put-together" look. But if long, straight hair has always been a woman's great pride, why should she be expected to cut it to her shoulders or above her ears just because some people have a notion that women must wear their hair more conservatively as they age? By the same token, if a woman has not changed her look since the mid-sixties, when she first started wearing hip-hugging bell-bottoms, midriff tops, and long, straight hair parted in the middle, it might be time for an update. By itself, the attempt to hold on to one's younger look takes away from living happily in the moment, not to mention that a change in hairstyle can be so invigorating.

On the flip side, I don't buy into the idea that coloring your hair is a universal mandate once silver strands start to show up. Healthy hair, whether it's silver, gray, white, or variations thereof, can give you a strikingly elegant look that may be much more beautiful than anything you get from a bottle. Does this mean there's anything wrong with coloring your hair in later years? Of course not, especially if you use gentler, more natural processes.

Over the years, change was my hair credo. I've worn my hair dark, light, and several shades of red; long and straight, long and curly, long and shaggy; short and shaggy, short and straight; and most styles and cuts in between. At fifty, I've chosen a simple, uncomplicated, above-the-shoulders cut that lets my hair fall and move naturally. It's flattering, I think, and compared to the bygone eras of teasing, hair spray and mousse abuse, curling irons, hot rollers, perms, and multistep color treatments that fried my poor hair, it is at this stage the healthiest it's been since childhood. If my choice of cut has anything to do with my age, it is only a need for low-maintenance because of how busy I am. I get a haircut every two months, along with a one-step color process for brightening my dark hair to auburn. The only jobs left for me are the basics—shampooing, conditioning, and protecting.

I'll confess that my fascination with the transformational power of hair started as early as my interest in skin care, back in my childhood days when I was developing facials in our kitchen. Meanwhile, I turned our bathroom into a hair salon, experimenting on myself and my girlfriends. Eventually, I became proficient at setting and cutting hair and coloring techniques. My knowledge of the needs of hair increased dramatically when the blessing of steady acting work also meant way too many chemical and heat treatments. Then, thanks to my celebrity endorsement contract with Jhirmack, my ten-year association with their hair-care scientists and product-development experts allowed me to receive a wonderful education not only about ways to restore hair but about how to develop effective and necessary products. All of this experience has proven valuable to me for creating and running my own cosmetics company.

One of the clearest lessons to emerge for me is that the fewer chemicals put on hair, the better. This was corroborated by Dr. Peter Pugliese, who, when referring to anti-aging methods for hair, states, "Avoid overtreatment. A lot of women don't mean to abuse their hair, but they do."

Simple, straightforward advice—although it may raise some concern about what hair treatments you should give up. Compromise may be in order. If you color and perm your hair, for example, try doing just one or the other, or alternate treatments. If you've been getting a two- or three-step color process—like some of those gorgeous mixed highlights or color weaves—maybe you can adapt it to one step. You can also talk to your hairdresser about more natural, less damaging products. Incidentally, it's advisable not to have your hair cut or color-treated when you have a cold or are feeling under the weather—which can change your hair's texture and its chemical reaction to the coloring process.

If you use a handheld hair dryer, like many of us do, you can help your hair by never using any setting hotter than medium. If you perm or press your hair to straighten it, you can take breaks by trying braids, hair extensions, or setting your hair wet in rollers for a smoother look.

As to what type of products are best for basic hair care and how often you should use them, the answers will vary widely depending on your hair type and its condition. Here are some variations, challenges, and suggestions:

- *Oily hair. Challenges:* Unless freshly washed, oily hair can look dirty or greasy, as if slicked down with gel, which means your scalp can be oily too, making skin breakouts more common. *Suggestions:* Take heart; oily hair is less prone to breaks or splits and tends to become less oily as you age. Shampoo often with cleanser made especially for oily hair. Apply shampoo twice and clean your scalp by massaging in shampoo. Skip conditioner. If you need to use a detangler, choose a low-oil product that offers extra body and use it only on your ends.

- *Dry hair. Challenges:* The results of overtreating, heating, and chemicals are dryness, split ends, and a dull, strawlike texture. *Suggestions:* If it's any consolation, few of us are generally born with dry hair, although over time, we dry it out. Unlike damaged skin, however, hair damage is easier to repair. Warm oil treatments and protein-enriched hair masks are beneficial for dry hair, as are leave-in moisturizing conditioners that you can keep on while you're around the house or under a hat if you go out to exercise. Use acidic shampoos and vitamin/protein-enriched conditioners every three or four days; be careful not to wash so often that you dry out your hair more. Anti-aging help from hormone replacement may also help. For milder cases of dandruff or seborrhea, over-the-counter products are effective. If the condition persists or worsens, your dermatologist may recommend a prescription treatment.

- *Fine hair. Challenges:* Also called "baby hair" or flyaway hair, fine hair can be hard to style, sometimes hanging limp and flat. *Suggestions:* A good layered haircut can give you thickness you never knew. Add to that the use of a penetrating, conditioning shampoo with extra body—often helpful—and you'll see visible improvement. No need for extra conditioning—which may soften your hair to further limpness—except for a ten-minute moisturizing, volume-enhancing conditioner once every other week. Unless your hair and scalp are also oily, avoid products made for oily hair. If your hair is oily as well as fine, intersperse the use of products made for oily hair with conditioning, extra-body shampoo.

- *Thin hair. Challenges:* Sparse, fragile, easily broken hair, sometimes thinning to the point that the line of your scalp can be seen, thin hair can be quite confounding because the causes are not well established. *Suggestions:* Handle your hair gingerly and look for a style that doesn't require heat, chemicals, teasing, or hair spray on a daily basis. A layered cut can add the appearance of volume. Acid-balanced, neutral shampoo should be used, only once a week. Conditioners may make your hair limp, so your best bet is a light conditioning detangler if you need it to comb out your hair without tearing it. Hair plugs, depending on the doctor's expertise and a person's hair type, have shown promising results. Although the current medications have had limited success, Dr. Pugliese promises that science is close to finding real help for men and women who suffer from thinning hair. In the meantime, have your hormones checked: Natural replacement may be a miracle cure for you. If not, invest in a high-quality wig that matches your real hair. Have it styled just as you would your own hair, and wash it with shampoo, not detergent. Take breaks. Wearing it nonstop will flatten your hair and deprive your scalp of healthy breathing room.

- *Coarse hair. Challenges:* Healthy, coarse hair can be so thick and wiry that it will do only what it wants to do, and on humid days, it can really get out of hand. *Suggestions:* If it's not dry, wash it as often as daily or every other day with a normal shampoo. Conditioners made specifically to relax coarse hair, or even a leave-in conditioning gel, can help. Frequent haircuts will definitely do a lot to keep coarse hair under control.

- *Thick hair. Challenges:* Maybe it takes you longer to get a comb through it; maybe it gets more tangled or matted in between washings. But don't complain, you have an abundance of hair! *Suggestions:* Pick a shampoo appropriate to your hair's condition—oily, dry, or normal—and wash every two to three days. Any and all conditioners are good. After you put on your conditioner in the shower, you may even want to gently comb it through your hair before rinsing.

If nature has endowed you with a mane of what is known as normal hair, you probably know what works best for you in terms of shampoo, light conditioning, and protection. To maintain optimum condition, heed Dr. Pugliese's advice and avoid overprocessing.

For everyone, keep your brushes and combs clean by washing them once a week in shampoo, not soap.

Unless you cut your own hair—which takes talent and agility—whenever you have it done, ask your hairdresser to give you pointers for styling it on a daily basis. With that advice, your own beauty instincts, and the healthy care you've been giving your skin and hair, you are almost ready for makeup and wardrobe. But first, let's address two beauty essentials that often get overlooked.

CARE FOR TEETH AND EYES

The beauty and health of your teeth are virtually one and the same. Providing for their basic care isn't an option, it's a must. If you aren't concerned by the prospect of ailments ranging from tooth and gum decay, jaw deterioration, and a host of other internal diseases that can begin with bad dental hygiene, just think about how poorly tended teeth detract from the rest of your beauty. That and the daunting cost and discomfort of having to receive professional dental treatment should motivate you to adopt some of the following basic habits for beautiful, healthy teeth and gums:

- Brush your teeth at least twice a day, making sure you replace your toothbrush frequently.
- Floss daily. (Okay, *try* to floss daily. This one's not my strong suit.)
- On a frequent basis, massage your gums manually, or use a Water Pik or electric toothbrush.
- Gargle with mouthwash, which will improve bad breath and may offer protection against mouth germs.
- See a dentist twice a year for a checkup and cleaning.

Preventive care isn't the only factor in the appearance and health of your teeth. Due to genetics or other conditions beyond your control, teeth may be crooked, broken, dark, or yellow, no matter how well you care for them. In such cases, however, there are some excellent remedies.

For starters, the latest bleaching techniques are very impressive. As a matter of fact, one of the fastest beauty makeovers is to get a new hairstyle and bleach your teeth. A popular bleaching treatment involves having your dentist make upper and lower plastic mouthpieces that you fill with bleaching paste and wear to bed for four to seven days. Your dentist can administer other bleaching methods in the office.

Another rapid fix is having your teeth filed: so easy you'll wonder why you never thought of it before. By simply filing teeth that are uneven at the edges, your bite can be aligned to even out shorter and longer teeth.

Slightly more time- and money-intensive are bonding and acrylic veneers. Bonding involves applying composite or porcelain material to teeth to fill in gaps or mend chips. Porcelain veneer works well for badly stained or poorly shaped teeth with a thin, natural-looking application that may not require the dentist to file down much of your teeth. Bonded teeth may need to be rebonded every five years, while veneers, if well made, should last four times as long.

Depending on the condition of your teeth, your dentist may first have to file them down significantly in order to create room for a porcelain crown—also known as a cap. Crowns should last twenty or more years, provided your gums stay healthy.

In case you've heard rumors to the contrary, you are never too old to wear braces. Maybe you never had an opportunity to get them when you were younger, or maybe your teeth have grown crowded and crooked over the years. In such cases, you have the option of invisible braces on the backs of the teeth—called lingual braces—or tooth-colored metal rather than silver. You can also be fitted with a retainer or similar removable orthodontic appliance. Most of these procedures will take from a year to two years for correction and improvement.

Special scaling and deep-cleaning techniques may be in order if you have receding gums or the onset of gum disease. Aging can play a role in the thinning of gums, as can hormone changes. To fend off gum tissue loss, remember that dental floss and dental picks are your friends.

With the care of your eyes, beauty and health are yet again intertwined. The majority of us in our forties and older will most likely experience a loss of elasticity in our eye lens that results in blurring of fine print and difficulty focusing at close range. The easy solution for some is to wear reading glasses. For those who already wear corrective lenses—whether for astigmatism, nearsightedness, or other refractive concerns—a dual approach may be necessary, such as bifocals or contact lenses combined with reading glasses. Other options include wearing bifocal contacts. You may want to also check with your optometrist to find out if you are a candidate for laser eye surgery. Many longtime glasses wearers are thrilled by the success of laser surgery and say their only regret is that they didn't do it sooner. Nonetheless, there are risks, as with most surgeries, and not everyone's eyes can benefit.

An ever-growing range of options is available in eyewear, and contact lenses can change the color of your eyes. Aside from the color options, the newer disposable contacts can be thrown out after a day or two weeks, thus requiring little cleaning or maintenance. A variety of substances are being used for eyeglasses as well, including treatments that reduce glare from computer screens; transitional lenses that darken and lighten to protect eyes from UV rays; and techniques to thin glass even with a strong prescription. The factors to consider in selecting eyewear, as with hairstyle, are what most flatters your facial features and body build, what best complements your personal style, and what functions with the demands of how you live and work. As long as costs aren't prohibitive, it's nice to have eyewear options to suit your changing needs and moods.

Whether you have worn glasses most of your life or have been graced with 20/20 vision since you were a child, regular eye exams as you age are important to check for such concerns as cataracts (lens weakening); glaucoma (buildup of eye pressure resulting in vision loss); and AMD (age-related macular degeneration due to retinal impairment, the leading cause of blindness in older adults). Early detection that leads to early treatment can prevent the loss of your precious eyesight.

Not surprisingly, all the preventative steps for taking care of your eyes are rooted in the whole-health practices we've been discussing all along:

- *Regular exercise.* Work out for stress reduction and to relieve buildup of eye pressure.
- *Good nutrition.* Eat a diet rich in natural antioxidants with supplements of beta-carotene and selenium.
- *Protection from pollutants.* Beware the usual suspects. Don't smoke, and do wear sunglasses on both sunny and overcast days to protect from UV rays and poor air quality. Pay attention to possible allergens, such as those that cause skin allergies, which can also cause eye allergies. Prescription drugs taken over a long period of time may also be culprits in vision changes.
- *Keep eyes moist.* For dry, itchy, or stinging eyes, try artificial tears and ophthalmologist-recommended eye washes. Avoid frequent use of eyedrops for reducing redness because they generally constrict blood vessels, something that isn't good for long-term eye health.

- *Replace eye makeup regularly.* Throw out those old mascara tubes and mildewed eye shadows. Take off your makeup at night—it's as important for eyes as it is for skin.

And lest we forget the commonsense wisdom of our foremothers: The kindest gift you can give your eyes, as well as your teeth, hair, and skin, is to get your beauty sleep.

WHOLE-BEAUTY CHOICES

So here you are. You're in the Beauty Zone, with clear, sparkling eyes, glistening-white teeth, shiny, lustrous hair, and soft, smooth, glowing skin. The only things left are makeup and clothes. Easy, right?

Not always. The reality is that with all the many roles that women must play over the course of our different daily and weekly activities, making choices about what to wear and how to put on our makeup can be fraught with questions and challenges. For those of us who live on the run, nothing can knock us out of the Beauty Zone faster than that dreadful rush to throw something on at the last minute. Having a wardrobe plan to fulfill whatever function you need makes sense.

Of course, clothing needs have gone far beyond mere function. To be well dressed in our day and age, we have to plan not only for weather, comfort, and protection, keeping in mind our specific activities and events; we're also expected to exude a certain sense of style, with some thought for both current style and, most importantly, personal style. And that's not all. The fact that we have fewer rules for what is considered appropriate apparel in so many different situations and for our different ages is liberating. But having that many more choices can be overwhelming too.

Have you ever pulled out virtually your entire wardrobe and stood there with everything strewn around your room, only to be moved almost to tears because not one article of clothing fit the bill? Maybe you've put on some weight and the majority of clothes in your closet are from an era when you wore a smaller size. Maybe you hurriedly bought some new clothes that did fit, but you brought them home and realized they weren't you at all. Maybe you have some favorite outfits that look wonderful on you but are starting to fall apart at the seams. If none of these things have ever happened to you, count yourself lucky. For the rest of us—women of every age—I offer the following guidelines that have helped me over the years:

- *Function first.* There are basic needs to everyone's clothing essentials, depending on where and how you live. These can include sweaters, jackets, and coats for cool and cold weather, raincoats for rainy weather, and shoes that can be worn in various climates. Socks, underwear, and sleepwear are staples for most of us. Other categories of clothing may be workout clothes and swimwear, work attire, casual everyday wear for running errands or around the house, and casual to dressy special-occasion outfits (what some of us used to call our "good" clothes and shoes). As you overview your current wardrobe, a constructive technique is to write down your different seasonal and lifestyle needs, then jot down the clothes you own that supply those needs. That way, the next time you're getting dressed for lunch with friends, your list can remind you of some of the options you have in your closet. If you don't have clothes that meet your basic requirements, this list may help you prioritize. So, rather than impulse-shopping and coming home with things you don't need, use your list to guide you to invest in the basics.

- *Find forms that flatter.* As with other beauty principles, the clothes you wear should be selected with thought to what accentuates your positives and detracts from your less favorite features. In a moment, we'll talk to an expert; in the meantime, add to your list of functional needs any features that you consider assets: maybe sparkling eyes, great legs, graceful shoulders, elegant neck, pretty ankles, sexy cleavage, or whatever you wouldn't want to cover up or take attention away from as you dress. Also jot down aspects of your figure that you don't wish to prominently feature.

When you do find pieces that look fabulous on you and that flatter your figure just the way you like, an economical, resourceful way to multiply your clothing choices is to take those pieces to a local dressmaker and have her or him copy the patterns. Compared to higher-end retail dress shops, a quality dressmaker may surprise you with the lower cost and greater access to richer, more exciting fabrics.

- *Imprint your personal style on the way you dress.* Think for a moment of someone other than yourself whose personal style in dress you admire. What do her clothes say about who she is? What adjectives do they bring to mind that are true to her? Now ask yourself what you'd like your clothing to say about you. What adjectives would you like to embody in a genuine way? After you've thought about how you'd like to dress, review your wardrobe to see if it's living up to that description. If not, perhaps you can think of ways to enhance or accessorize the clothes you have to better convey your individual style. To get you going on this process, here are some descriptions of looks and moods that may be aspects of your beauty persona:

> mysterious, exotic, sensual, earthy, sexy, artsy, sultry, innocent, cute, sweet, sophisticated, glamorous, dramatic, colorful, exciting, sporty, smart, charming, casual, classic, tailored, corporate, conservative, understated, elegant, graceful, dignified, healthy, traditional, clean-cut, feminine, fun, hip, cool, shy, discreet, demure, funky, wild, alluring, intelligent, sensible, humorous, whimsical, naughty, nice

Clothing can also reflect a sense of our ethnic or geographical heritage or those we wish to celebrate, drawing on looks from the Middle East, the Far East, Latin America, Africa, and Europe.

Explore what are—for lack of a better term—the different hats you wear over the course of the day. If you are running a household, raising your kids, and participating in community and school events, you may not have a need for a workingwoman's business suit. If you're in the corporate world, single, married, with kids or not, professional attire is probably a basic need. If you're retired and love to garden and walk, you might want more sportswear than tailored outfits. If you wear a uniform for work, what small accessories can you wear with it that communicate who you are, and what are your apparel needs in off-time? If you're single and would like to meet someone, you might want to look at your fashion choices to see what they're communicating about your availability, or lack thereof.

Professional clothing and costume designers use script descriptions to design looks that communicate who characters are. Though these characters can sometimes be written as stereotypes—much to the dismay of actors, in particular women and minorities who tend to be stereotyped the most—we can also use details of behavior and dress to make characters come to life. When I auditioned for the role of Pamela Barnes Ewing on *Dallas*, I wore blue jeans and cowboy boots with a cream-colored buttoned silk shirt slightly open at the neck underneath a camel corduroy single-breasted jacket. I also had on a necklace with a gold charm of the state of Texas with a diamond marking Dallas. My attire made such an impression on the producers that when they cast me in the series, they asked that I wear it for shooting the first episode.

There was a time when social class was identified through clothing. Thankfully, we have made some progress since the days when the saying "Clothes make the man" (woman, too) held true. I'm happy to say that, in today's culture, grace and social bearing are evaluated on other, less superficial qualities, such as one's entire demeanor—manners, kindness, intelligence, warmth, and consideration of others. Still, the taste and care with which we put ourselves together is often a factor in how others react to us.

Does this mean that you have to be wealthy to be well dressed? Not in the slightest. You can choose moderately priced, well-made articles of clothing that fit your figure and style, in keeping with simple, understated, classic design. If you do, you will appear much more expensively, tastefully dressed than someone who paid a lot more for a lavish outfit that doesn't fit or that broadcasts how much she paid for it.

- *Select colors and fabrics that reflect your personal style.* Though some schools of thought hold that our natural hair, eye, and skin coloring determine what colors we should wear in clothing, I believe that the best colors for you are those you love most. If you have no favorite colors but love them all, then by all means wear them all. At the same time, a wardrobe that runs the gamut of the color spectrum can be hard to coordinate. A compromise might be to determine three or four favorite colors and select clothes within those color families. You might keep a range of pinks for casual social attire, black and white for business or dressier occasions, and varying degrees of blue for sportswear and knocking around. Your choice of fabrics should be consistent with the look you'd like to convey. For instance, if your personal style is feminine and earthy, a flowing floral muslin might suit you better than a tailored navy wool gabardine.
- *Make whole-beauty choices to achieve a put-together look.* That magical ability to look effortlessly put together is in fact an art form that takes care, thought, practice, and a creative connection to all your senses. One trick is monochromatic dressing, which gives you continuity in color and fabric, coordinated with accessories in keeping with your personal style. This sensibility of creating a whole look and feel should extend to even your makeup and perfume choices. But don't be afraid to break the rules now and then in order

to have an authentic look. Maybe the traditional look is a single strand of pearls with your basic black evening dress, but if it reflects your artistic and colorful self, wear multistrands of colored crystal beads and matching earrings. Or if you find an accessory that you adore—a whimsical straw hat, a sexy see-through taffeta shawl, a pair of knockout high heels—then you can build an outfit around that accessory.

- *Practice low-maintenance with your wardrobe.* If frequent trips to the dry cleaner and the shoe repair are not practical for your budget or schedule, keep that in mind when you select new items, and look for wash-and-wear fabrics and shoes that won't wear down easily. One way to keep clothes smelling new is to use cedar hangers or cedar-chip sachets in your closet and herbal or floral sachets in your dresser drawers. Keep your clothes looking new the old-fashioned way—with a steam iron and spray starch. A portable clothes steamer is wonderful; hanging rumpled clothes in a steamy bathroom works too. For quick mending, keep a sewing kit with needles, basic colors of thread, straight and safety pins, and fabric tape. Neutral shoe polish is indispensable, and a suede brush can quickly revive worn-out suede. To prolong the life of your new leather shoes, take them to the shoemaker to have the bottom of the front sole reinforced with leather and the heel reinforced with rubber. If you live in a wet, cold climate, have the entire sole rubberized to weatherproof them. You'll be less prone to slip, more comfortable, and will extend the life of your shoes.

Remember the two sisters I credit as my book angels? The question that most concerned one of the sisters about her changing age was how to dress to appear youthful—without looking inappropriate. To address that concern, I sought the advice of the extraordinarily talented and insightful Vivian Turner, one of Hollywood's most in-demand wardrobe stylists. Over the years, I've learned so much and have been so inspired by the basics Vivian has generously shared with me: She draws from her experiences doing wardrobe styling for film, TV, commercials, print ads, and magazine layouts, and from the image and personal-wardrobe consulting she does for celebrities and other individuals. She also helps to design looks for special high-profile events such as movie premieres, awards shows, press junkets, and personal appearances.

So do we need to change how we dress as we age? Yes, Vivian says; in fact, she believes that women who don't change run the risk of looking older. "There are some women who continue dressing the way they looked when they were girls," she observes, "by following the trends in the younger women's fashion magazines that either aren't flattering on them or are inappropriate." Those youth trends, Vivian says, are for the young.

On the other hand, every woman can be youthful, no matter what her age. One of the best ways is to simply find a few youthful accessories, rather than a wardrobe of trends, to incorporate into one's closet and into one's life. For example, instead of shopping exclusively in juniors' departments when you're not a junior anymore, shop there for added youthful touches—a fun bracelet, funkier shoes with a more updated heel, a fashionable color of fingernail polish.

With those kinds of items, Vivian says, "You can be twenty or eighty and pick up fun younger accessories to add to your wardrobe to make it 'now' and bring it into the season."

Trying too hard to look young can cause some women to fall into the trap of looking like an old girl. Vivian suggests that our focus be on looking womanly in a way that's true to our sense of our own "woman-ness." Hence, one can become not an old girl, but a youthful woman.

Here's more of Vivian Turner's indispensable fashion savvy:

- To get the most mileage from your wardrobe budget, spend the most on your handbag and shoes. You can always find great pieces of clothing on sale, but don't cut corners with those two purchases. Vivian says that you can take any outfit—say, a pair of blue jeans and a white shirt—and turn it into something rich and gorgeous just by wearing a pair of beautiful loafers and carrying a smart, really well-made handbag.

- Dress from the inside out. Even when you're wearing the most elegant dress, you won't look elegant if you're wearing hose that dig into your waist and cause a roll, or panties that make a line across your bottom, or a bra that smashes your bosom, flattening you down or making you too busty. Vivian believes one should always start with well-fitting undergarments and hosiery. A staple is a nice smooth bra that flatters your bust, giving you a clean look that can't be seen under your clothes. You may want to invest in a wardrobe of undergarments that includes convertible bras (which can turn into strapless, halter-style, and racer-back), or different bras that fulfill those purposes, in colors of nude and natural. Panties such as thongs should be chosen for a smooth-looking bottom underneath pants. Waist-eliminating hosiery is now available in a style of panty hose that comes all the way up to just below your bra, giving you tummy support and smoothing your legs, hips, and bottom.

- When it comes to showing skin, there are no rules for age; use your own best judgment about whether it's appropriate for a given event and whether the skin you're showing is attractive. Vivian says that women who have lovely backs—with pretty skin and a smooth shape—should feel wonderful about wearing evening dresses cut low in back. For women of all ages who have gorgeous legs, show them off. A supermini cut may run the risk of making you one of those older girls; however, just above the knee is appropriate for all ages. If you have a great bustline and the skin on your chest and neck is appealing, V-necks or low-cuts that show collarbones are fine choices. Many of the old rules don't apply anymore, Vivian points out, since women in their forties, fifties, and older can be in better shape than women used to be in their twenties. Therefore, if you have a firm tummy and want to show some midriff, a two-piece bathing suit can look great on you, just as you'll look terrific tying up your shirt at a backyard barbecue.

- Dressing when you've gained a little weight? Vivian recommends that everyone have a small area in their closet of things to wear in such events. You may want to include a couple of dresses that are always forgiving (less fitted in places where we tend to gain weight); a pair of great trousers that are a little looser; jeans that aren't super-fitted; and perhaps a loose sweater to throw on, providing it's appropriate for the climate.

- To detract from body aspects we don't want to accentuate, Vivian shares some secrets for clothes that are slimming for heavier women and will work for dressing during pregnancy too. Longer pieces of clothing create longer looks, such as a longer tunic tied over flowing drawstring pants. Avoid clothes that stick or cling to the body, opting instead for fabric and styles that have movement. Again, when you're heavier, draw attention to your assets. If you have a lovely bust, show off your cleavage and throw color around your face with jewelry and makeup. As always, it's slimming to dress in darker tones and monochromatic tone-on-tone. Layering is great too—a long black jacket that comes to midthigh or longer, with a vest over flowing pants and a little tunic—great for slimming the middle. If too much slimming black becomes boring, Vivian advises a gorgeous colorful shawl or a bright-hued or jewel-toned sweater tied around your shoulders or waist. When you're smaller on top and bigger on the bottom, wear something tighter on top and looser on the bottom; if you're bigger on top and have great legs, wear something looser on top and more fitted on the bottom, as always, bringing attention to fabulous shoes.

- For big bosoms you'd like to play down, wear higher necklines, covering up cleavage. If you have a shorter neck, avoid turtlenecks, opting instead for deep V-necks or open collars. If you're very thin, dressing to reveal your arms and legs may not be the most flattering choice. Vivian stipulates that, unlike the models we see in high-fashion magazines, women really do look better with some meat on their bones—softer, more womanly, healthier, and more attractive.

If you're not sure what forms are most flattering to you, what your best assets are, what your personal style really is, or how to update your wardrobe, meeting with a personal shopper or stylist can be a meaningful investment. Many of the better department stores have sales staff trained to give you that kind of personal attention and information, free of any costs above what you may decide to spend on purchases.

When you've lost your way, are feeling overwhelmed by so many fashion considerations, or have a very limited budget, Vivian's best suggestion is that you do some research by buying several magazines that are appropriate for you. If you're a heavier woman, she says, there are magazines such as *Mode* that can serve you well. There are fashion magazines targeted to every age group, older and younger, as well as to women who work in business, in other capacities, and in the home. Vivian suggests that you assemble a scrapbook, notebook, or folder where you can organize the different pages that you cut out from magazines. Collect a variety of images related to all the looks you love—haircuts, makeup, clothing, accessories, anything that sparks your dressing imagination. You may want to divide your notebook into sections—special-occasion dressing, business wear, casual wear, foundation wear, whatever relates to your life. Then go back again to your wardrobe and review it to see if what you have works for the feelings, moods, and attitudes that have been emerging as themes in your selections. After that, you'll know what you need and can head out to the store. These days, many of the more moderately priced boutiques and department stores are selling affordable versions of top designers' new lines—even before the couture collections have hit the stores.

Moreover, Vivian notes that you can adapt some of the trends you see in the magazines without copying them exactly. If animal prints are popular, you may not wear the skintight animal-print bodysuit with the navel-plunging neckline, but you can pick up an animal-print scarf that makes your look that much more now and modern.

Once you put together looks you like, then you can begin to assess which ones are you. When choosing what looks are best for you, be realistic and tune into your senses about what classic feelings that fashion look inspires in you.

Within each of us, observes Vivian, can be different women—a woman who likes girly things, a woman who likes funky things, a woman who likes classic things, a woman who likes sophisticated and dressy things. Still, a theme will usually run through those different looks, a versatile, adaptive woman who knows when to be girly and when to be sophisticated.

In your research, again look for recurring themes—colors, necklines, women in magazines or in the media who have figures like yours or a personality like yours. Sometimes finding a new haircut can inspire the rest of your wardrobe. As we've said before, whole-beauty choices are important. Vivian feels that haircuts can sometimes make or break your look. "With all the hippest clothes on your body," she says, "if you're wearing old hair, your clothes aren't going to look cool in the least."

If you do invest in a stylist or consult with a personal shopper, your notebook is an excellent tool to communicate what your fashion desires are in pictures as well as words. When Vivian consults with clients who are looking to revamp or reinvent their wardrobes, before going shopping she helps them first clear out their closet to streamline their existing wardrobe. Many of us hold on to clothing and accessories from other eras because we're waiting for them to come back into fashion or to be able to fit into them again (whichever comes first). Vivian feels that getting rid of those clothes should be a priority—whether you put the unused items in storage, hold a garage sale, give them to a consignment store, or donate them to one of the many clothing drives within your community. If you must, preserve a small place in your closet for those articles you just can't bear to part with.

Once you've gotten the stuff out of the way that doesn't work or isn't you, you'll then be able to see the classic items that you should keep. And finally, you're ready to go build your new wardrobe.

When you're starting from scratch and need to begin a basic wardrobe, or if you're looking to put together a travel wardrobe, the following list of timeless/ageless fundamentals, regardless of budget, should provide you with some guidance:

A *suit,* preferably three pieces that include *trousers, jacket, and skirt or sheath dress* (whichever is most flattering on you) in black or other neutral color. A pretty *black cocktail dress.* A sexy *camisole* (perhaps in a charmeuse or sheer fabric for dressing up the suit with a pair of high heels). A crisp *white men's-style shirt* and a *black blouse* work with everything. Two or three *T-shirts* (short- and long-sleeve) are good to have in neutral colors (black, white, gray). A *tank top* for underneath your suit. A twin set—*cardigan and shell*—(any color) is great for changes in temperature. Basic wardrobe shoes include *high-heeled black pumps, business pumps* with a more sensible heel, nice *loafers or slip-on shoes, black boots,* and *sandals.* Don't forget that well-constructed *handbag* in great condition and simple *black belt.* Unless you live in a warm climate, a *classic winter coat* is a basic. We can all use a pair of *khakis or casual pants* and a pair of excellent-fitting *jeans.* For special occasions, one nice *dressy full-length outfit*—either a *long dress* (any color, but not prints or florals that go out of style more quickly) or a *flowing silk pantsuit* for evening wear.

Vivian knows women who shop once a year at sales to update their basics, then take Polaroids of all the different ways the pieces can be coordinated for quick reference. Throughout the year, they can accessorize with those now and happening extras—hoop earrings, if those are hot, or a lariat necklace, or a pair of beautiful gold sandals to wear with a little gold handbag. For dressing throughout the day and into night, workingwomen can wear walking shoes to work, slipping another pair into their bag for the office or later, or dressier scarves and jewelry for evening. Or, better yet, have a stash at work to be prepared for last-minute invitations.

When you've put yourself together in a more youthful, updated way Vivian Turner's million-dollar advice is to look in the mirror and say to yourself, "Honey, you're a babe."

And, finally, to complete your journey into the Beauty Zone, we come to the topic of makeup, an interest of mine that dates back to the days when I was barely tall enough to see all the fascinating cosmetics on my mother's makeup table. Over the years, I have refined a variety of makeup applications that depend on what I'm wearing, the occasion, and how much time I have to apply them. While age doesn't play a significant role in how I dress, I have found that it does when it comes to the way I wear makeup. More and more, I find that the more natural and more basic, the younger and fresher I look. Most beauty experts concur that the heavier your makeup is, the more pronounced lines and wrinkles can be.

For natural, fresh, simple, and fast, the *Five-Minute Makeup Routine* is timeless and ageless:

1. With a sponge, dot *foundation* on your cheeks, forehead, eyes, nose, and chin, and blend gently with your fingertips; be careful not to stretch or pull your skin.
2. Blend *concealer* under your eyes.
3. Blend *cream blush* along your cheekbones.
4. Brush a touch of *beige or natural-toned powder eye shadow* on your eyelids; if you want more contour, brush a slightly *darker-toned powder eye shadow* in the crease above your eyes.
5. If you use an *eyeliner pencil,* draw a fine line just above the lashes of your upper lid, then smudge the line with a brush or cotton swab.
6. Curl your eyelashes, holding to the count of five, then apply *mascara:* Brush upper lashes up and down, and lower lashes lightly side to side.
7. With a brush, apply *powder* to your whole face, except under your eyes.
8. Finish up with lips the way you love them—*lip liner* with *lip gloss, lipstick,* or both.

One of the best ways to learn new makeup techniques or to review some that have been used for years is to pay a visit to department stores in your area whenever cosmetic companies are offering free makeovers. Ask questions about how you can accomplish the same professional look they've given you at home, without all the different tools they've used. You can also ask which cosmetics are most complementary to the way you dress or to specific outfits. Usually, they're happy to give you the information you seek, whether or not you purchase anything. Chances are that these better cosmetics representatives know that the nicer they are to you, the more likely you are to make a purchase—if not at that time, then later.

Makeup, perfume, skin- and hair-care product samples are terrific to collect and keep in your purse, makeup bag, or travel kit. I love packing all these little beauty items into one neat makeup bag that's always with me in my purse, giving me a sense of preparedness. There are days at work when a ten-minute break in the ladies' room lets me feel as though I've taken a shower and gotten dressed and made up all over again.

Whatever it is that gives you that well-prepared sense of confidence, I invite you to embrace it and employ it—not just for today and tomorrow, but for a lifetime of beauty.

Practical Steps for a Lifetime of Beauty

Since we've covered a great deal of information in this chapter, it's important to echo a familiar theme from earlier chapter summaries: The best way to make real beauty changes is to implement these steps slowly, choosing areas of focus one at a time.

GIVE YOURSELF A WHOLE-BEAUTY CHECKUP

Take some time over the next few days to examine your current beauty and health habits and attitudes. (Questions to ask yourself: Do I practice skin care and hair care that incorporate gentle cleansing, moisturizing, and protecting? Do I have regular exams for teeth and eyes? Do I have a sense of authentic beauty? Does my makeup and wardrobe reflect my personal style and pride in myself?) If you discover from this process that there are aspects of caring for your beauty that you'd like to change, make a list and note which changes are the most important and the most realistic for you at this time.

EMBRACE BASIC BEAUTY PRACTICES

You may be encouraged by making a list of the things you already do for your whole-beauty health that you may take for granted. (Putting on plastic gloves when you wash dishes, applying hand lotion throughout the day, brushing teeth, styling your hair, wearing protective lipstick.) After you've completed your list, note ways you can improve upon the basics. (Try an enriched moisturizer, apply a facial mask once a week, simplify your makeup routine, streamline your wardrobe.)

ESTABLISH A PERSONAL BEAUTY DAY

Whether your choices for facials, massage, nail care, and hair care are those you do yourself or receive from a friend or professional, this is a wonderful way to make a weekly ceremony of caring for yourself. If, for example, you choose Saturday as your beauty day, start planning for it earlier in the week, say on Sunday or Monday.

CREATE SHORT-TERM AND LONG-TERM BEAUTY PLANS

As you review the main sections of this chapter—skin, hair, teeth, eyes, clothing, and makeup—note items you'd like to explore now and those you can investigate in the future. Include in that list any professionals you'd like to see right away, soon, or at some later date—dermatologists, aestheticians, hairstylists, personal shoppers, makeup artists, dentists, optometrists. You may want to review Vivian Turner's suggestions for creating a notebook of beauty ideas that inspire your sense of personal style.

It is really our vision and
hope for the future that
draws us forward. Our cells keep
replacing themselves daily, and
we create a whole new body
every seven years. . . .
If we can change the consciousness
that creates our cells, then
our cells and our lives improve
automatically, because health and
joy are our natural state.

— CHRISTIANE NORTHRUP, M.D.
WOMEN'S BODIES, WOMEN'S WISDOM

CHAPTER SIX

YOUTHFUL MATURITY—

UNDERSTANDING HORMONES,

ANTI-AGING, STAYING SEXY

*Aging with Intelligence and
Grace in the Twenty-first Century*

THE PROCESS OF AGING WAS ONE THAT I USED TO FEEL WAS BEYOND MY CONTROL. WHAT I COULD CONTROL, AS I viewed aging, were my own choices and responses toward the natural changes that it brings. But now I find that the distinctions between what we can and cannot control are beginning to blur, and my honest reaction is one of ambivalence.

When I began thinking about the philosophies I hoped would guide *Living Principal,* I was very clear about my feelings toward birth, living, growing older, and dying—a natural process that I felt I could depend on as surely as I depend on the sunrise and the sunset every day. But the rapid progress in the science of anti-aging has produced some confusing and conflicting feelings about how I should respond.

As we discussed earlier, the aging process is no longer thought to be as inevitable as it was just a decade ago; we have already found the means to halt or delay it up to twenty years. Within another decade or two, we're told, we may find the technology to make death itself a matter of choice. From the relatively short time ago when I sat down to begin writing the first chapter of this book to the moment that I now write this one, science has served up some staggering new understandings. Some of the remedies, supplements, and treatments that will improve my quality of life are ones I hope to explore. On the other hand, some radical technologies in the pipeline give me pause—perhaps as part of just feeling emotionally and intellectually stunned that there is even a choice.

As we take a look at some of the possibilities, it's important to emphasize that all of them are matters entirely of personal choice. I should also say that my personal attitude toward aspects of aging differs significantly from scientists who, by training, study mostly disease, disorder, and pathology. From their perspective, aging cells are deficient cells that need to be repaired; hence, you might conclude that aging individuals are deficient and need to be repaired. Such an onus placed on age makes me uncomfortable. Moreover, I think that in our human journey, aging moves us closer to wholeness, not further away from it. With the resources of wisdom and experience that our years have given us, many of our values have become more grounded. We have so much more to give of ourselves as our awareness grows of wanting to be here not merely to complete our biological functions but to make a contribution to the world that is our home. I believe that older, in a multitude of respects, is better.

Which brings me again to the concept of youthful maturity, one of the ways that I have resolved some of my ambivalence. If we can exalt and appreciate the maturity that aging offers while we preserve our own natural youthfulness and innate zest for life, then we can thrive in the best of all worlds. Youthful maturity can be attained, as we discussed earlier, simply by modifying our attitude toward aging, toward ourselves, and toward living. It can be attained through all the whole-health lifestyle practices we've gone through so far, in ways that allow us to be in balance physically, mentally, emotionally, and spiritually. Add to those practices some of the treatments and technologies from the science of antiaging, and we can enhance our youthfulness without giving up the growth that our maturity has helped us gain.

The attainment of youthful maturity, by the way, isn't something that has to happen at any prescribed age. Some girls in their teens and women in their twenties—physiologically youthful—can have a maturity of values and wisdom beyond their years. Women in their thirties typically have not had a significant impact from aging and are still generally youthful in appearance and energy; they may be simultaneously gaining maturity from giving up aspects of their younger lifestyle as they make choices that will determine their future. By our forties and fifties, officially considered our midlife, youthful maturity might reflect more personal growth, along with conscious efforts to stay youthful in mind, body, and spirit. By our sixties and seventies, many of us hopefully attain an even greater degree of maturity and wisdom thanks to accumulated life experiences. At the same time, we have many more options to remain youthful in attitude, looks, and health. In our eighties, nineties, and beyond, as we reach the pinnacle of our maturity, we can continue to be youthful and healthy in mind, body, and spirit—but with a different emphasis on our lifestyle and goals.

Again, I don't believe there is a set time for these passages to occur. Rather, I agree with anti-aging experts who look at the difference between our functional age (how well we function physically and mentally) and our chronological age (our actual physical age). There are, after all, some chronologically aged sixty-year-olds who are biologically more youthful than some thirty-year-olds.

Dr. Christiane Northrup underscores the potential for longevity when she points out that the several hundreds of trillions of cells in our body are constantly, naturally replacing themselves, so that every seven years we have, in fact, a totally new body. I'm not a scientist, but I have observed such a cycle in my own life: Instead of big changes taking place every decade, my personal transformations have occurred more regularly every seven years. It's thrilling to recognize that within the cells of our own bodies we have our own built-in anti-aging capabilities.

How to best channel those capabilities, as Dr. Northrup observes, lies in our own choices about how we want to age; in our beliefs about aging; and in the way we direct our consciousness to direct our cells, which, as we've talked about, are profoundly influenced by our internal voice.

Changing your beliefs about aging may not be easy, given our youth-driven media and the ageism that flourishes in so many aspects of modern life. Again, attitude is everything. Instead of buying into the idea that a particular age makes you over-the-hill, if you believe that you can be as youthful as you choose to be, you've already embarked on an anti-aging self-transformation. Next, consider Dr. Northrup's suggestion that our hope and vision for the future help us to create ourselves as we desire. She asks readers to imagine specifically what their lives would look like if they were in optimal health. You might take that one step further and ask yourself: *If I could be the embodiment of youthful maturity, what would I be like?*

The power to visualize optimal well-being so as to direct our cells toward that real future is a natural, anti-aging gift we all share. And yet, surprisingly, the question of how we'd like to age isn't one many of us have pondered. For some, it can be frightening to imagine what we'll be like once we get beyond that proverbial hill, as if the moment we step past whatever age looms ahead of us we'll plunge over a cliff into the unknown of older age. Others arrive at the feared age as though the belief that aging is a curse has indeed become a self-fulfilling prophecy.

Though I'd given some thought to becoming middle-aged, the question of how I wanted to age in my senior years was something I'd never taken the time to investigate. Then one day Harry caught me off guard by asking, "What do you think you'll be like when you're seventy-five?" Without thinking, I answered, "I'll have silver hair and a great ass." (Thanks to all those butt exercises!) Harry laughed, probably relieved to know that I had weathered the aging challenges of my forties and felt good about the positive changes that the years to come might offer.

But his question provoked me to think about the future choices all potential seniors will face. How do we resolve concerns about the environmental and population-control issues that the more radical anti-aging technologies raise? By employing artificial means to extend our lives, aren't we interfering with the natural order? Do our attempts to defy death mean that we are, in effect, playing God?

These are questions that have been asked by such scientists as Dr. Peter Pugliese, the expert from whom we heard earlier, in our discussion of skin. In *Skin, Sex and Longevity,* Dr. Pugliese addresses such concerns in sound, simple terms. First, he points to a range of scientific findings that assert aging is not part of the natural order at all. Whereas science once assumed that we were genetically programmed to decline, he reports, "some scientists now feel that life span is controlled not by aging genes but by longevity genes. There is no such thing as natural aging, any more than there is a natural tumor, or a natural broken leg."

Do these findings allow us to conclude that humanity is destined to achieve immortality? No, explains Dr. Pugliese, because of the laws of physics that govern our universe, humankind cannot live forever. Notable among these laws of physics, he writes, is the Second Law of Thermodynamics, a law that holds that every entity and system of the universe, including the universe itself, eventually must run down:

> The Second Law of Thermodynamics states that entropy always increases. Entropy is the term used by scientists to describe the state of disorder, or loss of energy. This means that everything must eventually run down because nothing can maintain an ordered state without constant input from outside energy.

Only the soul, says Dr. Pugliese, is immortal. When examined in this logical context, an anti-aging approach that enhances the quality and length of human life does not interfere with the natural order of the universe. What's important, I believe, is to pursue responsible avenues of human antiaging at the same time that we pursue responsible avenues of environmental and planetary anti-aging. Since human-made pollution contributes mightily to our own aging, it's clear that the environment plays a key role in the quality and length of lives. Therefore, if we're seeking ways to care for only ourselves, without seeking ways to better protect and care for our air, earth, water, and fellow humans, our efforts will be limited, if not ultimately fruitless.

If we remember our responsibility to all life, including our planet's, we can reasonably view anti-aging advances not as science's attempt to play God, but as a way to best utilize the gifts God has given us.

To help navigate the information onslaught from this new and exploding field of anti-aging, I'm fortunate to borrow not only from the expertise of Dr. Peter Pugliese—whose studies of the connection between skin, hormones, sex, and longevity are considered by many to be visionary—but from that of Dr. Uzzi Reiss, an internationally renowned anti-aging specialist, obstetrician/gynecologist and leader in the clinical application of natural hormones, nutrition, mind/body principles, and the author (with Martin Zucker) of *Natural Hormone Balance for Women*—a groundbreaking, comprehensive guide.

In addition, I'm honored to present the observations of Dr. Allen S. Cohen, who is heading up, together with my husband, Dr. Harry Glassman, a full-service anti-aging-medicine practice that has evolved as an offshoot of my husband's work as a plastic surgeon. As a leading anesthesiologist who is an integral part of the success of the surgical procedures that Harry performs, Dr. Cohen has long seen the positive impact that the self-improvement and youth enhancement of cosmetic surgery can have on the way individuals feel and look. Inspired to explore other anti-aging improvements, he has expanded his medical expertise to become certified by the American Board of Anti-Aging Medicine and has become a most knowledgeable and, I might add, sensible voice on this science.

Much of the publicity about anti-aging focuses on the attempts to extend our ultimate life span from 120 years to 140 years or more. But the real promise of this science, says Dr. Cohen, is its potential to extend our current average life span from seventies to eighties and even nineties, and for improving the quality of those added years. After all, it's not sensible to extend life span without extending our functional lives by improving our abilities to better function and take care of ourselves in our later years. Even if we are able to improve our functional lives for only four, five, or seven years, that can hold enormously positive social consequences. As only one example, consider the huge reduction of medical and nursing-home costs for our aging population that such anti-aging measures can provide for families with elderly members and for society at large. If we could enter a nursing home between eighty-seven and ninety-three, instead of seventy-seven and eighty-three, and remain functional for another decade, it would benefit everyone—starting with ourselves.

Moreover, suggests Dr. Cohen, anti-aging may relieve, not contribute to, overpopulation and taxation of the environment. How so? Because, he explains, people who live longer by making healthier choices tend to improve a national economy by more distribution of prosperity in social structures that are not overpopulated. And healthier, wealthier nations tend to take better care of the environment, even with personal choices.

As anti-aging medicine prolongs the functional lives of those who would otherwise be entering nursing homes, it can likewise make dramatic improvements earlier on. With such current treatments as human growth hormone, we are already seeing individuals in their sixties and seventies feeling and looking twenty years younger. We're seeing even more far-reaching possibilities for those of us beginning anti-aging treatments in our forties, and rather than attempting to undo aging, we will be able to delay the onset of many age-related discomforts and diseases. Dr. Cohen offers this commonsense logic that we're never too young to take care of our health or our aging: "Good health is like a savings account for your later years."

What would a visit to a practice specializing in anti-aging medicine entail? Dr. Cohen says the evaluation should include all of the following studies:

- A thorough medical history and physical exam to look for any disease concerns, individual and familial; also findings from a gynecological exam, recent mammogram, and pap smear.
- Lab tests for hormonal levels, blood counts, and thyroid and other metabolic functions.

- A bone scan showing bone density, fat content, and other concerns.
- A series of psychometric readings (H-scan) that evaluate reaction time, motor functions, visual acuity, hearing, pulmonary functions, ability to distinguish shapes and colors, memory, and sequencing.

Using all the data, the anti-aging specialist would then determine our functional age (how well we function) relative to our physiological age (our actual physical age). From that, a course of treatment would be devised with specific guidelines for each individual in the following five main areas:

1. Diet: Besides weight-loss needs for anti-aging, an aspect of alarming concern is high insulin, which leads to adult-onset diabetes, a problem of epidemic proportion in the United States.

2. Nutriceuticals: The term used for an anti-aging vitamin, mineral, and nutritional supplement plan. Antioxidants and coenzyme Q-10 are staples, as are some of the new supplement programs (available without a prescription) that address the chronological requirements of a woman's body.

3. Exercise: Anti-aging doctors agree that added exercise is lifesaving and life-extending. Dr. Cohen notes that besides the benefits we've already discussed, exercise enables us to burn calories more efficiently, improving bone strength and bone tissue.

4. Hormone supplements: A key component (more on this soon).

5. Relaxation techniques, meditation: As a way to relieve stress and promote well-being, these are powerful anti-aging medicines—whether it's transcendental meditation, progressive relaxation, yoga, self-hypnosis, twenty-minute deep breathing, massage, reflexology, acupressure, or any form of mental, physical relaxation done two times a day for twenty minutes. This includes prayer, as studies have shown that people who pray, drawing from their religion and their faith, have better abilities to heal. It includes all conscious approaches to relaxation and stress reduction—even taking a vacation!

Depending on the patient's individual concerns, further discussion may take place about aesthetic anti-aging options, the kinds we've been talking about in skin and beauty care and that we'll be talking about in the next chapter with regard to cosmetic surgery.

Beyond the thrust of current treatments, Dr. Cohen and his colleagues will continue to look at causes and cures for the diseases of aging. Interestingly enough, even though most scientists agree that aging isn't a normal, inevitable process, there is not a great deal of consensus as to the one cause of aging, or the one secret that can unravel the riddle that may lead to the proverbial treatment for youth everlasting. Earlier theories, such as the "wear and tear" theory—which says our organs wear out from use—have been determined incomplete. Another theory has to do with waste accumulation, which attributes aging to the backup of metabolic waste. Another theory is studying what's called our rate of living, by looking at links between aging, amounts of energy consumed, and metabolic rates.

The theory that aging is triggered by declines in our immune system has not been supported; after all, Dr. Cohen asserts, the leading killers are not infectious diseases. It is with the theories that deal with understandings of the damage caused by free radicals in the oxidation process and with the recognition of the links between aging and hormones that we have had the most amount of agreement.

For the future, Dr. Cohen and other anti-aging scientists will pay attention to stem-cell transplants and to what Dr. Peter Pugliese sees as the most promising investigation on the horizon: the molecular/genetic research being done with telomeres, the protective compounds at the ends of chromosomes that are needed to protect DNA from damage during cell division. Over time, telomeres become shorter and more frayed as a result of cell division, causing chromosomal damage, decline, or destruction, which leads to our own damage and destruction. However, it is predicted that with the proper utilization of an enzyme called telomerase, telomeres can be rebuilt, thus allowing us, writes Dr. Pugliese, "to set the biological clock back to Day 1!"

Will we live to be six hundred years old? Not yet, because to get that proper utilization, we need to overcome some practical stumbling blocks. So, for the time being, Dr. Cohen believes that kind of age attainment remains in the realm of science fiction. Where he sees the kinds of results that we can already call "turning back the clock" is in research about hormones.

Early on, when many scientists had concluded that the slowing down of hormones was a result of aging, Dr. Pugliese was ahead of the curve by positing that perhaps it happens the other way around—that aging is brought on by the failing of hormones. This could explain how the body chooses to begin the wasting-away process—with a decision in the brain not to send hormones anymore, giving the body the message to age and waste away and make room for the next generation.

Science has begun to agree with Dr. Pugliese, lending much power and steam to anti-aging options in hormone replacement, a subject in which Dr. Uzzi Reiss is no less a visionary. Rather than laboring to explain the causes of aging—which are many and complex, says Dr. Reiss—he frames the process in simple terms as to what the goals of anti-aging should be. If we had the ability to retain the body composition of a twenty-five-year-old—"with all the good enhanced and the bad decreased"—we wouldn't age. Therefore, with anti-aging, our goal should be to maintain and raise the levels of what we do want and lower levels, as much as possible, of what we don't want.

What do hormones have to do with the process? Everything. In *Natural Hormone Balance for Women*, Dr. Reiss writes:

> Hormones are molecules that serve as messengers in an amazing system of inner intelligence that organizes your physiology. Life itself is based on this inner intelligence. There are countless hormones generated within the body, many of which we don't yet clearly understand. They are secreted by glands—such as the adrenals, ovaries, and thyroid—that are governed by higher centers in the brain.

Traveling through our bloodstream, hormones make up the communication connection between our brain and the DNA command posts of all our cells. While science is only now beginning to unlock the wonders of our incredibly intricate hormonal system, what we do know, notes Dr. Reiss, is that the glands produce greater or lesser amounts of different hormones at different times of the day, month, and stage of life, and according to your activities. And we do know that nearly all of them start to decline after we reach our mid-twenties.

Dr. Reiss believes that unhealthy aging is primarily a hormonal issue. His metaphor is that hormonal imbalance, like accelerated aging, is a sorrowful melody of decline; while hormonal balance, like youth itself, is a grand symphony of progress.

DIFFERENT WOMEN, DIFFERENT REPRODUCTIVE JOURNEYS

Up until the last century, notions of longevity and rejuvenation for most women would have been quite foreign. Women in those times often were preoccupied with multiple pregnancies and births and with raising the children who survived. Life expectancy for women was shorter; many died by the age of fifty, some without even having reached menopause.

But for the modern woman, writes Dr. Reiss, "life is a whole new game." We can choose to delay the age we have offspring and opt for fewer children than our foremothers did; some of us don't give birth at all. Meanwhile, our reproductive systems, like the rest of us, are impacted by all the many unprecedented environmental and internal stresses we've been talking about. To further tax our adaptive skills, we have a multitude of other choices to make about work, relationships, sex, and marriage, not to mention enduring the faster pace of life, increased travel, and relocation to places far from where we were born and/or raised.

"The new reality has brought overdue choices and liberation," writes Dr. Reiss, "but with a price: hormonal chaos, increased risk of disease and so-called 'female problems,' and accelerated aging."

Here are some examples that Dr. Reiss has observed of how some women, regardless of age, may experience such hormonal chaos:

- Acne or highly oily skin and hair
- Severe PMS and migraines connected to the menstrual cycle
- Irregular periods and abnormal bleeding, severe menstrual cramps, fibroid tumors, endometriosis
- Cyclical emotional roller coaster—anxiety, rage, depression
- Postpartum depression, hair loss, inability to lose weight gained during pregnancy
- Postpregnancy increase of PMS symptoms, anxiety, mood swings, water retention, increased craving for sweets
- Loss of skin color and tone, grayish skin hue, prematurely aged appearance, poor overall muscle tone
- Painful, tender, swollen, or cystic breasts
- Sagging breasts and loss of fullness
- Hair loss from the head, brows, lashes, armpits, body, and pubic area; hair growth on the face
- Excess weight unrelated to increased caloric intake or not easily reduced by added exercise
- Loss of sexual desire, lack of energy
- Loss of sense of femininity, not caring about one's personal appearance
- Loss of passion in professional or personal creative pursuits
- Poor vaginal lubrication, dry eyes and skin, brittle nails
- Difficulty sleeping
- Foggy thinking, hot flashes, night sweats, loss of body thermostat with wild swings of hot and cold
- Osteoporosis
- Memory loss
- Loss of coordination, stability
- Increased insecurity, worry, indecisiveness, social isolation, resistance to new ideas
- Decrease in metabolic functions such as kidney, bladder, and immune functions

Though some women may experience few of these symptoms in their lifetime, shockingly, many view imbalances of such hormones as estrogen and progesterone as just "normal" female concerns associated with different life stages. To that, both Dr. Reiss and Dr. Pugliese argue that none of us would consider an insulin imbalance or a malfunctioning thyroid normal, would we? No, and most of us would be quick to see a doctor. Why then should we consider hormonal imbalances normal? Why should we hesitate to seek help, especially in light of the remarkable health and anti-aging benefits of medically supervised natural hormone replacement?

Unfortunately, one of the reasons for the hesitation, says Dr. Reiss, is because of the widespread practice of prescribing pharmaceutical versions of hormones that don't match our own—including some of the most frequently prescribed estrogen products, containing estrogens extracted from the urine of pregnant horses. The difference between what our body produces and these conventional substitutes aggravates the imbalance rather than helping it. Furthermore, the studies linking estrogen replacement (ERT) with increased risk of breast cancer have focused on the pharmaceutical hormones, not natural hormones. Reassuringly, Dr. Reiss concludes, "The scientific evidence overwhelmingly shows that estrogen hormonal prescriptions do not increase your risk of dying from breast cancer, and in fact, reduce the risk of fatal breast cancer."

To this Dr. Pugliese adds these statistics:

> The data is very strong showing the risk of fatal heart disease in women over 50. Taking estrogen from age 50 to 75—that is, for 25 years—will reduce the risk of heart disease by 48% and the risk of hip fracture by 49%. The risk of breast cancer for the same period with estrogen therapy is 21%. The risk of uterine cancer is higher but with progesterone replacement it is much less.

While the estrogen our body makes is a combination of three compounds—estrone, estradiol, and estriol—many of the pharmaceutical versions contain fragmented estrogen made up only of estradiol, the most aggressive form. If taken without balance from other hormones, estrogen dominance ensues—something Dr. Reiss warns against.

Meanwhile, many of the commonly prescribed progesterone substitutes are actually progestins, similar to but not exact models of the progesterone our body produces, with side effects that include an increased risk of heart disease due to constricted arteries. Because one of the vital duties of our own progesterone is to balance estrogen, a natural progesterone supplement is obviously preferable.

None of this is meant to vilify pharmaceutical companies; rather, it should inspire questions you might ask of your health-care provider as to whether natural hormones might be options for you. It should be said that some women respond better to the conventional hormonal substitutes.

So where do natural hormones come from and how are they different?

In *Women's Bodies, Women's Wisdom,* Dr. Northrup explains that natural hormones are "derived from the hormones found in soybeans and yams, but their molecular structure is modified in the laboratory to match those found in the human body exactly. That is why they are also referred to as bio-identical hormones."

As all these doctors would tell you, hormonal balance is as different for each individual woman as she herself is different. Fine-tuning the balance of your hormone supplements can take time, sometimes patience, your skills of observation to become familiar with your body's fluctuations, and, particularly, what Dr. Reiss calls your "partner" in attaining natural hormonal balance. That partner is a doctor who is knowledgeable about natural hormone supplements and who is open to your concerns and interests. Have your doctor test your hormone levels, but be aware that you may test in what's considered a normal range, even when you have all the signs and symptoms of imbalance; or you may show a deficiency when you don't have any symptoms. It's safest to be tested twice in the same month to obtain the most accurate reading. In either case, supplementing with natural hormones can be beneficial.

While DHEA, melatonin, and pregnenolone can be purchased at health-food and homeopathic stores, you should use them according to the dosage prescribed by your doctor. The other natural hormones require prescriptions and must usually be obtained from a compounding pharmacy. Also known as formulary pharmacies, these dispensers of prescriptions are able to customize medications for a patient's individual needs and provide combinations of therapies that are not available commercially. Some compounding pharmacies specialize in customizing nutritional supplement formulations as well as natural hormone replacement. That way, explains Dr. Soram Singh Khalsa, "When we treat women with natural hormone replacement therapy, we use individually compounded hormones for that woman's particular body that are made to her specifications—kind of like fitting a dress."

COMPOUNDING (FORMULARY) PHARMACIES

You can call Professionals and Patients for Customized Care toll-free at (800) 927-4227 to locate a compounding pharmacy nearest you.

The Compounding Pharmacy of Beverly Hills will mail prescriptions overnight. Your doctor can phone them at (310) 284-8675 or fax (310) 284-8680. The toll-free number is (888) 799-0212.

Women's International Pharmacy is also highly recommended. Their phone number in Madison, Wisconsin, is (608) 221-7800 or toll-free (800) 279-5708.

Natural hormones come in a variety of forms—creams, gels, capsules, patches, sublingual drops, and vaginal rings, among others. Your doctor can discuss your options and recommend what form he thinks is best for you, in addition to proper dosage.

Dr. Reiss strongly advises that you make sure two key concerns are addressed before you begin supplementing with hormones. First, he says, we are all too stressed and too stimulated. And we know that the higher our level of cortisol, the stress hormone secreted by the adrenal glands, the shorter our life expectancy. We need what he calls an exit from that stress, along the lines of Dr. Cohen's various relaxation methods. Second, before starting hormones, make sure you've taken the steps necessary to reduce sugar and highly processed carbohydrates (those foods that we don't need) in your diet in order to reduce the high levels of insulin that the pancreas secretes to control blood sugar levels. Not only do these two factors accelerate aging, as we've already discussed, they will also interfere with overall natural hormone function.

With those two concerns addressed, you may discover that you don't need hormone replacement; or, if you do, you'll be able to better assess your needs.

By the way, one of the common misconceptions about supplementing with natural hormones is that it's something needed only for women in menopause. Not so, says Dr. Reiss. As you saw in the list of symptoms, you can be anywhere from your twenties to your late eighties to experience hormonal imbalance and thus to benefit from natural hormone balancing.

WHO SAYS MENOPAUSE IS A FOUR-LETTER WORD?

For most of our lives we've heard about the dreaded menopause, also known as the "change of life" for women. Reports of hot flashes and hormonal rages make us fear our own natures, as though our bodies are walking time bombs set to explode at a preordained moment we can't control. Many of us have an image of being normal one day but hormonally crazed the next, a state in which we must remain for the rest of our lives. In reality, the liberation of not having PMS, cramps, sore breasts, and monthly weight gain can be a big relief, thus making menopause anything but a four-letter word.

Dr. Reiss reports that while the average age of menopause is fifty-one, a woman in her thirties can reach menopause, as can a women in her late fifties. The medical measure for whether a woman has reached menopause is when she does not menstruate for twelve straight months, but there can be other causes for the cessation of menses. Dr. Reiss also associates menopause with persistent signs of estrogen deficiency. The level of deficiency may vary based upon different factors, including what stage of menopause a woman is in. The three stages Dr. Reiss describes are onset (the first few years of period cessation), midmenopause (around three to eight years past cessation), and late menopause (around fifteen years past cessation). Some experts focus on estrogen replacement in the earlier stages, when fluctuations are more volatile. However, Dr. Reiss sees benefits in natural estrogen supplements for all age groups, noting in *Natural Hormone Balance for Women*: "Even a woman in her eighties can experience estrogen benefits to the bones, hair, vagina, breasts, mind, mood, and overall well-being."

While we've heard more about menopause, what we haven't heard much about until recently is the hormonal roller coaster of the process that leads up to the change, the stage known as perimenopause—meaning "around menopause"—which can last anywhere from a few years to over a decade. For women who don't know the signs, or who experience them at a relatively young age, it can be devastating to suddenly find themselves with plummeting hormones. To go from having an active, passionate sex life to feeling completely devoid of interest in a partner or even in yourself can be an unexpected nightmare.

Although intensified PMS (which may relate to a progesterone deficiency) may be experienced during perimenopause, much of the stage leading up to menopause has to do with an estrogen deficiency or estrogen fluctuations. Dr. Reiss explains that during our reproductive years, a week after ovulation, the body decides whether it's pregnant. If not, levels of estrogen and progesterone drop, leading to menstruation. In perimenopause, he says, the drop is steeper and faster.

Again, it's important to acknowledge that there are women who seem to breeze through these stages, maybe have a hot flash or two, and get on with their lives. For others, the journey may have challenges. Let's look at the ways that supplementing with different hormones can help, not only for crises, but to retain high levels of the things we want and to diminish levels of what we don't.

Estrogen: Made in part in the ovaries, this hormone is so critical to all aspects of reproductive, physical, mental, and emotional health that it may impact more than three hundred tissue systems in the body. Estrogen plays a key role for sexuality and sensuality, feminine energy, vitality, and youthfulness. Estrogen deficiencies encompass symptoms such as loss of sensuality; insomnia; mental fogginess and forgetfulness; depression; hot flashes, night sweats, and temperature swings; dry skin, eyes, and vagina; joint pain; migraines; sagging breasts; weight gain; and a racing heart. Excess estrogen can be seen in such signs as breast swelling and pain, clear-minded but hot-tempered or snappy moods, pelvic cramps, and nausea.

The benefits of natural estrogen replacement include mental rejuvenation; improved mood; better sleep and higher stamina; protection from weight gain; decreased risk of arthritis, bone and cardiovascular disease; improved sex drive; fuller breasts; improved skin tone and color; and no more night sweats or hot flashes.

To address excess estrogen—the operative word being "balance"—doctors will look to other hormone supplements, particularly progesterone, which is estrogen's natural balancing partner and safeguards against a buildup of estrogen.

Progesterone: Known as the hormonal harmonizer, progesterone is released by the ovaries after ovulation to help sustain pregnancy. Of progesterone's many important jobs, a vital one is generating new bone tissue. That is why progesterone deficiency in most menopausal women can contribute to osteoporosis. Low progesterone lowers the seesaw that raises estrogen to excess. Besides severe PMS, progesterone imbalance can cause symptoms such as irregular periods, heavy bleeding, fibroids, cystic breasts, and anxiety.

Natural progesterone replacement is something Dr. Reiss usually recommends for women who are supplementing with natural estrogen. The benefits include contributing to the formation of new bone tissue, helping to raise HDL (the good cholesterol), and protection against cancer of the breasts, uterus, and possibly ovaries. It can dramatically alleviate symptoms of postpartum depression and PMS; act as a natural diuretic; cut down on cravings for carbohydrates and sweets; reduce breast tenderness and pain; and reduce anxiety.

Testosterone: Men have it in spades, but we have it too, though in much lower amounts. Produced by our ovaries, testosterone levels decline after our mid-twenties, fluctuating along with other hormones. While supplementing with testosterone can definitely improve all aspects of sexuality—from how you feel about your sensuality to enhancing your experience of the sexual act—Dr. Reiss points out the benefits it can hold for all aspects of our strength, vitality, and emotional well-being.

Human growth hormone: Made by the pituitary gland, HGH is considered a treasure trove for anti-aging possibilities. Because it influences all our cells and myriad growth factors within our bodies, including the optimum operation of other hormones, symptoms of HGH deficiencies can be summed up by most of those we associate with accelerated aging and poor physical, emotional, and mental health. The balance can help restore health, youth, and well-being to all those areas. Interestingly, one of the best ways to boost your own level of HGH, without supplementing, is to exercise—a means by which studies say you can increase HGH up to 20 percent.

As with all hormone supplementation, HGH should be used conservatively, with careful medical guidance. Supplementing with natural HGH, for women and men alike, can bring new strength, vigor, and enthusiasm to life, an observation Dr. Reiss reports from personal experience in his own anti-aging program.

DHEA: Made by our adrenal glands—as is adrenaline and cortisol—DHEA has grabbed almost as much attention in recent years as HGH. Though they're available without a prescription, natural supplements of DHEA should still be used under medical guidance. Not a star but rather a supporting player in anti-aging, DHEA, Dr. Reiss says, can help control stress (one of its natural jobs), improve energy and mood, and benefit our immune systems. While research is still ongoing, other health benefits are expected from DHEA, but there are also areas of risk. To get the lowdown, talk to your internist, GP, gynecologist, or endocrinologist.

In addition to the fact that meditation and deep breathing have proven to reduce stress, new studies also indicate that such practices are a natural way to boost your DHEA.

Melatonin: This hormone is released by the pineal gland in our brain, which is in charge of our body's biological clock. Levels of melatonin rise with the dark and decrease with light, the sleep/wake cycles we call our circadian rhythms. Since sleep disturbances are common among aging individuals, particularly women whose other hormonal imbalances may impact sleep, supplementing with melatonin (available without prescription) can be beneficial for sleep and anti-aging in general. Among the other benefits of melatonin are: reducing the effects of jet lag, slowing down the graying of hair, and combating anxiety.

Some of the herbal supplements we discussed in regard to nutrition can also help improve sleep. Dr. Soram Singh Khalsa notes, "We find that a lot of menopausal women have a reverse day/night sleep cycle." He describes the symptoms of waking up exhausted (the way you'd like to be when you go to sleep), feeling revved up at ten P.M. when you're on the Internet chatting, and getting to bed at midnight when you can't relax or sleep. Among other things, Dr. Khalsa has found a program of regular acupuncture highly effective in treating insomnia by restoring the body's natural sleep rhythm.

Pregnenolone: Made by the adrenal glands, pregnenolone helps in the development and operation of other hormones and is considered a team player in your overall hormonal balance. Dr. Reiss suggests its use to individuals who want a total hormonal replacement program or to address memory and stamina problems. It has also helped women with difficult PMS that other treatments haven't alleviated.

I hope that this overview of the potentials of natural hormone replacement has given you some helpful general information to begin your own investigation. If any of these possibilities appear meaningful to you—to address deficiencies and/or for the longevity benefits you may seek—I heartily urge you to make an appointment with your doctor, have a hormonal profile, and discuss the options so you can get started.

In preparation for your appointment, you may want to spend the next weeks taking note of any hormonal fluctuations, as well as any of the symptoms of deficiencies that we've been discussing. As we've said all along, self-knowledge is truly a key to whole-health, just as it is a key to your happiness and fulfillment in regard to our next topic:

As a card-carrying baby boomer, I can attest to the fact that our generation has a different attitude toward aging than our parents had, different even from those who came of age in the 1950s. Instead of accepting that our time has come and gone, baby boomers have decided we're here to stay. We want to continue to look and feel young, living dynamic, longer lives. In this respect, we're very much leading the way in the anti-aging revolution that's taking place today. As the generation that came of age during the sexual revolution of the 1960s, we also have a different attitude toward sex than our elders did. Instead of accepting the old cliché that people in their middle and older years are supposed to stop having sex, or stop enjoying it, baby boomers aren't buying into that idea. We know what it means to be turned on—not just turned on by sex but turned on to being alive. And we understand that the life force that is expressed through sexual intimacy helps keep us feeling alive and young.

From an anti-aging standpoint, this turns out to be a good thing. Just as we have seen that supplementing hormones can make us look and feel younger, improve our skin and tone, elevate feelings of sensuality, and increase sexual drive, experts let us know that it also works the other way around: that increased sexual activity spurs the hormones that make us look and feel younger, improve our skin and tone, and let us continue to feel more sensual.

A healthy, active sexual life, in fact, is a leading factor in longevity. We should emphasize that a healthy, active sexual life does not refer to the practice of indiscriminant, irresponsible, or unsafe sex. Experts even believe that longevity is enhanced when emotional intimacy, love, commitment, and/or marriage are part of the sexual equation. Not that all those aspects are required for having good sex. Many top sexual therapists assert that for single women and men, having sex with yourself can give you a healthy, active sexual life that will contribute to living longer. At the same time, longevity studies have shown that individuals who live the longest, and stay healthier and more youthful, are those who are involved in fulfilling, long-term, monogamous sexual relationships into their later years. (We should all be so lucky!)

Dr. Pugliese points out that animals which have short sexual life spans die off more quickly. This includes species that may have sex only once or twice, or at peak reproductive stages, as if nature has hardwired them to die the moment their procreative work is done. The longest-living species, humans among them, have long sexual life spans, with ongoing sexual activity that can continue past reproductive primes. Nonetheless, in terms of evolution, we too are hardwired to procreate, making sex a part of our innate drive to perpetuate the survival of the species. It is so connected to our will to live that the cessation of sex has been observed to be a cause of aging and death.

Conversely, cultural attitudes about age can impact negatively on our sexual drive. Unfortunately, stereotypes that we see enacted around us send negative messages about our sexual viability as we get older. There are men whose fears and insecurities about aging manifest in efforts to stay young with affairs or younger trophy wives; they sometimes replace their spouses not once but twice. Some women may follow a similar pattern. Other women, fearing that age has made them less desirable, or worrying that their husbands have lost interest, retreat into denial, simply giving up or giving in, buying into society's destructive notion that older women are unsexy. It's an attitude that needs to be consciously altered.

Is there anything in our physiology that renders us incapable of having healthy sexual lives past a certain age? Not really. We know that women may undergo physiological changes through perimenopause and menopause that may impact sexual interest and the ability to enjoy sex, issues we know can be addressed with hormone supplements and other means. Moreover, Dr. Pugliese tells us:

All of this considered, a woman still has the same physical capacity for orgasm at 80 that she had at 30! . . . The vagina of a sexually active woman changes little over time, so that a 60-year-old woman who has sexual activity at least twice a month can readily produce adequate lubrication for normal intercourse.

Actually, he goes on to say, many of the concerns of aging women—such as thin, contracted vaginal walls, vaginal atrophy, and scarring—can result from being sexually inactive.

Dr. Uzzi Reiss concurs, explaining that, like the muscles of the rest of our body that we keep fit through exercise, regular use improves the tone of the muscles that we naturally exercise during sex. Can that help the loss of elasticity and the looseness that happens as the result of multiple vaginal deliveries—not to mention the growing size of babies being born these days? Somewhat, says Dr. Reiss, as can practicing Kegel exercises, which involve repetitive contractions of the p.c. (pubococcygeous) muscle. Dr. Reiss suggests that you practice stopping urination when you are in midstream, as though someone just walked into the bathroom. Once you've practiced isolating and contracting the p.c. muscle, then you can make a habit of repeating the contractions and holding them. Dr. Reiss recommends that you work up to the 10-10-10 method—ten repetitions, held for a count of ten, done ten times a day. While you're at it, he says, to add more challenge and more benefits, you might do a full-body contraction, squeezing and tightening your thighs, butt, abs, and biceps along with your p.c. muscle.

Dr. Christiane Northrup writes that Kegel-type exercises are very effective in strengthening the floor of the uterus and in helping alleviate (90 percent of the time) a huge problem for many women that is known as mild urinary stress incontinence. Beyond hormones, p.c. exercises, and healthy sexual activity, there are surgical options for more serious issues of incontinence (with relative degrees of success), as well as for lifting internal organs that may have moved or fallen with childbirth or the force of gravity.

Dr. Reiss says that some women request surgery who wish to surgically restore the tightness of their vaginas, usually out of an intent to please mates who feel that this may aid their ability to maintain an erection and increase sexual gratification. The less invasive approaches already discussed are preferred by Dr. Reiss, who also notes that there is a device your doctor can give you known as a weighted vaginal cone, that can be used to strengthen and tighten vaginal muscles as an alternative to surgery. However, he says, this is an individual's choice.

Dr. Reiss's main concerns are the social pressures that make women feel inferior about their bodies and their sexuality. Using the example of douches, products that were developed along unscientific lines, he stresses again that the key to health and anti-aging is the preservation of our body's resources—in this case, the naturally acidic habitat that enhances the health of the vagina. Dr. Reiss states that before developing feminine products, their makers should first study what he calls the "unique, static, sacred, balanced, homeostatic environment that has evolved from hundreds and thousands of years ago." Unfortunately, many of these products aren't made with an understanding of the acid environment so necessary to prevent the growth of most bacteria. As a result, overly alkaline douches with the wrong pH balance, whether they make women feel clean and fresh or not, can lead to vaginal and urinary infections. For this reason, it's important to make sure that any product you use has been tested and recommended for healthy pH balance.

Amid all the choices for caring for our gynecological whole-health, Dr. Reiss reminds us to maintain all the good that nature has given us, to get up every morning and ask ourselves, "How can I maintain the gloriousness and beauty that I already have?"

For a woman who has had a hysterectomy, maintenance of hormonal levels is usually answered by supplementation. Otherwise, there should be no impact on her life span, or on her ability to enjoy and maintain a happy, healthy sex life.

With the incredible discoveries of science, our capacity for fertility has been extended into our forties and even fifties. Theoretically, a women of any age can have a baby—although later reproduction is without a doubt more taxing on women's bodies, making it harder to bounce back and contributing to aging.

As we move away from questions about how physical issues may impact sex, we should look at some of the psychological and emotional issues that are probably more important for our attainment of a healthy, active sexual life. For most women I know, it's every bit as essential to be turned on mentally, emotionally, and in all our senses as it is to be physically aroused. If we're not, there will be times when libidos will flatten beyond recognition, when no hormone supplement, advanced sexual technique, or erotic manual can make us feel sexy.

This brings us to the all-important question, what is sexy? And, more to the point, what can we do to make ourselves feel sexy?

In the last century, as we struggled to dig ourselves out of the rubble of the sexually repressed post-Victorian age, the word "sexy" seemed only fitting for "loose" women or for sex symbols. These days, every woman can be as sexy as she wants to be, in her own individual, deeply personal way.

In *Women's Bodies, Women's Wisdom,* Dr. Northrup encourages women readers to reclaim the erotic in their everyday lives by connecting or reconnecting to their own feminine sexuality. Many women will tell you that they don't have to reach orgasm every time for satisfaction and that intimacy and all-over physical affection are their primary desires.

As we learn to tune in to our senses in order to find out what turns us on and makes us feel sexy to ourselves and sexually attractive to our partners, it's vital that we speak to ourselves lovingly. Our internal voice can help us either light the flames of passion or douse them in an instant. If a woman's internal voice has been beating her up all day, it's likely that when she climbs into bed at night, sniping at herself that her age has made her devoid of sexiness, she won't stop when she sees her husband eyeing her with interest. Instead of that making her feel better, she may go through internal self-flagellation that sounds something like this: *Oh, what does he want now? How can he be attracted to me, I'm so unappealing, what's wrong with him for even being interested? Okay, I'll just endure it and let him get it over with as fast as possible. Oh, but what if he expects me to act like I'm enjoying it? How can I? Oh, I'll have to fake it. Or maybe—yes, I do have a headache, and I'm so tired I can probably fall asleep before he gets across the room.* Even if her husband were her fantasy dream man, rippling with muscles and testosterone, it wouldn't make a difference. As long as she's not appealing to herself, she won't feel appealing to anyone or find him appealing to her.

Such a response is much more common than many of us would imagine. What can help her, as always, is to change her internal voice; instead of focusing on her lack of libido, she can encourage herself to indulge her passions in other areas. Sometimes passions experienced in nonsexual ways flow nicely to other senses, leading to an improved sex drive.

It may also help a woman, suggests Dr. Pugliese, to talk to her spouse, let him know that she's going through a difficult time, and ask for his support. Age and change, as we all know, raise emotional issues for us all, male and female.

Clearly, the attainment of a healthy, active, monogamous sexual life isn't easy. Long happily married, Dr. Reiss bemoans the challenge of monogamy: "You have to give up so much. And yet if through monogamy you develop this intimate amazing relationship and companionship with someone, all the hardship looks so little." There will be times of open, dry space, he says, but when you do come together, the intimacy that you've developed together over time will enhance the act of sex.

The best sexual relationships, all the experts advise, are those that are cultivated mutually, with give-and-take, communication, and consideration of the needs and limitations of each individual. For some couples, getting sexy together is as basic as remembering to set aside time to do it. You do have to make a conscious effort, say Doctors Northrup, Reiss, and Pugliese, especially as you get older. Many of us are exhausted, overworked, and stressed—not the most erotic influences.

How then to make the time and ensure that the mood isn't missed? Magazines and the Internet are full of juicy morsels of advice. Gleaned from their headlines and from our experts, here are just a few ways to get sexy, sexier, and sexiest:

- Not turned on by how your partner touches you? Try touching the way you like to be touched.
- Discover how you like to be touched by touching yourself. Do you like gentle, light, sensual caresses? Do you like harder, rougher, more vigorous touching? Do you like both?
- Get turned on without demanding that sex culminate in orgasm or intercourse.
- Get turned on by giving pleasure as much as from receiving it.
- Don't get into the IOU mentality. It's true, say the experts, that the desire to please your lover usually inspires his desire to please you. But the idea that you're doing it as tit for tat, so to speak, can be a turnoff for you both.

- Celebrate your male and female differences. Women are absolutely aroused by smell, says Dr. Pugliese, and can even smell testosterone. Colognes, scented candles, and other pleasing aromas are powerful for women. Men, on the other hand, are much more visual—so dressing seductively and in a way that makes you alluring will get him revved up.
- Other differences: Men want to get where they're going via a direct path. Women love to linger, languish, and luxuriate, like an unfolding, suggestive erotic story, like music that takes time to build to its climax.
- Men like to feel in charge. It's part of their hardwiring.
- Perk up the routine. Lovemaking out of the bedroom is one way—in the shower or living room, on the kitchen counter. Cars have always been sexy places to neck.
- Surprise is wonderful, says every expert source. Without his knowledge, send the kids to their grandparents or to some friends for a sleepover. When he arrives home, greet him in something silky and provocative, or nothing at all.
- Indulge your fantasies, together or by yourself. Act out roles of love slave, dutiful student. Play doctor and nurse. Meet in a public place and pick each other up, as if you've only just met.
- Talk dirty. ("Bad boys and naughty girls have more fun," according to one list.)
- Romance, poetry, flowers, candles, music, wine, and small thoughtful gifts never lose their luster.
- Wake each other up in the middle of the night for spontaneous, passionate lovemaking.
- Foreplay is great sex.
- Self-love is great sex.
- Laughter and a sense of humor make for more closeness in relationships and in sex.
- Have sex before marriage to make sure you're compatible (Dr. Reiss).

- Try Tantric sex, which involves delaying gratification over the period of several days while spending lengthy sessions touching, kissing, giving each other massages or hand baths; the waiting is worth it (Dr. Reiss).
- Experiment with erotica, light porn, sex toys, edible panties, lubricants, something called "Egyptian Magic"—a butterlike substance that can be eaten or absorbed naturally into the skin—massage oils, sexually intimate board games, or strip poker: whatever enhances pleasure in a loving, giving way.
- Besides the sexual improvements from hormone replacement, enhancements such as the topical use of testosterone on a woman's clitoris can be extremely stimulating. ("Better than I ever dreamed sex could be," some women tell Dr. Reiss.)
- Honor your relationship. Every day, recommends Dr. Reiss, do three things—something for yourself, something for your relationship, and something for your partner.

Finally, as we conclude the topic of anti-aging, we should mention a few other factors that effect a sexier, healthier, more vital, longer life. Dr. Pugliese emphasizes that work, a sense of purpose, meaningful projects, and ways to move toward productive goals will keep the fires going personally and sexually. We need to keep turned on to learning, he observes; our minds need to be exercised as much as our bodies do. I'll add that companionship, support systems, and a sense of community matter immensely. We must have a strong will to live and to live well.

One of the things that can never be taken for granted in marriage and romance is having a foundation of friendship. It's a turn-on to me that my sexy, romantic, brilliant husband is also my best friend.

And so, when I asked him if he would help me write the next chapter, he most kindly obliged. Even though we've been talking about him in his personal role as my husband, you'll be meeting him next in his professional capacity. Let's continue on to the area of his remarkable expertise.

Practical Steps for Attaining Youthful Maturity

In reviewing the highlights of this chapter and offering practical steps you can explore, let me say how fortunate I feel we are to be living at the threshold of new possibilities for improving quality of life for all of us. It's also encouraging to note that the main principles of anti-aging embody many of the whole-health practices you may have already begun to incorporate.

CELEBRATE YOUTHFUL MATURITY

Whatever this term means to you, take the opportunity to feel good about yourself for having lived and learned for as many years as you've been on this earth. You may contemplate at this time what aspects of your youthfulness are apparent and what aspects you would like to rekindle. What aspects of your maturity make you proud? In what ways would you like to become more mature?

GIVE YOURSELF AN ANTI-AGING CHECKUP

Using the five categories of treatment emphasized in anti-aging practices—diet, supplements, exercise, meditation, and hormones—gauge how well your lifestyle incorporates practices for health in these areas. Again, if you see an anti-aging need, choose one area at a time to focus on.

TAKE AN ACTIVE ROLE IN ATTAINING NATURAL HORMONAL BALANCE

This step reminds you of the age-old truth that knowledge is power. The more you know about your own body's fluctuations and the more you understand about hormones, the better equipped you'll be to work in partnership with your doctor to achieve maximum benefits—for health, happiness, and longevity.

TAKE AN ACTIVE ROLE IN ATTAINING SEXUAL HEALTH

This is an opportunity to remind yourself that this amazing, natural human capacity may not always just happen; it may require some conscious planning, inspiration, and encouragement on your part. You may want to review the chapter's section on sexuality and follow any one or more of the suggestions offered there. And remember one of the principles we covered early on—have *fun*.

Some say the soul informs the body.
But what if we were to imagine for
a moment that the body informs the
soul, helps it adapt to mundane life,
parses, translates, gives the
blank page, the ink, and the pen
with which the soul can write
upon our lives? . . . Its purpose is
to protect, contain, support, and
fire the spirit within it, to be a
repository for memory, to fill us
with feeling. . . . The body is the
rocket launcher, in its nose capsule
the soul looks out the window into
the mysterious starry night
and is dazzled.

— CLARISSA PINKOLA ESTÉS, PH.D.
WOMEN WHO RUN WITH THE WOLVES

CHAPTER SEVEN

LESS IS MORE—EXPLORING

COSMETIC SURGERY

Respecting and Enhancing the
Work of Mother Nature

NTERNATIONALLY RENOWNED, PUBLISHED, AND WRITTEN ABOUT EXTENSIVELY AS ONE OF THE MOST SOUGHT-AFTER COSMETIC surgeons practicing in the United States today, Dr. Harry Glassman brings together the very finest traits any woman might look for when choosing a surgeon. He is also a man of true personal integrity, a caregiver and a healer in the best sense of the words, and, I would like to add, one of the kindest human beings I've ever known. To his practice, the NOVA Surgicenter in Beverly Hills, he brings another attribute— though subjective in nature—that can make all the difference in a patient's attainment of her desired results: an artistic, aesthetic sensibility that honors the work of Mother Nature by understanding the meaning of "less is more."

We talked about those principles in the following Q&A:

Q: What defines the practice of cosmetic surgery?

Dr. Glassman: Cosmetic surgery is a division of plastic surgery, which itself has two divisions—cosmetic surgery and reconstructive surgery. The latter is the art of restoring the abnormal to normal, while cosmetic surgery is the surgical art of taking something normal and enhancing it.

Q: What does "less is more" mean to you?

A: "Less is more" applies to several issues in cosmetic surgery. First, above all else, it means the pursuit of a natural, nonsurgical appearance. Aesthetic enhancement should follow the guideline of normal anatomy rather than adhering to the adage "more is more!" Second, it refers to timing. Cosmetic surgery should not be excessive or pursued prematurely. It means the right operation at the right time in your life. "Less is more" is also about not waiting too long. When the aging process is taken on in smaller increments, the long-term goals of the patient and surgeon are more easily attained.

Q: How do individuals determine the right operation and the right time?

A: If a woman is unhappy with the way she looks, but unsure of the exact reason, she can compare a recent photograph to one taken about five years ago (or even more). She can then see and articulate the difference that she is bothered about. If it is not an aging issue but the shape of one's nose, for example, a woman usually knows exactly what it is she would like to change.

One of the greatest things that has come along in plastic surgery is the tool of mirror imaging. The surgeon uses a computer program that captures the image of the patient preoperatively on the screen with a digital camera, then manipulates the image in a way that's consistent with the anticipated surgical plan. Never before have we had this kind of an opportunity to preview for someone what we expect her to look like throughout the process and educate her about the operation. It's an indispensable tool. When a surgeon says, "I'm going to raise your eyebrows," it conjures up images of a surprised look. And yet when it's done subtly, in such a way that's normal, it's a very youth-enhancing thing to do. Therefore, with mirror imaging, a patient can see if the expected results are in keeping with personal expectations at that time, then make a much more informed decision. The use of mirror imaging is becoming much more widely available and is something to ask about when meeting with a prospective surgeon.

Q: What other questions should be asked?

A: It is the due diligence of a patient to find out about a surgeon's background, experience, education, training, licensing and certification, and areas of expertise. Those questions can be explored by asking direct questions or by asking around. Getting recommendations from your other medical providers is a good idea. It's important to make sure that your prospective surgeon's aesthetics are a match with yours. Because most cosmetic surgery is elective, it's mandatory to get detailed information about the expected costs and about the financial policy of the office. It's imperative that a plastic surgeon review any medical risks, what scarring to anticipate, recovery time, and any possible aftereffects.

Dr. Glassman reminds readers, "Plastic surgery is not like getting your hair cut. While it offers wonderful benefits, it is still surgery, often major surgery, and should not be taken lightly. Surgical risks vary from operation to operation and depend on the physical condition of the patient." Clearing up a common misconception, he underscores the fact that because a procedure is done with a laser, it is no less invasive. When most people think about having eye surgery, for example, in which the surgeon uses scalpel or scissors, it sounds grotesque because it involves "going under the knife," with incisions and blood. When they hear that the procedure can be done with a laser, they may naively think it's as simple as having a beam of light shone on them to solve all their problems. Actually, he points out, the beam is used just like a scalpel: Cutting is done with light as the sharp edge. Which method will depend upon the plastic surgeon, his preferences, his experience and expertise, and the many pros and cons of each particular operation. Dr. Glassman notes that cosmetic surgeons must be multifaceted in their approach in order to apply concepts and treatments in ways that best fit the patient's individual needs.

It is vital, advises Dr. Glassman, to be clear about your motivation for having surgery. The underlying reason for anyone to have cosmetic surgery is to feel better about yourself. Prospective patients have asked him, "Do I need to have my face done?" His answer is that no one *needs* to have a face-lift. It is more a question of *wanting* than needing. But if you're less than happy with, or even ashamed of, aspects of your appearance, then the fulfillment of your want can become fundamental to your well-being. Clearly, cosmetic surgery that improves self-esteem can be transformational not only externally, but internally as well.

I've seen countless women (and men) become more empowered individuals as a result of empowering their bodies through the options cosmetic surgery gives them. The key seems to be in having realistic expectations, like those you can attain through the mirror-imaging tool. Those hopeful, realistic expectations should no doubt be weighed against any guilt you may have about what some may consider a preoccupation with vanity, or guilt about spending money on something for you and you alone.

My take on vanity is that it's as much a part of what Mother Nature gave us as our natural features and assets. Throughout the natural world, in fact, most animals and plants have traits of vanity. Have you ever noticed how delighted your pets are after being groomed? And what about the competitive display of beauty among the different species of flowers?

Dr. Glassman's attitude is that you needn't apologize or feel guilty for doing anything that makes you feel better about yourself, will beautify you and your life, or will add to your self-esteem. If you have concerns that can be addressed in a straightforward, uncomplicated approach and you are prepared to handle the costs, risks, and downtime associated with the surgery, he suggests that you avail yourself of the opportunity.

Give yourself permission to follow the principles of less is more. Just because we have so many options doesn't mean we should rush to do them all at once.

Come up with a priority plan with your surgeon to make changes subtly and gradually. To echo that famous old ad campaign, "Only your hairdresser knows for sure" whether or not you color your hair—mounted in an era when the use of hair dye was thought to interfere with Mother Nature's plans!—the practice of less is more can be so natural and authentic that only your cosmetic surgeon will know for sure. Many people will wonder where you went on your vacation to give you such a glowing, restored, rejuvenated look.

Make choices that are right for you. If the idea that you must age by letting nature take its course is deeply ingrained in you, don't force yourself to have cosmetic surgery because all your friends are doing it or because your spouse or another family member thinks it's a good idea. Only you can make that determination. Know that if surgical options make you uncomfortable, there are some less invasive alternatives to consider, examples of which we will touch on in the following section.

FROM HEAD TO TOE—

A GLANCE AT COSMETIC SURGERY OPTIONS

D r. Glassman explains that most women pay visits to plastic surgeons with targeted concerns. Let's start from the top and move down as we look at a variety of the most commonly discussed areas:

Brow-lifts, face-lifts, and facial implants: When the sagging of your forehead lowers your eyebrows or crowds your upper eyelid, a brow-lift is the one of the best options to rejuvenate your look. In the past, the operation involved a much more invasive incision across the top of the head, while now, thanks to the endoscope—an instrument with a light and a camera—it involves only four to six tiny incisions in the scalp. In addition to raising the forehead, plastic surgeons can also access the muscles that cause the frown lines between eyebrows and remedy those to a great extent. A brow-lift is an operation that can be done alone, in conjunction with eyelid surgery, or in conjunction with a face-lift.

Like other major surgeries, a face-lift is by no means an operation to be approached one-dimensionally. With multiple layers and multiple approaches, there are many techniques that must be applied to an individual's face, based upon anatomical considerations. The basic steps entail making inconspicuous incisions in the hairline and inside the ear; removing any excess fat by liposuction (more on techniques in a moment); tightening the deeper layer of the face and the platysma muscle, a superficial muscle that forms the vertical bands on the neck, and pulling on the skin gently, not severely, retailoring the skin so it fits the skull, the neck, and the jawline better than it did before.

Dr. Glassman uses the analogy of looking for the best way to make your bed: "The bed has multiple layers to it, the sheeting, the bedding, the duvet. You wouldn't want to merely pull on the top cover to make your bed, because there would be a lot of wrinkled stuff underneath. You would want to first smooth out the lower sheet, then pull and tighten the upper sheet, and then the blanket." By working one layer at a time, he explains, the surgeon doesn't rely on any one layer to take up all the slack. In the past, pulling the skin was the basic procedure for face-lifts. Today, the vast majority of individuals seeking face-lifts have multidimensional problems that should be addressed with a multidimensional approach.

Facial implants play a major role in the restoration of the youthful face, addressing the aging process that may make the face thinner and longer with the loss of baby fat. When a person's face has become gaunt, pulling on it will create the artificial, surgical look that is to be avoided. Instead, cosmetic surgeons use small prostheses of silicone implants for the midface, the lower part of the cheeks, and sometimes the chin. Either as an individual operation or in combination with others, facial implants done in a "less is more" fashion are virtually undetectable.

As for facial scars, many respond well to scar revision, in which scars are removed surgically and sewn up. Some scars are amenable to resurfacing techniques such as dermabrasion and chemical peels. Some scarring can be improved with fat grafting, a process that has other effective applications as well, or by laser resurfacing—which can be used only on the face, not on the neck or chest, where peels are options. Unfortunately, very severe acne scarring does not yet have a full surgical remedy.

Chemical peels are administered in a variety of strengths by dermatologists, aestheticians, and cosmetic surgeons. Peels can improve many facial concerns—fine lines, poor skin texture, some discoloration, some acne scarring—but they can't tighten loose skin or make much of a difference with more pronounced wrinkles. Similar capacities are seen in dermabrasion, a form of sanding of the skin, and in microdermabrasion.

Laser resurfacing can be very effective for several purposes. While multiple types of lasers are being used for resurfacing, the carbon dioxide laser is most common. The setting of this laser can be changed to either act as a scalpel (for eyelid surgery) or to evaporate the water in the cells of the outer layer of skin. Once that water has evaporated, the outer layer of skin is charred, basically, and wiped away with wet sponges almost like debris, which leaves a raw surface of the dermis—on which the cells will then grow and repopulate the skin.

Eyes: One of the earlier signs of aging occurs around the eyes. There may be an accumulation of excess skin on the upper eyelids that obscures the natural form of the eyelid, giving a droopy, tired appearance and making the application of makeup and eye shadow difficult; or the lower eyelids can develop bags and puffy areas toward the nose. A blepharoplasty for the upper eyelids would remove the extra skin and excess fat, hiding the scar in the fold of the upper eyelid and, most importantly, preserving the natural shape of the eyelid. Very careful planning and execution are key to ensure that the person is fully capable of closing and opening her eyes.

In the area under our eyes, the lower eyelids, there is a membrane that is stronger when we're young and holds back the fat that acts as a shock absorber under the eye. As women age—some as early as their teens and twenties, but most more noticeably in their thirties and forties—the membrane weakens and lets the fat merge forward—which is what we call bags under the eyes. For this concern, a lower blepharoplasty is designed to remove or redistribute the excess fat and to remove the excess skin.

Wrinkles under and around the eyes cannot be solved with upper and lower blepharoplasty because pulling tightly enough to remedy the wrinkles risks changing the shape of the eye. There are several options to address wrinkles such as crow's-feet or the fold between our eyebrows. First, a quick explanation of how they form: Simply stated, these wrinkles evolve from the interaction between the superficial muscles of the region and your skin. Over an extended period of time, the impact causes the skin to fold perpendicular to the direction of the muscle is pulled. One option is to weaken the effect of the muscle and skin by injecting Botox (from a plant bacterium) into the vertical frown lines, the transverse lines of your forehead, and the crow's-feet. (It can also be used for the plastysma band in your neck.) It's safe, effective, and lasts up to six months or longer, as long as it's done by an excellent surgeon or dermatologist. (Botox doesn't work for wrinkles around the mouth because the weakening or paralysis of the muscles would change the expression of the mouth.) You could also fill the wrinkles with soft-tissue augmentation materials, such as injected collagen, or you can alter the skin with a chemical peel or laser resurfacing.

While laser resurfacing is the procedure of choice for removing lines around the mouth, improving all-over skin tone, and supporting cosmetic surgery, Dr. Glassman considers Botox the most efficient way to address lines around the eyes. Laser resurfacing may be more permanent (lasting ten years or more) but requires surgical procedures and a relatively extensive recovery period.

Nose: Nasal surgery was developed in Europe in the early part of the twentieth century and has changed dramatically over the last thirty years. Before we talk about your options, it may interest you to know how the development of this operation fits in the context of the rest of the practice.

In the early days, plastic surgery was done in a cookie-cutter fashion. If a surgeon studied with Dr. A, he applied Dr. A's technique; if a surgeon studied with Dr. B, she applied Dr. B's technique. When the anatomy of the patient and the particular surgeon's technique was a good marriage, results were fine. But in cases when there wasn't a good marriage, the results were unacceptable both aesthetically and functionally. Hence, a change was pioneered in the modern era of plastic surgery that puts an emphasis on individually customizing surgeries—such as rhinoplasty (nose job)—in order to preserve normal anatomy and function.

What this means today is that you can have a less surgical, more natural-looking nose. The process your surgeon must use to determine the best nose is almost like putting together a jigsaw puzzle to assess the needs of your personal anatomy.

Ears: An operation to pin back protruding, prominent ears, the ear job (otoplasty) is often done for children after the age of six, when ears are fully developed, or for women and men of any age.

Mouth: Unlike our ears, which are not affected by signs of aging, the mouth changes over time: lips get smaller and thinner, sometimes even longer. Several things can be done to restore the youthful appearance of the lips.

1. A mouth that's too wide or hangs down too low can be shortened to expose a little more of the upper teeth by making a small incision at the base of the nose and inside the base of the nostrils. Next, a portion of the upper lip is removed and the lip raised.
2. Thin lips can be augmented with artificial fillers, like Gore Tex (a woven synthetic used in weatherproofing) or SoftForm, or with an injection of collagen. Natural tissue transplants, cultivated in different ways, are also options.
3. Too-large lips can benefit from a lip reduction: The excess tissue is removed from the inside of the lip, while the outside lip is rolled inward.

For the smile lines around the mouth and the vertical lines across the top of the upper lip, there are two different lines of treatment: The first approach is to fill them, and the second approach is to press the lines. Collagen forms—ranging from bovine collagen to collagen from cadavers or collagen harvested from your own body—are used as fillers, along with other soft-tissue fillers that can be investigated by you and your doctor. The use of collagen can be expensive, as it must be reinjected periodically. For some women that may mean twice or three times a year; for others, collagen can last up to a year and a half. Administered properly, again by a cosmetic surgeon or a dermatologist, collagen is a wonderful, safe alternative to more invasive surgeries.

Pressing these wrinkles can be done with varying degrees of success by sanding the skin (dermabrasion), peeling it, or using laser resurfacing. While laser resurfacing is very effective in removing the lines around the mouth and across the top of the lip, sometimes the process can leave a discolored, lighter patch of skin, depending on pigmentation.

Neck: Another common area of complaint, as it's often one of the first places where visible signs of aging occur. Three things may be happening to your neck at the same time: accumulation of fat, accumulation of excess skin due to gravity, and laxity of the platysma muscle. Which surgery is appropriate depends upon those three things. For example, if your problem is fat, then liposuction will address it. If the problem is fat and the laxity or thickening of the platysma muscle, then liposuction and tightening of the muscle are in order. If all three concerns are present—fat, loose platysma muscle, and excess skin—that person is a candidate for a lower face-lift or a neck-lift, in which the fat is removed, the muscle treated, and the extra skin removed from behind the ears.

Liposuction: Used in conjunction with many cosmetic surgeries, liposuction was developed in France in the late 1970s and brought to the United States shortly thereafter by Dr. Norman Martin, a colleague of Dr. Glassman. At that time, liposuction involved the insertion of a broad, hollow metal tube into the fat and hooked up to a suction device. Before liposuction, the only way to remove fat was to surgically extract it, which left a series of long scars. The advent of liposuction was remarkable and has since evolved with a number of advances in the technique.

The tumescent technique, the first of these advances, involves injecting fluid into the fat to soften it and prepare it for removal. The process constricts the blood vessels in the area so there's much less bleeding. Another advance has been the development of smaller instruments which allow the fat to be drawn in a more subtle manner, taking longer but resulting in fewer irregularities or ridges. Another advance is the introduction of ultrasound—the emission of high-frequency sound waves that vibrate the fat at such a rate that it melts prior to removal.

The first two techniques are now essentials, although ultrasound remains controversial because the high-frequency waves sometimes cause protracted pain or burning in the area. It should be used, however, in cases where traditional tumescent might not be effective.

Arms: One of the most common complaints is laxity on the back of the upper arms. What's entailed in surgery will again depend on whether the problem is fat or excess skin and fat. When the concern is about fat, this is a wonderful area to improve with liposuction. A tiny incision can be made in the back of the elbow and the whole back compartment of the upper arm treated. With some individuals, the skin is so loose in the region that they are candidates for a operation that involves the removal of fat and skin with a seam that goes from the back of the elbow toward the back of the underarm. Since it leaves a visible scar, you must ask whether that is an aesthetic improvement over what you already have. If you're someone who is never going to wear a short-sleeve shirt again because your arms are so saggy, the scars may be a welcome improvement.

Breasts, torso: We might divide the concerns here into broad categories of women whose breasts are uneven, too large, too small, or too low. For women whose breasts are too large, there is usually a medical problem, not only cosmetic. They may have functional concerns because the weight of their breasts causes orthopedic problems—back, neck, or shoulder pain. They often have skin rashes under their breasts and difficulty participating in athletics or buying clothing. Under those circumstances, the operation called for is a breast reduction. The excess skin and breast tissue are removed, the diameter of the areola is reduced, then the nipple and areola are placed at a higher level on the breast. When a woman with very large breasts has fat that really stands out, liposuction is used as an adjunctive tool to improve the peripheral of the breast.

While breast reduction has been performed consistently for more than fifty years, the modern era of breast augmentation began somewhat later, in the early

1960s, when silicone breast implants were developed. Since then, that has been the predominant method of enhancing breast size. Along the way, saline breast implants became the second form of implants to be used. Whether to use saline or one of the multiple types of silicone—shapes vary with manufacturers—is up to the patient and surgeon. There are also different surgical approaches as to where the incision should be—whether it should be on top of or under the muscle—decisions that will be addressed in a very detailed consultation between the patient and the physician.

Some controversy remains about silicone breast implants and whether they increase the risk of autoimmune disease, although studies over the past ten years have failed to produce any scientific evidence of increased incidence of such diseases among women with silicone implants. The implants are still in debate legally and politically, but many surgeons, Dr. Glassman among them, have concluded to their satisfaction that they are safe. Provided a women understands the controversy and is willing to accept the risks (not only of this operation but of any operation), and the surgery adheres to FDA guidelines, it is perfectly fine, says Dr. Glassman, to use the silicone breast implant.

If you have any hesitancy, saline implants would be your option. Saline implants can be excellent, though they can have more wrinkles and ridges and are not as lifelike as silicone. At issue is whether a woman has enough covering tissue; if so, saline is a fantastic alternative. But when someone has very thin skin or very little breast tissue of her own, hiding the flaws of a saline breast implant is difficult.

When it comes to cosmetic surgery of the torso and body, by the way, use of the mirror-imaging tool is not as effective as it is for surgeries of the face. Dr. Glassman recommends that you select photographs to show your surgeon what size you desire. He notes that when someone says she wants to be a B or a C cup, that could be interpreted differently by different people. With photographs from magazines or lingerie ads, say, you can achieve visual agreement.

Even so, some women opt for adjustable implants—made of silicone and saline—which include a valve that is inserted under the arm or to the side of the breast. This allows greater or smaller amounts of saline to be adjusted after the surgery, until the patient and the doctor are satisfied, at which time the valve can be removed and the implant remains intact.

When women have concerns about unevenness in the size of their breasts, many are very embarrassed about it, even though it is a remarkably common occurrence, says Dr. Glassman. Many are reassured to know they're not alone. Whether or not surgery is warranted is based on if their asymmetry is significant.

If one side is dramatically larger than the other, you can reduce the large side, augment the smaller side, or do both. The decision will be based on the problem, the preference of the patient, and what's in her best interest.

Breasts that are too low can be addressed in association with some of the other surgeries. For example, if a woman wanted to be larger and higher, she might opt for an augmentation and a breast lift at the same time. The breast lift is similar to the breast reduction, but instead of removing breast tissue and excess skin, the surgery just removes the excess skin. While it leaves the breast tissue intact and raises the height of the breasts, it's not a match for what Mother Nature can do—attach the breast to the chest wall with a series of ligaments that cosmetic surgery has not yet been able to duplicate.

A promising new technique, Dr. Glassman notes, is called a laser bra—whereby the excess skin is removed and the remaining skin treated with a laser to tighten it as would a bra, giving it a more youthful tone. The goal—although its development is in very early stages—is also to prevent premature sagging of the breasts after the procedure.

Other targeted concerns in the realm of the torso can be addressed with liposuction. This includes eliminating fat that may hang on the underarms and sides of the body, as well as on the back, protruding from evening gowns or undergarments.

Abdomen: Depending on what the needs and complaints are, you have a few choices for improving tummy tone and tightness. Women who have gained a few pounds but have retained fairly youthful skin and muscle tone are candidates for tummy liposuction. When the skin becomes excessive or muscles have lost tone—usually as a consequence of pregnancy—then women may consider a mini tummy tuck or a major tummy tuck. The procedure will depend on how much skin needs to be removed and whether the navel needs to be relocated. In both of the operations, three steps are involved: The fat is removed; the muscles are tightened; and the extra skin is removed with an incision above the pubic region from one hipbone to the other, while the upper skin is pulled down and stretched flat. If you want to remove stretch marks in your lower abdomen, they would be discarded in a tummy tuck. If you had stretch marks on your upper abdomen, they would be improved but not eliminated.

This procedure has not changed much over the years, except for recent developments that use endoscopic surgery, which allows for tinier incisions for liposuction and can tighten the muscles, though its use under these circumstances doesn't remove the skin.

Legs: When improvement is sought for overall shape of the legs or lack of muscle tone, two forms of surgery are explored. The first is liposuction, and the second, a newer procedure, is called a body lift—where, in addition to liposuction, the excess skin is removed to tighten the remaining skin.

The body lift—for people whose serious loss of tone can't be helped by liposuction alone—is virtually a tummy tuck on the back. Developed by Dr. Ted Lockwood, who practices plastic surgery in Kansas City, the body lift emerged as a technique for legs when he continued a tummy tuck all the way around to the back, like a very wide belt around the waist. Removing excess skin and fat from the whole lower portion of the body, a body lift tightens the legs as well as the abdomen and buttocks.

As plastic surgeons don't do vein stripping or cauterization, most of the procedures for removing varicose veins and spider veins fall under the specialties of vascular surgery or dermatology. Dr. Peter Pugliese recommends nonsurgical measures that may diminish milder vein concerns. Again, if these are an issue for you, avoid wearing tight or constricting undergarments or jeans. Wearing light support hose can be helpful, along with incorporating more walking. Though he reports mixed results in laser treatments for spider veins, Dr. Pugliese is impressed with a nonsurgical technique for varicose veins called sclerotherapy, or injection of a sclerosing, or hardening, fluid into the veins.

Buttocks: Tightening the butt, removing fat, or reshaping the derriere are among the concerns many women ask about. Options include liposuction and body contouring—liposuction combined with the removal of skin, such as that used in the Dr. Lockwood approach. (While some surgeons augment the buttocks with implants, Dr. Glassman neither approves of nor performs the procedure.)

Is there a point at which an individual is too old for a particular procedure? Dr. Glassman notes that the main consideration about age-appropriateness for surgery is physical health and the ability to undergo surgery. The other concern might be with older individuals who wish to have liposuction, which depends a great deal on the skin's elasticity.

Cosmetic surgery is not an alternative to diet, nutritional supplements, exercise, the maintenance of skin care, or repair that might be achieved with hormonal supplements. Cosmetic surgery is a recourse when all those measures have been pursued without improvement, or as a complement to improvements you've already made.

In preparation for surgery, Dr. Glassman suggests an action plan to deal with both emotional and physical needs. First, get yourself psyched up about the pending surgery. Because there is a lot of anxiety involved, getting yourself excited is important. It's best to plan surgery at a time when you are not stressed with factors like moving to a new home or job, or going through a personal crisis.

For your physical regimen, homeopathic vitamins and herbs can be taken that will help the lymphatic drainage essential to decrease scarring and bruising while facilitating better healing and a faster recovery. Topically, in advance of surgery, focus on maintaining skin in its optimum presurgery condition—cleaning and hydrating, as well as having facials and skin treatments. Make sure to avoid the sun, as tanning makes the skin less elastic and more difficult for a surgeon to handle. Even when you've decided to do cosmetic surgery for you and you alone—good for you!—you probably shouldn't withhold this information from your spouse or significant other; a support system of some kind is important for recovery and healing. As for friends, acquaintances, coworkers, and others with whom you come into contact regularly, Dr. Glassman believes that you should decide from the beginning how you're going to talk about having had surgery. Right out of the gate, he says, choose one of two things: to be candid, or to be discreet. There is a growing trend to share the excitement with others. After all, being proud of how you look and how you take care of yourself is what's it's all about. As always, however, it's a matter of choice.

Stay tuned to new developments in cosmetic surgery, which are happening all the time. In the very near future, an integrated use of hormones and plastic surgery for anti-aging techniques will take the field to unprecedented capabilities of improving and beautifying our lives.

In the meantime, I'd like to thank my husband for sharing the gift of his professional wisdom for this chapter, as I turn to a subject near and dear to my heart: how we can improve and beautify our lives in a less scientific but just as transformational way.

Practical Steps for Exploring Cosmetic Surgery

As with previous chapter summaries, I'd like to emphasize how important it is not to be in a hurry to pursue these steps all at once. Particularly in the case of cosmetic surgery, we should recall that these procedures are all elective. These steps are offered for you to explore now, in the near future, or at some later point when they are appropriate for you and your lifestyle.

EXAMINE YOUR ATTITUDES TOWARD COSMETIC SURGERY

Look at what may be complex or even conflicting attitudes toward options for improving your appearance. If you're ambivalent, you may want to ask whether the advantages available to you outweigh the concerns: To help you resolve any conflicts you may have, you might want to review the principles of "less is more" from this chapter and see how this applies to you.

DO YOUR OWN HOMEWORK AND LEGWORK

Even before you consult with a plastic surgeon (review the suggestions in this chapter and in Chapter 5 for finding professionals right for you), take some time to develop a sense of what you'd like to achieve with cosmetic surgery. (Example: Collect photographs to show your doctor what you hope a breast enhancement might do for you.) When you consult with plastic surgeons (it's wise to have second and third meetings before surgery as well as second or third opinions), have a list of questions ready. And remember to ask about mirror imaging.

BE OPEN TO ALTERNATIVES AND NEW ADVENTS IN PROCEDURES

As you familiarize yourself with options you may wish to explore at a future date, remember to consider less invasive procedures that may be options for you now. (Examples: In lieu of a face-lift, you might opt for collagen and/or Botox, a chemical peel, or laser resurfacing.) Also stay tuned for the promise of new procedures that science is bringing us all the time.

The question, "What's in it for me?" is the internal dialogue of the ego. Asking, "How can I help?" is the internal dialogue of the spirit. The spirit is that domain of your awareness where you experience your universality.

— DEEPAK CHOPRA
THE SEVEN SPIRITUAL LAWS
OF SUCCESS

CHAPTER EIGHT

THE SPIRITUAL NATURE

OF BEAUTY—TENDING

TO YOUR SOUL

MOST OF THE HEALTH AND BEAUTY CHOICES WE'VE DIS-
CUSSED SO FAR HAVE BEEN EXTERNAL AND INTERNAL
enhancements to improve the quality of our physical life. We've talked about our internal voice and about ways to stay connected to all of our senses to improve our whole-
health, not only physically but mentally and emotionally as well. Something we haven't
yet discussed, which is just as important to me, is the quality of our spiritual life.

For each individual, having a rich and meaningful spiritual life can be defined differently. To me, it begins with an understanding that a spiritual life is in
great part an inner life—I don't mean the way we observe characters in film and
literature, where we regard inner lives as thoughts, feelings, and motivations. In
this context, I'm referring to our inner life as that part of us where we experience
our universal connection to all life.

Though our inner spiritual life is profoundly personal and intimate, that's
not to say it doesn't translate outside and extend itself to others. I believe that our

true beauty springs from our spiritual inner life, because that's where our generosity of spirit comes from.

Most of us can recall meeting someone whom at first glance we didn't find to be an astoundingly beautiful woman or an extraordinarily handsome man. But within the space of less than an hour, maybe minutes, we were so taken with this person's spirit—an air of sincerity, self-knowing, peacefulness, generosity, inner happiness, genuine interest, humor, and goodness—that we found the person incredibly beautiful. It gave us pleasure just to look at this person and to be in the presence of his or her spirit.

Spiritual beauty can be found in our own inner lives, in our perception of others, and all around us. It exists in our relationships with ourselves, with family and friends, with nature, with all living things. Spiritual beauty exists in the way we treat ourselves—that's including exercise and food and the kindness we extend to our bodies—because that's where we live. I believe we experience spiritual beauty in our connection to this planet and to the God within ourselves.

That spiritual connectedness is our umbilical cord to the state of being alive. We all experience times of stress, isolation, and loneliness when we feel that our umbilical cord to the planet has stretched too thin, when we feel the need to better connect on a spiritual level. When we have that need, many of us are able to reconnect in our places of worship, where we find inspiration and contact with others who care about connectedness.

Sometimes when I feel the need to connect, I might turn to a meaningful piece of writing, such as *A Manual for Living.* Even a passage will suffice, although rereading the whole book makes me feel really connected. And then there is the place that I consider my very own place of worship—my garden. To feel connected, I don't need to do any actual gardening; I can simply go from plant to plant, flower to flower, smelling them, looking at them, greeting them, and basking in the wonder of this extraordinary planet that creates and supports these beautiful living plants and flowers, which in turn support insects and other living creatures—and that bring me such joy. There's a real community in my garden, members of the congregation of what I call my church; or what our rabbi's wife refers to as my temple.

When I was much younger, I wasn't very aware of my need to have such a spiritual connection to living, growing things. Then I discovered it one day, as if by accident. This was many years ago, when I'd first left home and moved to New York in hopes of being an actress. Instead, I found myself modeling to support my acting habit, but finding work as a professional model wasn't going so well either—mainly because I'm not five feet eight and willowy, which came as a shock to me. The work I was able to get, in commercials or modeling fashions for petites, was sporadic. That meant living pretty much hand-to-mouth, sharing a tiny, bare-bones room at the Barbizon Hotel that boasted one sink, one closet, two single beds, and possibly a wooden chair—my roommate and I may have removed the chair to make space to walk around each other. We had to go to another floor to bathe and use the bathroom, where a sign read PLEASE WASH AFTER USING. Actually, I still have that sign, as I later stole it (I take full responsibility for that indiscretion of my youth) as a reminder of the journey that has been my life.

My journey in those days was hard. Feeling lonely and displaced, neither I nor my career was faring well. Even eating was a challenge. Basically, I could afford to eat twice a day, as long as that left enough to cover transportation. Since taxis were out of the question and the subway was harder to navigate, riding the buses worked best for me. To save money, I walked whenever I could, being careful not to wear out my only two pairs of shoes. But when I was very tired at the end of the day, sometimes I would treat myself to a bus ride—even if it meant not eating.

Such was this particular day. Totally exhausted, I decided that instead of eating dinner that evening, I had to take the bus. And as I was walking toward the corner where I would catch my bus, I passed a neighborhood market that was open to the street where fruits, vegetables, and little plants were for sale. I stopped for a moment to look at one of these plants, sitting in its small plastic green cone. No flowers, no buds, just a tiny green plant. For a moment, I just held it. Then I put it down, turned to go, and got almost to the bus stop before turning around again and going back to buy the plant. And holding it, I walked and walked and walked as the streets darkened and evening turned into night, until I got to the Barbizon.

I put my plant on the sill of the one minuscule square that represented a window, and I loved that plant, looking at it each morning when I woke up, watering it, talking to it. It flourished and so did I. And when I finally got a well-paying job that meant moving to Europe, I made my girlfriend promise that she would take care of it for me. That little plant meant so much to me that as soon as I was able to return to the United States, I went back to New York specifically to get my plant—only to find that it had died. Not because of my friend's neglect but because I had left it, because I couldn't take it with me to Europe. I was devastated. And yet I had discovered something essential about my spiritual need for connection.

Part of this love, I now realize, was instilled in me from watching my maternal grandmother on her farm, and was further nurtured by my father, who taught me so much when I was young about planting and growing vegetables and flowers. Having discovered how deeply felt this love was in me, ever since that experience in New York with my first plant, wherever I've lived, my plants have been part of my family—even in my first very own apartment, which contained one bed and one hanging plant.

In churches and temples, in gardens and neighborhood markets that sell plants, however we find our connection—and there are many ways to care for our inner lives—getting in touch with our spiritual beauty is as vital to looking and feeling our best as the act of breathing. It's so easy to feel disconnected in today's world. In our information age, we are bombarded by digital minutiae coming at us faster and more furiously than we can process, in forms that are more and more removed from real life and real time. We deal with computer screens, voice messages, and e-mail. Contact? Yes, but I think it's a poor substitute for the real thing. Have we forgotten the beauty of sitting down and handwriting a letter, pouring our soul onto that paper to give to someone we care about? And what about the excitement of receiving a letter in the mail, recognizing the handwriting, opening the envelope, and reading words that came not only from that person's heart and mind but from the pen in his or her hand. It's so intimate—the thoughts and affection that they're sharing with you. It's so beautiful.

True, we can receive an e-mail that is funny, thought-provoking, personal, and even inspirational. But for spiritual beauty, the electronic connection, at least for me, loses a little in translation. The true intimacy and beauty of simple things like lovingly handwritten letters tend to be overlooked as objects of value. Returning to those things, the basics, for connection helps us return to ourselves, where our spiritual beauty lies.

When we think about our life in hindsight, it seems to me that its meaning and beauty are made up of what are the pearls of our existence. Those are the moments of living that we can draw together to complete our pearl necklace of memories, the times when we were most in touch with the moment, connecting with something or someone. That something can be a sunrise or a sunset you behold when you're all alone, a moment so beautiful that you wouldn't want anyone to speak because the silence is perfect. Or the sight of a bird flying free in a blue sky. Or the sight of a child learning a word for the first time, when you can see behind that child's eyes the recognition of discovery. Or the connection to a puppy who feeds from your hand, whose gratitude you can see on its face when it curls up to sleep. So much of what we experience is unspoken if we're truly in the moment. Those are the pearls that bring spiritual beauty. And if you don't have those moments that you can draw together at the end of your life, it's hard to imagine that you have lived—or that you have lived, in spite of challenges, with a full inner life.

For many of us, the experience of falling in love brings forth those moments in a dramatic way. After all, love is the ultimate human connection. We all seek it. We want self-love, we want to be loved, and we want to love. There's nothing like the spiritual beauty of being in love with another person, being in love with a new friend or an old friend, being in love with your mother or father, sibling or child, being in love with your puppy or your kitten . . . or your llama!

What makes a person spiritually beautiful? Perhaps that can be answered by whether you believe that each of us is born with the ability to be good or bad, and that our journey in life is to cultivate the inherent goodness within each of us. If you believe that for yourself, then you're already on that path of spiritual beauty.

We're all capable of being our better selves or our not-so-better selves. There are times in our relationships with others when we learn the difference. For example, when you see someone you know who is capable of annoying you and your first reaction, inside your head, is: *I can't stand her, she's a fool!* Then you pretend to earnestly look in her face and, in your most socially appropriate way, with false sincerity, say, "Hello, how *are* you?" as if you cared. You're missing the point. Yes, you're being courteous and civil, but that's not a human connection. The alternative is to recognize in your internal voice that, yes, you think that person is a fool, but also share with yourself that you sense this is a person who is lost or needy or in pain. And perhaps by saying, "Hello, how are you?" your courtesy could improve the moment in that person's life. Then you have extended generosity of spirit instead of false courtesy. And only you know the difference; only you know the spirit in which you spoke.

Everyone is capable of acting, acting kindly, acting friendly, or acting happy. But when we're none of the above, if it's not real you will eventually reveal your true face. But when it comes to your actions and your gestures—whether physical, verbal, emotional, or spiritual—if they evolve from the desire to be a good person and wanting to share that goodness with the world around you, then I think the spiritual beauty that inhabits you will be revealed outwardly.

Does this mean that we have to bring people into our circle of experience who have a negative impact on us? I don't think it does. I think that how we respond to other people is a choice. If someone has a negative impact on us and we choose to stay in that situation—whether it's employment or romantic or platonic relationships—and we consistently allow that person to consistently behave the way that they do to impact us negatively, we have to know that is our choice. They're not as much to blame as we are. If we choose to work with people who have a positive effect on us, and to build relationships with those who bring out the best in us and those who enhance our virtues, that, too, is a choice. We can control only ourselves, and we can't blame our actions on others.

When we choose not to have those people in our lives, the act of forgiveness may be important for our spiritual lives in order to free ourselves. But forgiveness doesn't mean you forget. Forgiveness means that the act, whatever it was, is less important than freeing yourself and moving on—you can forgive and move on with that person or cut that person loose from your life, forgiving that person and yourself for allowing it to have happened. Forgiveness, I have found, is very often twofold—involving both the person you are forgiving and yourself.

If some of this sounds unfamiliar, yet the idea of exploring your own spiritual beauty is something you're interested in, you can begin right now. You can start within the next hour, when you encounter someone that you see on a daily basis: Look at that person closely, truly look at her. Not at how she did her hair or jewelry, or what kind of suit and shoes she's wearing, whether her suit is pressed well, or if her shoes are polished or worn. Simply look into her eyes, not to be judgmental of who she is, but to observe her human condition. And if you observe her human condition to be very happy, you can practice being spiritually beautiful by commenting on how happy it makes you to see her happy. Or if your observation is that this is a person in pain or suffering, offer generosity of spirit and ask, in an appropriate manner, if there's something wrong and whether you can be of help. Offer only with sincerity—not if you're not prepared to give that help. The more often you offer yourself to someone in need, the more natural it will become. And the more you'll understand the spiritually beautiful human condition.

Throughout the ages, all the great prophets, philosophers, and leaders of spiritual belief—regardless of religion or denomination—have shared the teaching that our spirit is revealed at some point in our lives by everything that we do, by the sum of our actions. Being connected isn't something to isolate on one day of the week when you worship; instead, pursue it throughout the days, weeks, and years that number your life.

So the next time you spot a stranger in a car trying to turn from a side street onto a main thoroughfare in bumper-to-bumper traffic, instead of refusing to give up an inch of your slow progress, wouldn't it be nice to let him in? Odd as that may seem, that's generosity of spirit. Those are the moments that you accrue. On those days when I would certainly like to keep going, I stop, because I know how that person must feel. And in that moment when he turns into traffic and waves acknowledgment, it feels so good. We don't know each other, but we just connected, we had a moment of shared generosity. If he doesn't acknowledge it and I feel tempted to yell out a four-letter word, I can choose to do that and completely defy my own act of generosity and connectedness. Or I can choose to recognize that he hasn't made the spiritual connection but I have, that I shared and exhibited generosity of spirit.

Looking around me, at my loved ones, friends, and colleagues, I observe so many different expressions of the generosity of spirit that lead to connectedness.

I have a girlfriend who absolutely connects when she is riding horses. When she is on the back of her horse and they are galloping or jumping, it's one of the most spiritually beautiful, connected, and joyous sights I've ever seen. Their spirits float. She has a relationship with God through her horse.

I have another girlfriend who, there is no doubt in my mind, sees God in her two boys. Though she attends regular religious services, worships, and prays, I know that she connects on a spiritual level every day of her life, just looking into the faces of her sons and giving thanks for them.

Another girlfriend has a passion that is separate from her profession—her ability to paint watercolors. When she paints, it is as close an act of spirituality and worship as anything I've ever seen. The spiritual nature of beauty is palpable in her joy and connectedness when she paints, and when she gives her paintings as gifts. She truly gives a piece of herself, her spirit, her joy.

Some of us connect through creativity; others connect by responding to that creativity, or we connect by being both creative and responsive to others. Listening to great music is an immediate connection for me. When we hear an artist such as the virtuoso Itzhak Perlman, how can we not hear spiritual beauty? When we listen to someone who plays or sings from the soul, how can we can not hear that spiritual connectedness?

Moving our bodies, breathing, meditating, dancing: All are ways that allow us to get in touch with feeling spiritually beautiful.

Sometimes humor and laughter can connect us spiritually. Sometimes shared sorrow gives us a connection that goes beyond words.

I have friends who connect spiritually through philanthropy, charity, or volunteering. I know people who offer generosity of spirit as animal-rights activists or who connect by adopting pets who might otherwise be put to death. Others I know look for the connection in their umbilical cord to the planet, by taking even small steps to care for and protect our environment. Though recycling may mean you have to load up your car and drive to a location that's not so convenient, it can be enormously satisfying. Your inner life can be beautified by remembering to turn off lights and other energy sources when they aren't needed; by not overusing water for bathing and household cleaning; by driving less and walking more; by buying a bicycle to get around town; by participating in local environmental cleanups; and by teaching your children to respect the only earth we have so it can support us and them, their children, and all our generations to come.

Generosity of spirit takes so many forms. I have some friends who would get up in the middle of the night and drive a hundred miles if I needed their comfort, but who would no more write a check for charity or volunteer at a homeless shelter than go to the moon. We don't need to judge who is more generous or who is more connected. We have enough judgment without needing to do that. What matters is simply that we give, however we can.

In our Western culture, the idea of karma is frequently misinterpreted to mean that if you do good deeds, eventually something good will happen to you. Karma's true principle is that in the midst of giving, you are receiving. If your giving is sincere, the joy you receive from the act of giving is your karma.

I've found that the most important acts of goodness are done without witness. It's not the grand gestures that touch me most, it's the people who go through life day by day doing heroically simple and kind things. It's not the people who are cajoled into donating that big check as a tax write-off, it's the people who on a daily basis give a dollar, whether it's a true dollar or a measure of their time, energy, effort, or love.

How we cope with challenge can be a place where we discover our spiritual beauty. The difficulties of our lives don't change who we are, they reveal who we are, so that in moments of the most intense grief or duress, pain, or loss, who we are is most revealed. We will know ourselves, whether we are courageous or weak, negative or positive, optimistic or pessimistic; if we are forgiving or blaming, arrogant or humble, grateful or ungrateful, connected or not.

Will having a healthy spiritual life inform us as to what our purpose is here in this life? I can't promise that. I think that, not unlike the ocean's tide, our sense of purpose has an ebb and flow. It waves in and waves out, which can be said of every sense and emotion we have in life. There may not be any point in most of our lives where we arrive, and from then on, in every single moment of every hour of every day, we can be sure of our purpose. But I do think that as we get more in touch with what brings us joy, and what gives us that universal connection, we find a peace that evolves and gives us a stronger foundation. And so when the waves are out and we're not altogether sure of our purpose, we have the inner peace and the security to know that the waves will come back in.

I would like to close by sharing with you an experience that I had in my early thirties. In my own desire to do more to connect spiritually, I began visiting the children at the Shriners Hospital on Easter weekends. I chose to go on Easter because I was told that, for whatever reasons, this was a holiday when very few visitors ever showed up. It seemed that the children were particularly despondent during this time, knowing perhaps from television and from talking to one another that other children got to go on Easter egg hunts or other festive outings that they could not attend. So I decided that I would go to the Shriners Hospital each year and take Easter baskets and be an Easter bunny of sorts. I was a novice at this, and naive about the condition of the children.

What I did not realize was that there are a number of children there who have neither arms nor legs. These children were confined either to a bed or a basketlike bed, or hanging device, so that they would not develop bedsores. They lived a very internal life.

Not realizing this, I arrived at the Shriners Hospital with baskets filled with goodies. And on top of each basket, the very top gift, was a big bright Frisbee. Back then Frisbees were absolutely what kids wanted to play with. I figured the children would just love these Easter baskets that also had Frisbees.

So there I was, ushered into the ward with a trolley bearing all these baskets topped with big bright Frisbees, looking around and seeing that the ward was filled with children who could not possibly ever use a Frisbee.

The oldest boy in the ward was named Tony. He had no legs, was missing his entire right arm, and had a stump where his left arm would have been. And as I stood there, dumbfounded at the error I had made, trying to think of what to say to explain this enormous oversight, Tony spoke up and said, "Oh, Miss Principal, thank you so much for the baskets! And thank you, we can all wear the hats."

Tony had spiritual beauty in the truest sense, because he knew they were Frisbees. And he knew my mistake was well intentioned. So I went to each of the kids and put the Frisbees on each of their heads. Then I lay down with them in their beds and took Polaroids and taped up the pictures in places where they could see themselves in their hats.

In all my life, I don't think I've ever met anyone more beautiful than Tony.

Practical Steps for Tending to Your Soul

Throughout this chapter are several practical examples and suggestions that I hope will offer you choices and inspiration for embracing the spiritual nature of your beauty. Rather than repeating them here, I hope you'll feel inclined to perhaps read this chapter more than once or use it as a reference when looking for ways to feel connected to others and to your spirituality.

I'd like to take this opportunity to thank you for coming on this journey with me and for welcoming such a personally meaningful topic in this next-to-last chapter.

Before we end, there is one more important subject I'd like to share. Think of it as dessert!

Just do it.

NIKE AD CAMPAIGN

CHAPTER NINE

TEN MINUTES OF JOY

THIS PRACTICE WAS ONE OF THOSE THINGS I STUMBLED ONTO SEEMINGLY BY ACCIDENT, BUT WHICH ALSO GREW OUT OF A need to maintain connectedness with myself, with the earth, and with the potential for each day.

We've talked already about how easy it is to get caught up in the day-to-day minutiae, the trials and tribulations of life, the information bombardment, the stress, the work, the pressure. Our to-do lists are ever-expanding: driving our kids from place to place, getting to the grocery store, making dinner, meeting the demands of our boss, keeping employees happy, being a good wife, a good mother, a good friend, a good daughter. It's endless. It's so easy to lose sight of the joy of being alive. It's so easy to stop having fun!

Some years ago, I found myself in a stretch where I'd lost sight of joy, even though I didn't put it to myself in quite such frank terms. It became apparent to me one hot, sunny day as I was driving down Wilshire Boulevard, in bumper-to-bumper traffic, late for an appointment. By chance, or not, I happened to look over toward one of the big office buildings, and there I saw a lovely young woman who had come out, obviously on her lunch break, and had found a place on a little square of grass out in front. She was sitting in a little sliver of sunlight with her lunch in her lap and her face uplifted as she ate her sandwich. She looked absolutely joyful.

There I was in my nice air-conditioned car, thinking that this young woman on her short lunch break was having a lot more fun than I was. I thought how wonderful it was that she had sought out that little ray of sun on that little patch of grass to enjoy her sandwich, looking up into the sky, rather than simply sitting at her desk. She took that short amount of time to give herself that simple pleasure and joy. It made me ask myself: *Why can't I do that?*

One evening shortly thereafter, I was on my way home feeling all the heaviness of work and stress that had been building up. It seemed that the days had blended into weeks and months without fun, that the press of life was relentless, and that the most pleasure I got was in going to sleep, for those few hours, before getting up to start the grind all over again.

When I arrived at my house, it was still light out—which was unusual—and without consciously thinking about it, I did something I'd never taken the time to do before. After dropping my stuff inside, I opened the back door and went outside, where there was a hill and a little pondlike pool. I sat down in a chair and watched the light change over the hill for about twenty minutes. And in those twenty minutes I was transformed, just from the enjoyment of watching the light change on the plants and the occasional flower, seeing the birds put the day to rest, and listening to the sounds of the coming night. Where I lived at the time was very rural, so rather than listening to traffic, I heard the sounds of nature.

That spontaneous activity gave me a sense of joy and tranquility that I hadn't felt in weeks, maybe months. Remarkably, it had happened in twenty minutes, and I had done very little. But it made a tremendous difference in my mood then, for the rest of the night, and even the next day.

So the following evening, when I was driving home from work and it was already dark, I found myself thinking about those few minutes the night before and wondering what I could do to reproduce that feeling. Thinking that maybe there was something else I could do to have that same quiet joy, I drove my car to a safe spot where I could look out over the city on the San Fernando Valley side of Los Angeles and watch the lights come on. It was, again, a few minutes of happy respite.

From the inspiration of that young woman out on her lunch break to those two nights of stumbling onto my own fun grew a concept called Ten Minutes of Joy.

Ever since then, I try to find a way, every day of my life, to be in the moment for ten joyful, undemanding minutes. Everyone has a different way of going about this. For me, that's the key—that it not be demanding. I can't tell you what will give you joy, but I am more than pleased to provide some examples that have given it to me. As you peruse these moments, maybe they will prompt you to discover your own.

Recently, I was at work on the set, where the pace is always busy and bustling, with a frantic atmosphere of hurry up and wait, and work, work, work. We were shooting outside in over-100-degree heat. Away from the main shooting areas, I discovered a pool house on the property, so when the cast and crew broke for lunch, instead of going with them to eat, I went into the pool house by myself to sit in the cool and eat a piece of chocolate. For ten minutes I sat in solitude, looking out the window at the trees and light clouds in the sky, eating my single square of chocolate, which I made last for the entire time. It was a wonderful respite that I thoroughly enjoyed—the cool, the quiet, the solitude, and the pleasure, all of those things, and I found them in the pool house and the chocolate.

On typically overloaded days, I can usually look forward to Ten Minutes of Joy just walking in my garden, sometimes in silence, sometimes talking out loud to plants and flowers that I've been nurturing for over a decade, experiencing happiness to see them healthy and blooming and sharing themselves with me.

Some days, Ten Minutes of Joy is curling up on the floor with my dogs, feeling their warmth, resting, listening to their heartbeats. Not long ago, on a particularly stressful day, I tended to one of my dogs who had been on a restricted diet after having surgery. I went out and got a type of dog food that she's not normally allowed to have and hand-fed the pellets to her, one by one. After each bite, her tail wagged in anticipation of the next one. It was so joyful to see her getting better and her appetite restored, enjoying this indulgence and sharing it with me.

I don't try to organize or micromanage Ten Minutes of Joy. Writing down what I do isn't important either, because it would be a poor impostor of just being in the moment.

What I have done, especially in the beginning of my practice, is to make the conscious decision to seek out joy. Sometimes when I think I've forgotten, suddenly the ten minutes will come upon me when I least expect them. I may park the car and have farther to walk than I'd anticipated and, with time to spare, might come upon something as mundane as a bench. Without any planning, I can decide to sit down for a few moments and people-watch. That can be joyful.

Sometimes being conscious is taking those moments to check in with yourself from time to time and ask if you've had Ten Minutes that day. If you haven't, and you forgot the day before, don't punish yourself or feel failed in the joy-seeking process; instead, ask yourself if you'd enjoy having Ten Minutes of Joy today or the next day. It's not another must-do or should-do, it's something that you desire or that enriches your life.

Your conscious mind may not know what will make you happy for ten minutes, but by doing it every day, you'll know. And then, as your life changes, what makes you happy might change.

Ten Minutes of Joy can be about slowing down, about getting off the main highway and driving through residential streets, looking at everything, taking it all in, imagining the lives in the houses and community.

Ten Minutes of Joy can be about just driving, rolling down the window, putting the music on a little too loud, and simply rocking out for ten minutes. Not thinking about work, not thinking about what I need to do next, just enjoying the music and the wind in my hair and on my skin.

Joy can be not taking phone calls for ten minutes and putting my face down on the cool glass of the desk and thinking about something that is joyful to me. Sometimes that's the only way I can manage during the day.

Cooking is joyful. There aren't many things I can cook in ten minutes, but even making a sandwich, just right, and then eating it slowly, can be joyful. It can be blissful to practice the art of making a cup of tea—whether it's for someone else, for yourself, or for the both of you—brewing it so it's just right, pouring it into a beautiful teacup, inhaling the fragrance before you ever taste it, and letting it cool off a few minutes longer so you can enjoy the anticipation of that first sip.

There are so many senses that can be served. Your ten minutes don't have to involve food or drink. You can find them in a plant, a ray of sun, a breeze, music, a memory. It can be time out, as I've mentioned before, to go into a ladies' room and have a minibath, washing your hands really well, brushing your teeth if you have a toothbrush and toothpaste, brushing your hair, and just taking ten minutes to refresh yourself. That can be joyful. Then you come out of the ladies' room feeling like you can take on the world again.

Spotting me after a refreshing break once, someone asked, "What did you do in there, take a shower?" I replied, "Well, yes, almost."

Sitting in silence and reading the newspaper for ten minutes: joyful luxury.

I have a dear friend who—due to the circumstances of her life—can only have one child. For my friend, her Ten Minutes of Joy come every night, after she has tucked her daughter into bed and watched her fall asleep. Then my friend spoons around her and experiences true joy by smelling the nape of her daughter's neck as she sleeps.

Instead of a chapter summary, I'll conclude with some simple suggestions that may help you on the path of experiencing Ten Minutes of Joy every day:

1. Put aside ten minutes in the afternoon for quiet time and a cup of tea or glass of water.
2. Any time in the day, find a way to go outside and experience nature for ten minutes.
3. Play with a pet, even if it's not your own, for ten minutes.
4. Ask a child a question and listen closely to the answer. You'll be surprised how joyful it can be to learn an answer through the eyes of a child.

5. If it's nice weather, lower your car window and crank up the music. Remember when this was the only way to drive?
6. Call someone you love who lives far away. Experience ten minutes of joy at the sound of his or her voice.
7. Buy a sandwich and offer it to a homeless person. Experience inner joy.
8. Instead of killing garden snails with insecticide, take ten minutes to pluck them and call snail ranchers to take them away. Or put on some nice music in your car while you take ten minutes to drive your recycling to the recycling center. Or, while eating a single square of chocolate, write a letter to a legislator about needed environmental protection you favor. Or do something good for the planet and experience universal joy.
9. Change the sheets on your bed, take a shower, and moisturize; now slide in naked.
10. Follow the instructions above, but with someone.

You can plan your joy, catch it in the moment, or let it catch you. Sometimes I find myself at the very end of the day, realizing I haven't had Ten Minutes, and I go looking for them. Best of all is when they come to me as I get into bed. As I described much earlier in my list of likes and loves, pure joy for me is knowing that everyone I love is sleeping sweetly, safe and sound. The dogs are in the bed with us, and I can hear them breathing. The phone isn't ringing. The house is quiet but full of the sounds and feelings of the surrounding serenity, and I spend those ten minutes connecting to gratitude, simply enjoying being alive just before I go to sleep.

THIRTY DAYS TO LOOK AND
FEEL TEN YEARS YOUNGER

O NE OF *LIVING PRINCIPAL'S* THEMES IS AN AWARE-
NESS THAT THERE ARE NO ONE-SIZE-FITS-ALL SO-
lutions or game plans for looking and feeling great. With that in mind, and with
the caveat that none of us needs any more must-dos on our daily list of endeavors,
I offer these planning suggestions as just that—ideas that may spark your imagination in practical ways that incorporate change in your life. This planning device
can help with making the myriad daily choices that can be so overwhelming. You
know the ones—when you've got an extra hour for yourself and you're stumped as
to whether you should exercise, meditate, take a bath, read, make a salad, meet a
friend, get a massage, or go buy yourself a new lipstick.

Again, trying to do it all, all at once, can be overwhelming and self-defeating.
I believe that if all you do is practice Ten Minutes of Joy every day, you will look and
feel younger within a week. Beyond that suggestion, I've mapped out a *30-Day*

Change Your Life schedule—with options to choose from on each of those thirty days. I think the simplicity will fit any lifestyle and any mind-set. It's just that easy. Simply try Week One (Level I—*The Basics*), then add Week Two (Level II—*Positive Motion*), then add Week Three (Level III—*Lifestyle Transformation*), and then add Week Four (Level IV—*The Works*). By day 30, you'll have changed your life.

WEEK ONE—LEVEL I—THE BASICS (DAYS 1–7)

A notebook or journal is an important tool to have in advance for Level I.

DAY 1 • LEVEL I

Take charge of your internal voice by paying attention to the way you talk to yourself (see pages 12–15).

HAVE TEN MINUTES OF JOY.

DAY 2 • LEVEL I

Three times today and every day, say loving, supportive things to yourself. Take a deep breath each time you do, and drink a glass of water.

HAVE TEN MINUTES OF JOY.

DAY 3 • LEVEL I

Acknowledge your likes and loves. Cheer yourself on today. Breathe. Drink more water.

HAVE TEN MINUTES OF JOY.

DAY 4 • LEVEL I

Recognize your likes and loves about yourself, keep it going. Drink eight glasses of water; breathe.

HAVE TEN MINUTES OF JOY.

DAY 5 • LEVEL I

Remember life lessons you've learned and ways you've changed your life positively before. Drink your eight glasses of water; breathe.

HAVE TEN MINUTES OF JOY.

DAY 6 • LEVEL I

Choose one lifestyle change you'd like to make for yourself now.

Use the 1–10 scale to decide on a priority (see pages 31–32).

Drink water; breathe.

HAVE TEN MINUTES OF JOY.

DAY 7 • LEVEL I

Get in touch with your primitive guide (see pages 19–22).

Today, resolve to listen more closely to its messages.

Drink water; breathe.

HAVE TEN MINUTES OF JOY.

WEEK TWO—LEVEL II—POSITIVE MOTION (DAYS 8–14)

Before starting on your first day of Week Two, know and have in advance what you'll need for diet, exercise and supplement plans.

DAY 8 • LEVEL II

(Repeat Day 1, WEEK ONE—LEVEL I)

Follow *30-Day Diet to Lose*, Supplement (see pages 107–24).

EXERCISE (EMPHASIS ON STRETCHING)

(SEE PAGES 134–42).

DAY 9 • LEVEL II

(Repeat Day 2, WEEK ONE—LEVEL I)

30-Day Diet to Lose, Supplement, Exercise (emphasis on toning and strengthening) (see pages 138–40).

PLAN A SPECIAL BEAUTY TREATMENT FOR THE END

OF THE WEEK (SEE PAGES 161–73).

DAY 10 • LEVEL II

(Repeat Day 3, WEEK ONE—LEVEL I)

30-Day Diet to Lose, Supplement, Exercise

(emphasis on aerobics)

(see pages 140–42).

CALL A FRIEND.

DAY 11 • LEVEL II

(Repeat Day 4, WEEK ONE—LEVEL I)

30-Day Diet to Lose, Supplement, Exercise (your plan).

READ SOMETHING TO INSPIRE YOU.

DAY 12 • LEVEL II

(Repeat Day 5, WEEK ONE—LEVEL I)

30-Day Diet to Lose, Supplement, Exercise.

SURPRISE A LOVED ONE.

DAY 13 • LEVEL II

(Repeat Day 6, WEEK ONE—LEVEL I)

30-Day Diet to Lose, Supplement, Exercise.

ENJOY YOUR BEAUTY TREATMENT.

DAY 14 • LEVEL II

(Repeat Day 7, WEEK ONE—LEVEL I)

30-Day Diet to Lose, Supplement.

HAVE FUN: GO TO A PARK AND
TAKE A HIKE OR BIKE RIDE.

WEEK THREE—LEVEL III—LIFESTYLE TRANSFORMATION (DAYS 15–21)

*In advance of starting Level III, you should have the
products you've chosen for your new skin-care regimen.
If you are considering starting hormones or changing
your hormonal-supplement plan, you must have had
a medical consultation and blood-test results
before taking hormones.*

DAY 15 • LEVEL III

(Repeat Day 1, WEEK ONE—LEVEL I)

(Repeat Day 8, WEEK TWO—LEVEL II)

Follow a new skin-care regimen (see pages 159–63).

Take hormones if that's part of your plan

(see pages 210–20).

DAY 16 • LEVEL III

(Repeat Day 2, WEEK ONE—LEVEL I)

(Repeat Day 9, WEEK TWO—LEVEL II)

Care for skin (see pages 151–71). Throw out old makeup.

(Hormones?)

DAY 17 • LEVEL III

(Repeat Day 3, WEEK ONE—LEVEL I)

(Repeat Day 10, WEEK TWO—LEVEL II)

Care for skin. (Hormones?)

HAVE A MAKEUP ARTIST GIVE YOU A MAKEOVER;

BUY NEW COSMETICS.

DAY 18 • LEVEL III

(Repeat Day 4, WEEK ONE—LEVEL I)

(Repeat Day 11, WEEK TWO—LEVEL II)

Care for skin. (Hormones?)

MAKE AN APPOINTMENT FOR A MASSAGE.

DAY 19 • LEVEL III

(Repeat Day 5, WEEK ONE—LEVEL I)

(Repeat Day 12, WEEK TWO—LEVEL II)

Care for skin. (Hormones?)

Make appointments for any medical updates
you may need or want—physical, gynecological exam,
optometry checkup, dentist, etc.

MAKE A SPIRITUAL CONNECTION WITH A STRANGER

(SEE PAGES 255–57).

DAY 20 • LEVEL III

(Repeat Day 6, WEEK ONE—LEVEL I)

(Repeat Day 13, WEEK TWO—LEVEL II)

Care for skin. (Hormones?)

ORGANIZE CLOSETS AND DRAWERS—

OUT WITH THE OLD, IN WITH THE NEW.

DAY 21 • LEVEL III

(Repeat Day 7, WEEK ONE—LEVEL I)

(Repeat Day 14, WEEK TWO—LEVEL II)

Care for skin. (Hormones?)

BUY SOMETHING BEAUTIFUL JUST FOR YOU—

FLOWERS, PERFUME, OR A NEW NIGHTGOWN.

WEEK FOUR—LEVEL IV—THE WORKS (DAYS 22–28)

DAY 22 • LEVEL IV

(Repeat Day 1, WEEK ONE—LEVEL I)

(Repeat Day 8, WEEK TWO—LEVEL II)

Care for skin, hair, nails.

(Hormones?)

GET IDEAS FROM MAGAZINES AS YOU EXPLORE

YOUR AUTHENTIC BEAUTY.

DAY 23 • LEVEL IV

(Repeat Day 2, WEEK ONE—LEVEL I)

(Repeat Day 9, WEEK TWO—LEVEL II)

Practice beauty care.

(Hormones?)

BE A SHOULDER FOR SOMEONE WHO NEEDS IT.

DAY 24 • LEVEL IV

(Repeat Day 3, WEEK ONE—LEVEL I)

(Repeat Day 10, WEEK TWO—LEVEL II)

Practice beauty care.

(Hormones?)

PUT A CONDITIONER ON YOUR HAIR

FOR TWENTY MINUTES.

DURING THE TWENTY MINUTES,

CALL YOUR MOTHER.

DAY 25 • LEVEL IV

(Repeat Day 4, WEEK ONE—LEVEL I)

(Repeat Day 11, WEEK TWO—LEVEL II)

Practice beauty care. (Hormones?)

READ THE MORNING'S NEWSPAPER.

DAY 26 • LEVEL IV

(Repeat Day 5, WEEK ONE—LEVEL I)

(Repeat Day 12, WEEK TWO—LEVEL II)

Practice beauty care. (Hormones?)

BE GENEROUS OF SPIRIT.

DAY 27 • LEVEL IV

(Repeat Day 6, WEEK ONE—LEVEL I)

(Repeat Day 13, WEEK TWO—LEVEL II)

Self-care for beauty and health.

(Hormones?)

TODAY, TRULY LISTEN WHEN SOMEONE SPEAKS TO YOU.

DAY 28 • LEVEL IV

(Repeat Day 7, WEEK ONE—LEVEL I)

(Repeat Day 14, WEEK TWO—LEVEL II)

Self-care for beauty and health.

(Hormones?)

HONOR FAMILY TODAY.

On day 29, review the past month. Assess what's working and what isn't. On day 30, look at the next month and select some goals. Choose to continue doing what is working, change what's not, and always remain open to the possibilities of the moment. Now, look in the mirror and say to yourself: "Honey, you're a babe."

Allen S. Cohen, M.D.

Born in New York City, Dr. Cohen graduated with Phi Beta Kappa honors from the University of Rochester before going on to graduate from New York University School of Medicine with honors from the Alpha Omega Alpha Honor Society. Following an internship at University of California at Los Angeles Hospital in internal medicine, with additional training there in general surgery and head and neck surgery (otolaryngology), Dr. Cohen completed the anesthesiology residency and served as chief resident in anesthesiology at UCLA in 1976. During the course of his current work in practice with Dr. Harry Glassman at the NOVA Surgicenter in Beverly Hills, Dr. Cohen has expanded his interest and expertise into the exciting new specialty of anti-aging medicine. In conjunction with Dr. Glassman, Dr. Cohen has spearheaded the development of one of the first full-service anti-aging practices in the nation. He is certified by the American Board of Anti-Aging Medicine.

Harry A. Glassman, M.D.

After receiving his undergraduate degree in biology from Franklin and Marshall College in Lancaster, Pennsylvania, Dr. Glassman went on to receive his medical degree from Hahnemann Medical College in Philadelphia, where he was president of the Alpha Omega Alpha Honor Society. Following his internship in Philadelphia, Dr. Glassman moved to Los Angeles to complete his general surgery and plastic surgery residencies at UCLA Hospital, along with other leading medical hospitals in the area, such as Wadsworth Veterans, Sepulveda Veterans, Rancho Los Amigos, and Harbor General Hospital. Since entering private practice in 1975, Dr. Glassman has gained international renown as a leader in plastic surgery, both reconstructive and cosmetic. He and the cutting-edge work of his Beverly Hills practice, the NOVA Surgicenter, have been written about extensively, and Dr. Glassman has been a contributing editor to several major publications on subjects ranging from geriatric dermatology and aesthetic plastic surgery to anti-aging developments within this field. A frequently featured lecturer, Dr. Glassman also contributed to one of his wife's earlier books, *The Beauty Principal.* Dr. Glassman's e-mail address is: *harry@glassmanmd.com,* and you can visit his website at *www.glassmanmd.com.*

Soram Singh Khalsa, M.D.

Dr. Khalsa graduated from Yale University and Case Western Reserve School of Medicine in Cleveland, Ohio. After his internship, he moved to Los Angeles and did his chief residency at the Hospital of the Good Samaritan. In 1977, after becoming board-certified in internal medicine, Dr. Khalsa entered private practice and joined the staff of Cedars-Sinai Medical Center. Over the past two and a half decades, he has broadened his training both in the United States and abroad by staying on the leading edge of therapeutics using homeopathy, acupuncture, and phytotherapeutics, which he integrates into his traditional practice of internal medicine. Dr. Khalsa is a founding member of the American Holistic Medical Association and a founding member of the American Academy of Medical Acupuncture. A past chairman of the Executive Steering Committee for the Complementary Medicine Department at Cedars-Sinai Medical Center in Los Angeles, he currently serves as the medical director for the East-West Medical Research Institute. You can visit Dr. Soram Singh Khalsa at his website: *www.khalsamedical.com.*

Peter T. Pugliese, M.D.

A native Pennsylvanian, Dr. Pugliese earned his bachelor's degree from Franklin and Marshall College and his doctorate from the University of Pennsylvania. Since 1978, after practicing family medicine for twenty years, Dr. Pugliese and his laboratories have investigated the mechanisms of aging skin and evaluated the biological efficacy of skin-treatment products. His work as a product development consultant has influenced the decisions of major cosmetic and pharmaceutical companies worldwide. Internationally renowned as an authority in the research areas of skin and longevity, as well as the relationship between appearance and sexuality, Dr. Pugliese is a dedicated educator and the author of more than fifty publications. His textbook *Advanced Professional Skin Care* has become the industry standard for skin-care practitioners. *Skin, Sex and Longevity,* by Peter T. Pugliese, M.D. (Reading, Penn.: Pugliese, 1998), is available at major bookstores and Internet booksellers. Or you can visit his website: *www.thepugliesegroup.com.*

Uzzi Reiss, M.D.

Israeli-born Dr. Reiss earned his medical degree at the Technion Institute of Technology in Haifa, Israel, and completed his U.S. residency in obstetrics and gynecology at the Albert Einstein College of Medicine in New York. He is one of the first doctors in the United States to become board-certified by the American Academy of Anti-Aging Medicine. After serving free clinics in New York and Los Angeles at the start of his career, Dr. Reiss entered private practice. Now, in his highly successful Beverly Hills practice, Dr. Reiss has become a leader in the clinical application of natural hormones, nutrition, mind-body principles, and other innovative methods, helping to optimize the health of thousands of patients. *Natural Hormone Balance for Women: Look Younger, Feel Stronger, and Live Life with Exuberance,* by Uzzi Reiss, M.D., with Martin Zucker, is published by Pocket Books (2001).

Carsten R. Smidt, Ph.D., F.A.C.N.

Dr. Smidt received his undergraduate degrees from Friedrich Wilhelms Universität Bonn, Germany, and the University of California, Davis. At U.C. Davis, Smidt went on to receive his master's in nutrition and, in 1990, his doctorate in nutrition and physiological chemistry. Since then he has spent the past ten years as a leader in the dietary supplement and medical foods industry, including four years at the Mead Johnson Nutritional Group, Bristol-Myers Squibb Company. Dr. Smidt currently holds the position of Senior Director of Pharmacology and Clinical Affairs at Pharmanex, Inc., Nu Skin Enterprises, in Provo, Utah, where he has worked for the past four years as the leading research scientist in product development. Dr. Smidt's professional emphasis is on identifying new nutritional product opportunities that are medically sound, safe, and effective and engaging in company and collaborative research—clinical, preclinical, and analytical studies—and his special research interests include the effects of diet components on the prevention and treatment of human disease, and the role of nutrition as an adjunct therapy for chronic diseases.

dessert recipes:
    banana-berry, 106
    honey apples, 105
DHEA (Dehydroepiandrosterone), 214,
    219
diabetes, 208
diet: *see* diets; food; recipes; weight control
Diet for Life:
    fat content of, 54
    guidelines for, 65, 67, 125–27
    sample menus from, 66–67
    in VP's daily routine, 35, 51
    see also recipes
diets:
    grocery list for, 65
    guidelines for following, 55–56, 63–65,
      155
    medical supervision of, 55
    see also 30-Day Diet to Lose; Bikini Diet,
      Diet for Life; recipes
Disease of Aging, The (Kugler), 49
doctors:
    choice of, 163–65
    supervision of supplement dosage by, 111,
      112, 113, 127, 215, 218, 219
    and weight-loss guidance, 55, 126
    see also cosmetic surgery; medical check-
      ups; psychotherapy
Dong Quai, 121
douches, PH balance of, 224
drugs: *see* prescription drugs

E

ears, cosmetic surgery for, 241
eating: *see* food; overeating; weight control
egg recipes:
    French toast, 101–2
    omelette, mini, 98
    omelette, vegetable, 98–99

    popovers, 104
    scrambled egg white, 99
elastin, 23, 153
environmental concerns, 158, 204, 205–6,
    207, 258–59, 269
Epictetus, 36, 252
essential fatty acids (EFAs), 112–113, 120, 121, 123
estrogen replacement therapy (ERT), 213–14,
    217–18
    see also hormones
exercise:
    aerobic, 137, 140–142, 144, 275
    and breathing, 38, 132, 138, 142
    excuses for avoiding, 130–31, 132–34, 143
    guidelines for, 135–38, 140–44, 274–75
    health benefits of, 25, 129–30, 174, 182, 208,
      219
    making time for, 134, 137–38, 144
    resistive/isometric, 132, 134, 136–37,
      138–40, 143
    and spirituality, 252
    stretching, 35, 132, 137, 139, 143, 144, 274
    for vaginal muscles, 223
    and weight control, 49
    see also Pilates method; weight training;
      yoga
eyes:
    cosmetic surgery for, 237, 239–40
    routine care for, 181–83, 197, 198, 277

F

face-lifts, 237–38
    see also cosmetic surgery
facial treatments:
    basic care routines, 159–60
    at home, 166–67, 197
    value of, 33–34, 166
    see also cosmetic surgery; skin; skin care
      products

Fairley, Josephine, 107

fat: *see* overweight

fats:

    as basic nutrients, 52, 53–54

    in diet recipes, 64

    see also essential fatty acids (EFAs)

Feel Fabulous Forever (Fairley and Stacey),

    107–8, 174

feet: *see* foot care

fiber, dietary, 53, 122, 157

fingernails: *see* nail care

fish recipes: *see* seafood recipes

food:

    additives, 63, 64

    appreciation for, 33, 36, 39, 42, 56, 63, 267

    basic nutrients in, 52–55

    and eye health, 182

    and hair health, 174

    "nonfat" packaged products, 54

    as primal pleasure, 49

    and spirituality, 252

    see also antioxidants; diets; nutritional sup-

      plements; recipes

Food and Drug Administration, U.S. (FDA), 55

foot care, 141, 154, 170, 171–73

formulary (compounding) pharmacies, 215

friendships, maintenance of, 36, 38, 275, 278,

    279

fruit recipes:

    apples, honey, 105

    banana and walnut breakfast, 102

    banana-berry dessert, 106

    banana bread, 100–1

    fruit and yogurt breakfast I, 102–3

    fruit and yogurt breakfast II, 103

G

generosity of spirit, 256–59, 279

ginkgo, 113, 122

ginseng, 122, 124

Glassman, Harry:

    as cosmetic surgeon, 206, 233–38, 240, 242,

      244–45, 247–48, 281–82

    as VP's spouse, 27, 28, 31, 32, 33, 204, 228

glucosamine, 121

    see also SAM-e

grace, as personal quality, 6

    see also youthful maturity

green tea:

    as antioxidant, 107, 112, 120, 157

    in weight-loss diet, 63

H

hair:

    and aging process, 23

    basic care for, 173–74, 176–79, 183, 196–97,

      278

    color, 175–76, 237

    and eating habits, 174

    loss of, 178, 212

    removal, 170

    and smoking, 150, 174

    styling, 174–76, 178, 179, 193, 198

hand care, 154, 171, 172–73, 197

health, whole-living approaches to, 19–44,

    108–14

heart disease risks, 213, 214

herbal remedies, 109, 113, 119, 120–22, 247

hormones:

    and essential fatty acids, 113

    and food additives, 64

    functions of, 210–11, 221, 230

    herbal help for, 120–21, 124

    HGH (human growth hormone), 24, 207, 219

    imbalances of, 211–13, 214, 216, 218

    "natural" *vs.* pharmaceutical, 213–15

    and physical aging, 119, 120, 121, 153, 209,

      210–11

replacement of, 177, 178, 207, 208, 210,
213–20, 224, 228, 248, 276–79
and sex drive, 14
hysterectomies, 224

I

implants:
breast, 243–45, 249
facial, 238
insomnia remedies, 113–14, 220
internal voice: *see* self-acceptance;
self-awareness
intuition, whole-health role of, 19–22, 28, 39,
48, 163, 251, 274
iron, as nutritional supplement, 120,
121

J

joints, protection for, 121, 138, 141

K

karma, concept of, 259
Kava Kava, 113, 121, 124
Kegel exercises, 223
Khalsa, Soram Singh, 108–14, 122, 215, 220,
282
Kugler, Hans, 49

L

Lebell, Sharon, 36
legs, cosmetic procedures for, 246
letter writing, 254–55
libido: *see* sexuality
*Life and Times of Judge Roy Bean,
The* (film), 7
life expectancy:
medical perspectives on, 4, 22, 206–11
psychological aspects of, 203–4, 228
and sexuality, 221–22

ways to extend, 49, 130, 134, 205, 209–10
see also aging process; anti-aging
life inventory checklist, 26–31
life-style changes: *see* personal changes
liposuction, 242–43, 245–47
lips:
cosmetic surgery for, 241–42
protection for, 154, 197
living ceremonies:
daily routines as, 41–42, 147–48
and special events, 42–43
value of, 32, 37, 38
Living Principal, fundamental ideas of, 3, 5–6,
201–4, 271
Lockwood, Ted, 246, 247
longevity: *see* life expectancy
love of self: *see* self-acceptance
lysine, 174

M

magnesium, as nutritional supplement, 111,
116, 120, 121
makeup:
basic routines, 183, 195
choice of, 183, 195–96, 276
mammograms, 41, 170
manicures: *see* nail care
Manual for Living, A (Epictetus), 36, 252
marriage:
comforting routines in, 33
sexuality in, 225–28
Martin, Norman, 242
massage, 33–34, 42, 163, 208, 277
medical checkups, 41, 138, 143, 170, 182, 197,
207–8, 214, 276, 277
see also doctors
meditation, 219, 229
melatonin, 214, 219–20
memory loss, 23, 113, 122, 212, 220

"tummy tucks," 245–46

Turner, Vivian, 188–94, 198

U

ultraviolet (UV) rays, 150, 151, 153, 174, 182

V

vacations, as self-renewal opportunities, 10–11, 208

varicose veins, 246

veal recipes:

    piccata, 83–84

    scallops in tomato sauce, 84–85

vegetarian recipes:

    green salad, garden, 93–94

    pasta with vegetables, 96–97

    spinach-mushroom salad, 92–93

    tomato halves with garlic, broiled, 90–91

    tomato salad, sliced, 94

    tomatoes, cherry, sautéed, 91

    vegetable plate, steamed, 89–90

    vegetable salad, California, 92

    vegetable salad, Italian, 88–89

    see also egg recipes; fruit recipes

vitamins:

    antioxidants in, 112

    as basic nutrients, 52, 53, 54, 119

    list of, 114–18

    as nutritional supplements, 107–10, 113, 121, 247

W

wardrobe: see clothing

water:

    as basic nutrient, 52, 54, 110

    daily requirement for, 55, 125, 155, 273–74

    and hair care, 174

    and skin care, 155, 157

weight control:

    importance for health of, 48–49

    practical steps toward, 125–27

    role of attitude in, 9, 13, 48, 49, 50–51, 125

    see also diets; overweight

weight training, 136–37

Women's Bodies, Women's Wisdom (Northrup), 214, 223, 225, 226

workouts: see exercise

wrinkle removal, 237–40, 241, 242

    see also cosmetic surgery; facial treatments

Y

yoga:

    choosing teachers of, 163, 164

    as exercise routine, 29, 35, 132, 137, 141

    as relaxation technique, 208

youthful maturity:

    and clothing choices, 189

    concept of, 3–4, 202–4

    steps toward attaining, 229–30

Z

Zucker, Martin, 206

Having gained world recognition for her role as Pamela Barnes Ewing on the hit television series *Dallas*, VICTORIA PRINCIPAL has gone on to establish herself as a phenomenally successful entrepreneur with her Principal Secret skin- and beauty-care line and her film and television production company. She has also emerged as a tireless activist on behalf of such organizations as the Arthritis Foundation, the Founder's Society of the ASPCA, and Victory Over Violence. Victoria Principal is the author of the bestselling books *The Body Principal, The Beauty Principal,* and *The Diet Principal.* She is fifty-one years old and lives in Los Angeles with her husband, Dr. Harry Glassman.